UNBROKEN SPIRIT

< > < > < >

UNBROKEN SPIRIT

My life before and after quadriplegia

Gilbert John

Second Edition, Revised and Expanded

edited by Zelda Leah Gatuskin

AMADOR PUBLISHERS, LLC
Albuquerque, New Mexico, USA

Edited by Zelda Leah Gatuskin

Printed in the United States of America
Second Edition, Revised and Expanded
First Printing, 2021
ISBN: 978-0-938513-68-1
Library of Congress Control Number: 2020946249

AMADOR PUBLISHERS, LLC
Albuquerque, New Mexico, USA
www.amadorbooks.com

ACKNOWLEDGMENTS

Many people have helped me through the long process of writing this book, and I am grateful to them all. I would especially like to thank the following people:

My mother, Mary Bowman John, who has given me encouragement, provided me with care, and shared her memories;

Mrs. Margaret Pargin and family, my adopted mother, who first gave me the idea that I had a story to tell and helped me start the process;

My uncle, J. Toney Bowman, who supported my efforts and researched ways that I could work more efficiently, leading me to the idea of obtaining a computer;

My niece, Monique Lynn John, who became knowledgeable about computers so that she could help me and has spent many hours working with me;

My friend, Archie Silago, who directed me to resources to obtain assistive technology and provided information and advice;

Kathy McWhorter, who through her work at the Career Services office found assistive technology to make my life more productive and opened new horizons to me by encouraging me to tell my story to a larger world;

Connie Munroe, who visited me many times to help me review, edit and organize the transcriptions of my audio recordings;

Mrs. Ela Yazzie-King, New Mexico Division of Vocational Rehabilitation, who found the resources needed to get the book published;

Jason Crye and Acacia Publishing, for editing and publishing the first edition;

Zelda Gatuskin and Amador Publishers, for editing and publishing the second edition;

To God who gave me plenty of patience and lots of faith.

—Gilbert John

EDITOR'S NOTE ON THE SECOND EDITION

This revised and expanded Second Edition of Gilbert John's *Unbroken Spirit* combines text from the first print edition (Acacia, 2010) with that of a manuscript the author provided to Amador Publishers in 2016. That manuscript included a version of the material published by Acacia, insertions and addenda to that text, and entirely new material. The Prologue and Postscript that bracket Gilbert John's life story in this edition are passages written after the book's initial release. —*Zelda Leah Gatuskin, 2020*

UNBROKEN SPIRIT — CONTENTS

Sometimes it's like magic. I time-travel right here in this beloved land. I can feel again the boundless energy and enthusiasm of myself as a fifteen-year-old boy. I know his heart and mind can once again saddle my horse and ride like the wind.

PROLOGUE

Many years later, way beyond my traumatic accident, it was like a dream. Waking up the next day, I could not believe I was not able to move any of my body parts like I used to. I was overwhelmed by the pain around my neck. During my stay in the hospital as I recovered from my drastic injury, I asked all of the hospital staff if they had ever come across a book about a Native American with a similar story who could be a role model for me. At that time I did not know I was the first one to think about writing this kind of literature.

First of all, I did not know where to start. I just collected the information in my mind. I learned a lot being in the hospital with a diverse population of nationalities and hospital staff. Writing this book was always on my mind. When I talked with my mom and dad they never said anything negative. But my grandma was against it because of our Indian culture and traditions. Even though I had concerns about that, the book I wanted to write was in my mind all the time. For the most part I kept it to myself. I knew that some would be against writing a book about a disabled person, for that was blocked by barriers of taboo and myth.

I had a strong idea to continue writing, a second book about a quadriplegic who lives on the Navajo Reservation in a lonely rural area, where everything is all scarce and it seems like he has distanced himself from the whole society. Where even going to get a cold glass of water to quench his thirst seems like a mile hike. Even relatives live a long distance away. This area is so quiet and calm, he can do a lot of thinking about anything. Late in the afternoon all he sees is little dirt devils that swirl around, or sometimes a stray dog or two looking for scraps of food or coming by just to keep him company. They will be around to visit for a day or two, then they go away to someone else's house. Only toward the evening time does it seem routine and not like a dream, when family members come home from work late in the evening, and all they do is cook supper and talk with one another about what happened during the day. Around that time he is tired and wants to go to bed. Seems like during the daytime he is a watchdog looking over the property, not wanting to go to sleep. If the weather is cool enough, he wants to go in and out of the house constantly to see who is out wandering around.

Before this, or maybe he is remembering:

During the day, he lies in his hospital bed hopeless and motionless. He can't move or wiggle a limb on his body, of course, but at night he believes in his dreams that he's whole again, and is able to do anything without any obstacles to get in his way or barriers to hurdle. He can go anywhere and everywhere he ever desired. This is someone who owned a 554cc Honda 4-stroke midnight-blue sparkly motorcycle, which had a windjammer shield that protected him from the wind, rain and dirt. In the story, the motorcycle is a brand new beauty that he spends most of his time washing and polishing. Its chrome sparkles in the neon moonlight like a diamond in the desert, while he rides on his reservation where he grew up as a young Navajo boy. He rides down his reservation dirt road with all the lights turned on, looking like an unidentified moving object. There's always a gentle breeze toward the middle of the summer night, perfect conditions. The kind of silent night cruising anyone can imagine, nobody around to distract them.

But in the early morning dawn, he's back in his bed in the rehab hospital and everything is frozen once again and a day nurse who just came on duty comes to his room and wakes him to do his morning vital signs. Now he's wondering if his dream was really true, because he is thinking more about the outside than life in the rehab center. Thinking about his dream, wondering if he really was out and about riding his beautiful motorcycle.

His dreams are very vibrant, and as time passes this dream becomes even more intense. At first it's just a dream and he recognizes that it was from the night before, but suddenly one night he finds himself actually walking down the hospital ward. He is fully aware that he is walking down the walkway near the turtle pond and out the entrance of the hospital. His motorcycle awaits him. Magically, it is parked in the visitors' parking area not far away from the rehab hospital. He gets on his bike and goes cruising into the neon moonlight, not knowing which direction he is going, just following the traffic. The ride becomes so real to him that he doesn't want to come back to a populated area.

He wakes up in his bed at seven in the morning in shock that his dream was not real. He thinks only of this most of the day, not noticing if anyone comes close to him. He is lying there trying to concentrate, his hair is in his face and tangled into dreadlocks. The nurse comes in and says, "Oh, I'm very sorry. I didn't position your pillow last night. You were already sound asleep in your dream world. You slept with your hair in your face, it's all tangled up."

He says nothing, but he's thinking that his hair is tangled from the ride when he was out cruising the night before. One time he comes back still wearing his helmet and black leather bomber jacket, and he has to hide it in the hospital room closet because the nurses are going to wonder where it came from.

Now his mother and father, and younger brothers and sisters, have been very distressed all along. Since he became paralyzed, it is hard to approach him or communicate with him, he has not been able to pull out of a serious depression. He has shut them out of his life. His siblings are afraid of him because he is unable to move by himself and they don't know how to be with him and they don't know how to communicate with him, whether he can talk or not. His mother has been talking to the doctors and the case workers at the hospital about what to do, because he is apparently unable to cope or to come out of his shell. He has gotten so stubborn since he's been sent away from the reservation to be physically rehabilitated in a different environment, among a different population where Spanish and English are spoken. That is the reason why he does not want to come out of his depression. One of the doctors tells his mom, "Don't worry, he will be alright again. It will take some time. He is severely injured. That is why he is wearing the body brace and the halo around his neck to keep his neck stable."

But as he continues to go riding in his dream world, and these dreams become more and more genuine, his stubborn mood begins to dissolve and he seems less withdrawn. In the mornings he is more pleased and much more communicative. His mother and father notice the change, but they can't understand it, and he won't explain it. It's not something that he can talk about in detail because he doesn't know if he will walk again. He thinks he may be losing his mind. But since the family is feeling the benefit of his improvement, his dreams are making their life together more comfortable and content. Now he is communicating with others and getting out of his room for a short period of time. He loves to go outside to smell the fresh air and look all around the hospital.

To his mind, he is ready to leave rehab. But his doctor says he can't leave the hospital till he is well enough. After that little talk with his doctor he does not want to talk to anyone, it has set him two steps back. Depression shadows him again.

He rides his bike in the Tohatchi area near his high school or a similar spot there at Chuska Boarding School, and there's an older man at a little gas station related to him from his father's side, who works the graveyard shift, selling gas only to midnight, and has a little deli shop. He gives him a free sandwich of his choice whenever he fills up his tank. The man watches him from outside of the gas station as he rides away on old highway triple six. Sometimes he sits on his bike and the man asks him how fast his bike goes. He responds, "As fast as you want it to go." "And how economical is the bike on gas?" He says one tank can last him a week. He can tell from the yearning in his eyes that the motorcycle is something the man loves and admires, hoping he might purchase his own one day. Not that he's jealous, but he never misses a chance to see the motorcycle ride so beautifully and smoothly and quickly in the neon moonlight. Sparkling like a diamond in the desert.

Well, there comes a time when our protagonist realizes that these voyages offer a way of escaping from his paralyzed circumstance, that he could just ride and ride on happily—it's what he loves most in the world better than anything else—until one nightfall he would go out into the middle of the reservation where nothing existed or he doesn't know the surrounding area, doesn't know which way is east or west, and he wouldn't take supplies or anything. He would just ride until he ran out of gas and then would die happy. That was always on his mind when he would ride his motorcycle and not tell anyone where he was going. He would just go riding down the path of the neon moonlight, as far as he possibly could go, and leave everything and everyone behind him. Sometimes that's what he hopes to do someday in the real world.

And one night he starts to do that. He just decides he's going to go with no destination in mind, with no idea where. He is going to ride away forever and never come back, not telling nobody. But then, as he is heading out toward a town he doesn't know much about, he starts to think about what he has in his life in the real world, how grateful he is for his family. Because, during the days, you see, he's changed. His siblings are less afraid of him, and they're communicating with him. And his mom continues to comfort him with conversations about how their cattle and ranch are still in perfect harmony. He is coming out of his depression gradually. It's been hard because he is so far from the reservation for the first time in his young teenage life, for a long period of time.

So here he has been selfishly doing the thing that he loves most, only for himself. Thinking that he could ride on and forget about the world and everything and everyone. But along the way he begins to realize what precious things he is leaving behind. He immediately turns his bike around, goes straight back to his reservation hogan and parks his bike outside. And when his father comes out to greet him, he says, "Here, are the keys." He gives up the motorcycle, which he no longer needs. He wakes up in the hospital, and he's frozen and realizing he's paralyzed again. But he has an entirely new foundation to build upon. Now he sees the light at the end of the tunnel and begins looking for a healthier and quicker recovery, a restored future for his life.

At the time, it sounds simple. But to live it is another chapter.

1
WELCOME TO MY WORLD

In Gallup, New Mexico, one Indian Summer day in 1957, a young Navajo woman stepped gingerly from her father's truck and went off to her job as an attendant at the Shalimar Inn. Her father waved to her and drove off to have coffee and catch up on the news with his old friends.

The young woman began her work day, but it ended quickly when sharp pains gripped her back and abdomen. She slumped into a chair until the pains receded, then told her supervisor that she was going to the nearby St. Mary's Clinic, as she believed that she was going into labor. She walked the short distance to the clinic and asked to see a nurse. The nurse in charge, a nun like all the other nurses at the church-sponsored clinic, gave the woman a referral to see a doctor at the nearest hospital for Native Americans. This was the hospital run by the Bureau of Indian Affairs in Fort Defiance, Arizona.

A government van was leaving to transport other patients, so the young woman was told she must get in the van immediately. She hesitated for a moment, wishing that she could tell her father that she was leaving, but then climbed into the van with five other Navajo patients to begin the forty-five-mile journey.

On the long trip over rough, washboard dirt roads, she thought of her husband. He was working for the Santa Fe Railroad in

Chicago at that time, and would not be able to get home in time for the baby's birth. She thought of her two sons, Lawrence and Delbert, and was glad that her mother and father and younger sister Julia were there to take care of them. She worried about taking time off from her job, as she needed the income to supplement what her husband was able to send her each month.

When she finally arrived at the hospital, the physician who examined her saw the roundness of her belly and thought she might bear twins. For three long days, she labored to bring her child into the world. Finally, at the end of the third day, she delivered a nine-pound baby boy.

That young woman was my mother, Mary Bowman John, whose Navajo traditional clan is *Naakai dine'é* (Mexican clan), and born for *Kiyaa'áanii* (Towering House People). I was that baby boy who fought his way into a new and unknown world filled with amazing and terrifying wonders.

Since my mother had no time to notify her family before leaving for Gallup, her father was surprised to learn that she had gone to the hospital when he returned to the Shalimar Inn at lunchtime that day. He drove home immediately to tell my grandmother. After I was born, my grandmother came to the hospital to see my mother and me. She told my mother that my brothers were fine, and that they were all preparing for our return.

When I was about two weeks old, my mom and I were finally released from the hospital and brought back to our home in Twin Lakes in a government vehicle. My family welcomed us: my grandmother, Asdzáá Ichii (Red Woman) Bowman, whose clan was *Naakai dine'é* (Mexican clan), and born for *Táchii'nii* (Red Running into the Water People); my grandfather, Sam Bowman, who was from the *Kiyaa'áanii* clan (Towering House People) and born for *Tódich'ii'nii* (Bitter Water People); my Aunt Julia, who lived with my grandparents; and my brothers, Lawrence and Delbert.

Soon, my family began preparations for my Naming Ceremony.

A shade house was built next to the main house by my grandfather and some of the other men in the community to accommodate the large crowd of people who would attend the ceremony. The frame for this structure was made from cedar logs, the walls and ceiling made from cedar branches. My grandmother invited the people of our clan, *Naakaii dine'é*, and some of her relatives who were born for *Tábaahá* (Water's Edge People) and their acquaintances, to participate in this traditional Navajo ceremony.

The clan system is one of the most important aspects of Navajo life. The clan into which a child is born establishes his or her identity. The child inherits his clan identity from his mother, and is born into her clan. When a Navajo introduces himself to another person in his tribe, he not only states his name, but he identifies his mother's clan, his father's clan, and where his people originated on the reservation. The mother's clan always comes first, and the father's clan second. Adherence to the principles of the clan system prohibits marrying or having a relationship with anyone from one's mother's or father's clans because they are all relatives.

The purpose of the Naming Ceremony is to give a child a harmonious beginning of life so that Mother Earth, Heavenly Father, and the Holy People will know that this individual exists on Mother Earth among the surrounding species. An infant boy's Navajo name must always be associated with a warrior name, as before my time the Navajos and other Indian tribes were always on the warpath against the Spaniards. For this reason, my grandmother, as the eldest woman in my maternal clan, gave me my name, Hashke' Yitaaswod, which means "He Ran Amongst the Warriors." Infant girls are given names beginning with "Bah," which means "to have a warm place," like a hogan. The first laugh of a Navajo baby is the most celebrated event, as it is the first sign of a harmonious and fruitful life.

The people who participated in the ceremony came to bless my birth, as they had blessed my brothers before me. Everyone who attends a Naming Ceremony receives a gift from the infant so that, in the future, the child will learn to share and not be selfish. If there is no other gift to be given, then natural salt rock is given to those present. In return, some of the people who attend the ceremony bring gifts for the child to show gratitude for a new life.

Very early on the morning of the Naming Ceremony, the men slay a lamb before the sun rises. The women prepare a feast. The newborn is blessed, and a pinch of corn pollen is placed on the tip of the infant's tongue to signify a new life being brought into the world.

In addition to my Navajo name, I was also given an Anglo name. A nurse at the hospital where I was born suggested the name of Wilbert Bruce John for me, and my mom agreed, because she had gone to school with several boys named Wilbert at Ft. Wingate Boarding School. When I was about two years old, my Aunt Caroline decided that I should be called Gilbert, after a medicine man from Steamboat Canyon, Arizona. She had worked with him at a jewelry store for many years and liked him. So from that time, I was called Gilbert by everyone except my grandpa. He called me Gibben, because he found it easier to pronounce.

2
HOME

Our home was forty-five miles from Fort Defiance, in a rural area we call *Bááhaztl'ah* west of Twin Lakes, New Mexico, below Cove Mountain. This area is located twenty-five miles north of Gallup, New Mexico, on the Navajo Reservation, the largest Indian reservation in the United States. The Navajo Reservation encompasses land in four southwestern states: Utah, Colorado, New Mexico, and Arizona. In ancient myth, the Navajo homeland is guarded and bounded by four Sacred Mountains, which also represent the four cardinal directions: East, South, West and North.

In the East lies Mount Blanca, which was given the Navajo name *Sisnaajini*, meaning, Dawn, or White Shell Mountain. Mount Blanca lies to the east of Alamosa, in the San Luis Valley of Colorado. In the south lies *Tsoodzil*, whose English translation is Blue Bead, or Turquoise Mountain. This sacred mountain lies in the area north of Laguna, New Mexico. San Paco Peak is the Sacred Mountain of the West. Its Navajo name is *Dook'o'oosliid*, which means Abalone Shell Mountain, and it is located near Flagstaff, Arizona. To the North is Mount Hesperus, which is a part of the La Plata Mountains of Colorado. Its Navajo name is *Dibé Ntsaa*, or Big Sheep.

My grandma and grandpa had two camps which they combined when they got married, a summer camp and a winter camp. During the summer, they would drive all the animals up the hills into the mountains to graze on fresh grass, sagebrush, cedar, pine trees and other plants that grew in the area. These natural herbs made them physically strong for the upcoming hard winter. There were a lot of rabbits and prairie dogs in the region. There was plenty of water for the flocks, collected from rain and melted snow from the previous winter.

Herding sheep and looking out for predators that might attack the flock was hard work, but at times it could be fun. The entire mountainside appeared to be covered in snow when the whole herd was there, because my grandparents owned over a thousand sheep and goats. Each year the animals would multiply as many newborns arrived in the spring. The summer camp was on top of the mountain, far from any other houses. The winter camp was in the valley below Cove Mountain. After our family moved back down to the winter camp, my grandfather constantly rode back on horseback to check on the hogan in the summer camp.

As was typical, our family lived without electricity, central heating, or indoor plumbing. Our home was a traditional Navajo dwelling: a medium-sized hogan, octagonal in shape. The frame was built with cedar logs, and adobe mud mixed with straw was used to fill the cracks. Cedar logs covered with adobe mud made up the ceiling. There was a hole in the center of the hogan to provide ventilation and an outlet for the smoke from the wood fires used for cooking and heating. The floor was earthen, which helped to prevent fires from the ashes and cinders that escaped. In keeping with Navajo tradition, the entrance faced the East to welcome the new day as the sun rose above the horizon.

Kerosene oil purchased from the local trading post was poured into glass lamps to provide light at night. Beds were thick sheepskin hides placed directly on the dirt floor. They were comfortable and warm on the coldest of nights. During the day, they were taken outside to hang over wooden posts so that they could air out. My mother and grandmother wove warm blankets from wool that was sheared from our sheep. They carded and spun the wool and wove the blankets for everyone during the summer months. My mother sometimes sold her blankets to the local trader for groceries and other necessary goods. In addition to the rugs and blankets, my mother used an antique foot-pedal Singer sewing machine to make quilts for winter warmth.

I grew up with a very loving extended family. My father, Joe John, *Haltsooi dine'é* (Meadow People), born for *Tódich'ii'nii* (Bitter Water People) came from the Coyote Canyon coal mine area. He was very concerned about providing for us, and therefore he was not at home very often. He worked for the Santa Fe Railroad in different regions across the country.

My aunts and uncles did not live with my grandparents because they were always away at school, at work, or serving in some branch of the military. Opportunities were scarce on the reservation. Children were forced to go away to Bureau of Indian Affairs boarding schools as soon as they reached school age. When they became adolescents, most were either drafted into military service or they stayed at home to help their families.

Some people we knew journeyed to different parts of the country to experience a different lifestyle. They took jobs as migrant workers or caregivers, or whatever they could find. Some people never returned because they grew accustomed to the urban way of life or they just did not want to return to their native culture and the hard life on the reservation. They became acculturated to the *bilagáana* (Anglo) society. Some did come back to visit, but the visits became less and less frequent, until the family and the old way of life became only a memory or a fleeting thought. Some families grew apart because the members moved to different communities and became ashamed of where they came from and how they grew up.

Most families on the reservation did not have running water, electricity, or decent roads to travel. Most homes had outhouses for bathrooms and kerosene lamps for light at night. Many families had to wash their clothes by hand in large tubs using a washboard and brush, and sweat lodges and sponge baths were the only means of cleansing their bodies. It may have seemed like a hard life, but this life was good for our family. We had grown used to this cycle of living on the reservation with little outside interference.

From time to time, we traveled with my dad to many different towns in California where he was working on the railroad. We usually traveled by train because my dad could get free family passes for us. Although my dad asked us to go back to California with him every time he came to New Mexico on leave, my grandparents never wanted us to go. One time we went to Needles, California for a month, and when we returned my grandparents told us they missed our little voices and our helping them with the chores.

When my dad was gone, my mom had to drive our old white Chevrolet truck over two miles of dirt roads to the highway in order to get her errands done. My dad always took care of maintenance on the truck when he came home so that it would be in good running condition for her. He worked on it almost every day when he was at home, and he always got new tires and chains for the winter months so that we wouldn't get stuck in the mud and snow. He instructed my older brothers on how to put chains on the tires if we needed them. It snowed a lot in the winters back then, and the old truck would move through the snow like a plow!

When the snow was deep, the animals would stay in the corral. My dad and grandpa would shovel the snow around the corral so that the animals could move around, and we fed them hay that my dad bought in bales up at the Chapter house near our home. The winter chores were difficult, and when I was young, I seemed to get in the way when I tried to help.

When the adults scolded me, I went outside to play in the snow with my dogs. My dogs and I loved to dive into piles of snow, though sometimes we scared the sheep and goats as they nibbled on their hay. I had fun roaming in the hills with the dogs. They would run after anything that moved, especially cottontail rabbits. I would try to help the dogs catch the rabbit, looking in every burrow and bush, but I didn't have the patience to keep looking so I would just let it go. The dogs' names were Blackie, Bullet, and Chubby. Any time we came back home from a trip to do errands, they were always happy to see us, jumping around and playing with each other, but two of them would always get into a fight because one would get more attention.

Some things I only remember from the stories my family told about me. My grandparents told me that I couldn't walk until I was fourteen months old because I was so chubby. When I started walking, there was no stopping me, and no turning back. I was mischievous and got into everything that I shouldn't. I wanted to be outside all the time so that I could play and eat the dirt, especially when it rained and the earth smelled so good!

Water from the rain and the melting winter snow backed up in the earthen dam near the house. I got soggy from going to the water and collecting tadpoles and frogs in a bucket which I took to my mom. My mom would say, "You're not supposed to bother those creatures! Take them back!" In the process of returning them to the water, I got muddier and soggier than before. One time, on my way home from the dam, I crawled into the chicken coop and began chasing the chickens. When the rooster began to run after me, I ran out of the cage. Then I opened the hatch of the rabbit pen and crawled inside to get out of the hot sun, and I fell asleep. Soon, my mom saw rabbits hopping around the yard, and she began calling my name. Her voice woke me from my nap, and I helped her to catch most of the rabbits and return them to the pen.

We also had turkeys on our land. When I tried to get near them, they would begin to gobble to warn the other turkeys of an intruder, and then they would all chase after me as a group. I ran as fast as I could, screaming at the top of my lungs when they began to attack me. The dogs barked at them and scared them away from me.

My brother had a big black and white pig that scared me. It ran after me and pushed me down with its snout as though I were something for it to eat. This pig was always hungry, as she had five little piglets to nurse. I tried to stay out of her way!

The best part of my young life was when I was not going to school. I loved to run to the top of the hills near my home to see everything for miles around. I played with rocks and stones, and once tried to build a house for myself. I never succeeded in constructing my own home, but I had a vision of the house I wanted to build: it would be the biggest and sturdiest house ever, and I would be the most famous rancher and livestock owner on the Navajo Reservation, like my grandfather. I planned to invite my cousins over for dinner, and there would be plenty of room for all of us. But I got tired of moving rocks and fell asleep near the dream home that I was building. In the end, it was a very small house—too small for my dog and me to get inside—but I had a great adventure. When I woke from my nap that day at my dream house, I saw a lizard-like creature beside me. I jumped up and looked again, and realized that it was my "grandpa," the horned toad. My grandma always told us about the Navajo traditional belief that the horned toads are our grandfathers.

My two older brothers helped my grandpa with his horses, so they were allowed to ride with him. There were three riding horses: one was white, one was brown, and the other one was a sorrel. My brothers went out to get the horses in the morning, but they sometimes had trouble mounting, so they led the horses beside a big rock, climbed on top of the rock, then jumped on the horses. When they brought the horses back to the corral, the horses were sweaty and breathing hard. My grandfather told them not to ride the horses so hard, but they loved to race as soon as they got out of sight, often arguing about who had won the race. Although they were hidden from view, we could hear the thunder of the horses' hooves and knew that they were racing again. I wished that I could ride with them, but I suppose that I was too small at that time.

When I was five years old, I was anxious to get into school and start kindergarten. I didn't have the slightest idea of what school was about, but I knew all about country life. I know I was only five because my birthday is in the middle of September. School started at the end of August and I had to wait until I was almost six to be eligible for first grade. It turned out that I was very happy about being at home the year that I was five! I had a lot more leisure time and lots of fun running after the sheep and the chickens.

One of my older brothers told me that I would have more fun at school because I would meet other kids from different areas. He would bring homework from school and show me what I would be learning when I got to school. I didn't fully understand the things he showed me, and I asked him many questions about it, but at that young age, it was too confusing to me, so I just made paper airplanes and experimented with flight paths outside, or I offered the papers to my grandmother as starter for the fire instead of kerosene. I was just too curious about all that was around me, trying to chase everything that moved, doing things I shouldn't have been doing, throwing rocks at innocent birds, running through the hills and cornfields and tearing things apart like a madman!

Today, as a grown man, I chuckle as I think of those days. I know that my mom laughs about these things, too. Sometimes she reminds me of the things I did when I was a boy, and she tells me the stories that were told about me. She probably thought I was a headache then because of all the things I did, especially those that were dangerous. It was hard for her to keep up with me and my younger brothers and sisters, and sometimes I'm sure she felt like giving up on me.

Aunt Julia is my mom's youngest sister. She lived with her mom, my grandma, right next door to us. She was single and had no children of her own, so she treated us like we were her own kids. But sometimes she had an attitude and did not want to be bothered by the noise made by energetic little kids because she liked sleeping late.

She had a pet goat named Tl'ízí (meaning "pet goat" or "kid") and she taught that little goat very well, just like a circus animal. She raised the goat from a newborn because the mother goat would not take the kid as her own. My aunt fed the kid milk through a regular-size baby bottle. The goat was housebroken, and she learned how to take a nap beside Aunt Julia. It followed her everywhere she went.

When my aunt would say, "Shake hands and say Yá'át'ééh " the little kid goat would lift her right front leg and baa. She taught the goat several different commands. For instance, she would say "Tl'ízí, go jump on the bed," and she would jump on the bed; "Tl'ízí, go outside," and she would go outside. This is how my aunt taught the little goat. I remember some years later Tl'ízí had three playful kids. Before my aunt departed for the boarding school in Utah, I didn't have any idea as to where Tl'ízí had gone or what my aunt had done with that animal. However, later on my mom informed me that Tl'ízí was attacked and killed by a bobcat while she was on one of her ventures to the top of the mountain.

My Aunt Julia went away to Intermountain Indian School in Utah. Her father signed her up to go there because he wanted her to get the best education possible. Some years later she graduated from high school and came back to visit the family a few times more. Then she enrolled in the Air Force Academy and moved to Colorado Springs. While she was there at school she met an Anglo guy who was studying to be a law enforcement officer. They were together at the academy and they both graduated the same year. She followed him back to Philadelphia and married him. My aunt never introduced him to the whole family, not even to her own mother. When she graduated from the academy, where she studied to be a registered nurse, she came back home by herself to the reservation to visit. This was the last time I saw her.

Before her return trip to Philadelphia, she quietly and gently pulled me aside and bent down to whisper in my ear. She asked me, "Do you want to go back home to Philadelphia with me?" In retrospect, I believe she asked because she knew that there were too many children around for my mother to handle and she was like a big sister to me. At that time I was only eight years old so I did not say anything, because I did not know what was going on or even where Philadelphia was. In addition, there were still many chores that needed to be attended to at my grandparents' residence, and my grandmother asked me not to go too far. She believed that going outside the borders of the Four Sacred Mountains would place me in danger and I would not be protected according to Navajo tradition.

3

GRANDMA AND GRANDPA

My grandmother's name was Marian Bowman. Her clan was *Naakai dine'é* and born for *Táchii'nii*. She was born and raised in the Rock Springs area (*Tse Chi' izhi*) near Gallup, where a large area of land was assigned to her when she was a little girl. When she grew older, she assigned that land to her youngest son. In this region, there were cedar trees, sagebrush, rabbit brush, and sandstone rock. Her family made winter camp in the *Naakai dine'é* community area, west of Twin Lakes in the foothills of Cove Mountain, so that their flocks could graze on fresh grasses. My grandmother said that her father had many wild horses, and that she had helped to tame them. My grandmother was a petite woman with light brown hair and a radiant complexion that made her look Anglo or Hispanic. Because of her complexion, her Navajo name was Asdzáá Ichii, or Red Woman.

My grandma constantly talked to us and taught us about the Navajo rituals that she performed as a little girl and continued throughout her life. Before the rising of the sun, she would wake to sprinkle white cornmeal to feed the Holy People and ask them to bless us with a harmonious day. As she went about her daily chores, she was always mindful of the goodness of the balance in all that surrounded her. In the afternoon, she again took time to sprinkle yellow corn pollen to thank Mother Earth and the Great Creator for providing us with life and the Earth's abundant nourishment. At dusk, right before the sun was setting in the West, she would sprinkle yellow cornmeal to show thanks for a day filled with honest hard work, goodness in balance, and a healthy, respectful life. This daily tradition, which had been passed on to her by her mother and grandmother, was handed down to future generations as part of the cycle of life. She always let us know that the continuation of the traditions was important. Sometimes she would literally "knock some sense into our heads" with the cane she used to help her walk and to stir the ashes in the cooking fire. It was her utmost desire that we would remember her teachings and keep the Navajo traditions.

She told us every living thing on this earth and the stars had been created by the Almighty. Also, all living things are sacred and that there are gods in trees, flowers, the earth, water and sky. Everything in this world was created by the Great Creator. They are put on this earth for a good reason, don't hurt them or mistreat them.

My grandma did not like electricity or running water in her house despite how difficult it was in the winter or summer, because of how expensive the bills were, just like today. The only thing that she really admired was her land because it sustained her sheep and goats. I used to love to ride my horse way up in the hills where I could look down in the valley and see a number of my grandma's sheep grazing. She had lots of sheep, the last I counted when I was able there were around eight hundred. Today I could only imagine taking care of that many heads of sheep. It was too much when I was younger.

My grandma had her share of chores. She fixed breakfast for us every morning, then, before sunrise, she drove her large flock of sheep and goats near the top of Cove Mountain where they grazed on fresh grass and trees. My grandma kept a watchful eye on the animals, and with the help of her dogs kept the coyotes and the vultures away from them. My grandmother made sure that no sheep was lost or left behind. She loved her flock, and I believe they loved her in return. She told us that owning her flock was her most important role in life—her prayer and her song. She believed that they were the reason she was placed on this earth. Her flock gave her life harmony by providing food, clothing and goods for trade. The wool that was sheared from her sheep with the help of her grandchildren was sometimes given to relatives who carded and spun the wool into yarn for her.

When my grandmother married my grandfather, she started working with cattle, helping him drive them to the Inter-Tribal Indian Ceremonial in Gallup. She and my grandpa and their sons, Dan and Dale, drove an old red and green pickup truck filled with camping gear. My grandpa was one of the well-known stock contractors for the rodeo at the Inter-Tribal Ceremonial in the 1930s and 1940s. My grandma loved and admired all her flocks and they were always around her. She would love the sound of the sheep and goats which brought her comfort along with the cows and the horses. Nothing could make her happy enough except to hear the noises of her livestock.

My grandparents had six children: three boys and three girls. My mother had a close bond with her parents, and we lived with or near them during most of my childhood. My younger brothers, Hilbert and Terry, sometimes sneaked out of my mom's house in the middle of the night to go to my grandmother's house. They took turns crawling through my grandma's window to enjoy the comfort of her home. My grandma took care of them from the time they were about ten or twelve years old.

Hilbert, who was older than Terry, followed my grandma wherever she went, even when she herded her flock to the mountains in the summertime. In the winter it was hard for him to go with her because it was so cold, so my mom kept him at home with her. Sometimes he would sneak out of the house to find my grandma, and my older brothers and I would search the hills for him.

After I started walking and knowing about things, asking a lot of questions, my grandma always used to gather us boys in her hogan around the light of the open fire and tell us about the beliefs of the traditional ways she was brought up, the Great Creator and the mythology of how the world was made. She would sing short songs but not all of it. She always told us, "I do not know where the bible came from, but in my day there was no bible, just the teaching of our traditional ways of our culture." As we grew older and curious of more things we asked our grandma many more questions about our culture, such as who is Changing Woman and where does she live. Grandma would not tell us who Changing Woman is, where she resides and what her name is. She'd go on with what she was doing for a little while and go to bed, while us boys were still eager to hear more from her about our traditional ways. If we asked her more questions, she would tell us to ask our grandpa and that he knew more about it and had more patience for the details of his story.

My grandpa was Sam Bowman. He was born and raised in the Bread Springs (*Bááháálí*) area, about twenty-five miles south of Gallup, New Mexico. His clan was *Kin Ya'áanii* and born for *Tódich'ii'nii*.

My grandpa was the only man around the house for most of my early years, since my father was away working on the railroad and my uncles lived far away at that time. Although he was only about five feet, five inches tall, he did heavy farm work by himself until my brothers and I got big enough to help him. His daily tasks included caring for his horses, cattle, and cornfield. He taught us responsibility and the value of hard work. Because we were able to produce more than we needed to sustain our family, he gave food to local men who helped him with chores like hauling wood, plowing, and cattle branding. Our family was more fortunate than some: we had sheep, goats, cattle, chickens, pigs, rabbits, and vegetables grown in the fields.

Early every morning, before sunrise, my grandfather would drive his wagon to get water for our family. We had to compete with other families who also needed water for their families and livestock. Sometimes he even camped out near the water well. I remember watching him haul water in fifty-five gallon wooden barrels every day. The well was located on a hillside across a large arroyo from where we lived, and my grandfather was diligent about getting our water before the well went dry.

My grandfather was married to another woman before he married my grandmother. They lived between the north side of Coyote Canyon (*Ma"ii teehitlizhi*) and Naschitti (*Nahashch'idi*) for a number of years, where they had four or five children. One day, he found out that she was living with a long-term illness that he had not known about because he was away tending to his cattle so much of the time. By the time he knew about her illness, she was too weak for a healing ceremony or to travel the fifty miles to the nearest hospital, and she passed away. After her passing, he took control of raising their children, with the help of relatives who cared for them when he had to tend his herds.

A few years later, my grandfather met my grandmother at a Squaw Dance near where she lived. She was twenty years younger than my grandpa.

My grandfather was like a second father to me because my real father was not around all the time. He taught me many things when I was young: how to saddle and ride a horse, what kind of horses were good for ranching and open range riding, and how to care for livestock. When I was small, I traveled on horseback to check on his horses where they grazed in the area around Tohatchi, Coyote Canyon, and Naschitti. He drew a picture in the sand to show me what his brand looked like, and when his eyes grew weaker, I could spot his livestock for him. There were cattle rustlers who would steal the calves that had not been branded and sell them to unsuspecting traders and individual buyers in Gallup and Grants. He told me one day that I would be the one who would take over his herd when I got older.

My grandpa lived on top of the mountain, the place he admired the most even though there was no running water or electricity. I guess what he liked was the small kerosene lamp and the heat from the wood stove. My brothers and I helped my grandma and grandpa; we'd chop wood, haul water and do other chores that were required. My dad and my brothers hauled wood for our grandpa so he'd be warm during the wintertime, and they would occasionally visit him to see if he needed anything.

For me and my brothers, Grandpa was a source of valuable information about our traditions. The visit to our grandpa way up in the mountains wasn't too far for us, because he would be happy to see us. We would catch him on the days that he was not doing anything to try to get the explanation about the creation of the world. Sometimes he would just get after us and ask why we wanted to know so much. He'd tell us, "Go back to your grandma and ask her. She knows more. She is full of stories that you boys want to know! Her dad was a medicine man."

The fact is, my grandma and grandpa didn't live together, so it was best to catch my grandpa in a good mood on a nice day. Maybe do a little chore for him here and there. We'd catch him off guard sometimes. He'd pull out a chair and start telling us how the world was created. He told us first that most of the traditional Navajo stories were only told in the winter time. He never gave us a reason. Some of the stories were spooky, so we boys would gather around him in a circle. He would talk to us gently. He sometimes lulled my little brother almost to sleep. When he saw this, he would raise his voice and say, "I can't tell you boys to listen to all of my stories while you are going to sleep, you have your own mom and dad to tell you that."

I would tell him, "No, grandpa, we like to hear from you because you are a patient man and older than our parents, and our parents are always on the go." He would tell us more on our next visit. He said, "For me to tell you these stories it will take me many days and nights. Some of the stories I will tell you involve songs, that's why it takes a long time. It would be best for me to tell you when you guys get a little older because this requires going into a sweat lodge. And like I told you, this will take some days and nights. I will tell you most of it when you are with your dad because some of the stories are hard to explain." I would tell him, "Why don't you tell us the easy part, the one we will remember throughout our lives?" He told us that he can't tell us any easy part because the story contains a lot of teachings and traditional ways.

We would bug our grandpa to tell us the story about the twin brothers who went to see their father, because when these two young individuals tried to ask their mom who their father was she wouldn't give them a straight answer. Finally grandpa gave in after he got tired of us bugging him all the time. My grandfather said, "I will tell you a little, not too much, because this is a very traditional, sacred and valuable story." He told us to listen and make sure we understood what he was telling us because this wasn't a joke or a fairytale story. We had to have a lot of patience to sit around and listen, it was going to take a long time, maybe a sleep-over at grandpa's.

My grandpa started talking about the twin brothers. The brothers often asked the mother, "Who is our father?" The mother always ignored the question and started to do something else. At last, the two young men set out to learn the answer to their question. They took a holy trail and journeyed on the sunbeams. It was the Wind that guided them, whispering his counsel in their ears. Their father was Johano-ai, the Sun-God. His beautiful house was in the East. It was made of turquoise and stood on the shore of Great Waters. There the Sun lived with his wife, White-Shell-Woman, his daughters, and his sons, the Black Thunder and the Blue Thunder.

Until the coming of the strange twin brothers, the wife had not known that her husband had visited goddesses on the earth. Nor would Johano-ai believe that the two gods were his sons until he had proved their powers by making them go through all kinds of trials. The young men came through each test unharmed. Then the Sun rejoiced that these two handsome youths were indeed his children, and he promised to give them what they asked. They said immediately, "We need weapons with which to slay the Anaye monsters." So their father, the Sun, gave them helmets, shirts, leggings, and moccasins, all made of black flint, for the power of flint came from Morning Star. When the young men put on this armor, the four lightnings flashed from their different joints. For weapons, the Sun gave each a mighty knife of stone and also arrows of rainbow, of sunbeam, and of lightning. So after they returned home, the brother-cousins slew the Anaye. After every victory, their mother rejoiced with them. In Navajo mythology the Anaye are demons, and some are still with us: Old Age, Poverty, Cold, and Famine.

This story was only supposed to be told in the winter time. Late November is close enough. That day when Grandpa was telling us the story, I don't know where the afternoon went. When he finished with part of the story it was almost dark and he told us, "You boys better go back home before your grandma comes looking for her flock. I don't want to get involved with her about it. Make sure you count every sheep and goat and take them home." Before we left we told him we would be back so he could tell us more. He told us that this is just a little part of the long story. He walked away scratching his head. I could tell by his uneasy posture as he went to feed his horse that he was unsure if he should go on with the long story.

During his older years my Grandpa's hair started thinning out on the top of his head, and he covered his head with a wig. The only time he took the wig off was when he was sure that nobody was around. At times my brothers and I would sneak up on him on a hot day when he was bathing outside in front of his house. We wouldn't let him see us, but he knew that we were close by, because our dogs would wander close to him. He would always yell at us, "Where are you foolish boys? Don't hide from me! I know that you are around here, my grandsons." But we would laugh and hide and not let him see us.

One clear spring day, right after breakfast, my Grandpa told me to get some wood and start a fire in front of his house, and then to get a large bucket, fill it with water, and set the bucket on the fire. When the water started to boil, my Grandpa brought out a piece of buckskin hide from a deer that he had hunted, killed and skinned the previous winter. Then he gave me the piece of old, dry, hard, stinky deer hide to put in the boiling water.

This dry, stinky deer hide meant nothing to me. It looked useless. Then my Grandpa took a long wooden stick and forced the hide deep into the boiling water. He instructed me to keep the logs burning under the water bucket at all times, so that the water would stay boiling at a high temperature. He boiled the skin for at least half a day. When my Grandpa decided that the skin was ready, he removed it from the bucket of boiling water and began to loosen and stretch the hide. He applied a combination of deer brains and water to the hide to help remove all the hair and excess flesh. He then picked and scraped the rest of the flesh and fat from the hide with his sharp buck knife.

To dry the skin, he carefully spread it out in the sun on a large pine log. He wanted the skin to dry for a few days, and he asked me to keep a watchful eye on it. My Grandpa said that he was going to tan the buckskin. He told me that it would take a lot of time and work, and he needed my help to gather up different herbs and tools to tan the hide. Tanning would soften the buckskin and eventually it would feel like a velveteen material.

Finally, the tanning was completed and the buckskin was ready.

What I didn't know was that this buckskin had been prepared so that my Grandpa could make himself a new wig! He had taken the hair from the mane of one of his favorite horses and carefully thought about how to sew the horsehair on the buckskin so that it would stay attached to the skin. He never sewed the wig in front of me, but once it was completed, I knew that I had participated in the process of making my Grandpa a new wig. To hold it in place on top of his head, he used a rubber band or a thin slice of an inner tube from a tire. Over his wig he wore a cap that resembled an Eskimo hat with earflaps that he always tied under his chin. He wore this hat year-round and never took it off, not even to wash the obvious sweat stains from it.

Rain or shine, hot or cold, Grandpa would be on his horse, and I would be on the lookout for him along the trails he'd ride on his way to watch his cattle. I loved riding along with him. When I was not doing anything at home, or sometimes when I was supposed to be doing something and wanted to get away from all the work that had to be done, I would sneak off before my older brothers could boss me around and dump the chores on me. I would take every chance I could get to ride or work with my grandpa. When I saw him I would catch up to him on horseback. He would average about twenty to twenty-five miles a day, riding his horse and checking on his livestock. I asked him why he had to ride so far instead of making a big corral and gathering them up and taking them back to where he lived. He said that with the land and the environment around here it made sense to let them graze and eat for free instead of investing in bales of hay. I told him that we could help him build a big corral on top of the hill so he wouldn't have to ride so far. I also told him he was getting too old to go down and check on his cattle. That was the most negative thing I have ever said to him. Without thinking about anything he got mad and told me that it was none of my business and that his cattle were used to grazing. After that I didn't mention his cattle to him anymore. I just helped him out a lot of times. As his body was aging so was his eyesight, which made him rely on me, which made me feel good that I was looked at as a grown man in a young body. I could recognize his brand and how his cattle ears where marked. I used to love helping him with his herd.

4

BOARDING SCHOOL ADVENTURES

This is a daydream-like vision way down in the Southwest, on the largest Indian reservation, where only the dirt devils and tumbleweeds roam. A young Navajo boy sits on a sandstone rock, looking at the horizon and the land he loves. Nobody can empathize with his thoughts and feelings, or understand why he holds a cedar twig in his hand. He might think of going away to school, or just living another day. He has been taught that there is always a Great Creator looking over him. A new adventure begins. This young Navajo child goes forward to take a step on a ladder, but he doesn't know where it may lead him. This is a white man's concept—to educate the Indians, to take away their language and the culture that they value, thinking that it is "for their own good."

My older brothers Delbert and Lawrence went to school at Twin Lakes Boarding School. It was built of cinderblocks, and was situated about two miles away from my grandma's home. The kids who lived in the dorm at the school were lucky in that they didn't have to worry about getting up so early to get to school. Even if you overslept, you could still get to school on time.

One year later, both of my brothers were transferred to Coyote Canyon Boarding School because they didn't register for classes until the school year had already started. I was very eager to go with my mom to pick them up for the weekend, but sometimes she would go without me because I was helping my grandma tend her flocks. She would go to the school and check them out so that they could come home and help with chores for a couple of days.

I always looked forward to riding in the back of the old white Chevy truck when my mom took me with her to pick up my brothers, especially on a dirt road, where we went over a dirt clump or a little hill and I bounced like a basketball. I liked looking at the trail of dust we left behind as we traveled on the dirt roads. A person could see a trail of dust in the air all the way down from my grandma's house to the main highway. As my mom drove faster and faster, the dust would rise and grow like a mushroom in the sky. I could feel the cool breeze and fresh air as it blew my hair back. Looking back at the trail of dust, sometimes I saw the dogs following us. I would yell at the top of my lungs, commanding them to go back home and take care of the house. They didn't follow us too far, maybe several hundred yards or so, then they would tire out and go back home. Sometimes my grandma would go with us, getting out at the store to visit her friends and relatives and coming home later. When we got to the school I would hide my face under the front seat. Even if the rest of my body was showing, I assumed that the attendants couldn't see me if my face was hidden. I hid because I didn't want to go near the school building!

On Sunday evenings, just when they had gotten used to being at home again, my brothers had to go back to school. I missed them when they were gone, even though we got into brotherly fights over insignificant things like toys and who should go first at anything.

I liked being at home when my brothers were at school because I could sleep late and be alone with my grandparents, getting all the attention that my older brothers stole when they were around. I had a couple of younger brothers and sisters, too, so being one of the oldest, I had no choice but to help around the house and give a helpful hand in caring for my siblings. At a young age, I learned about the concepts of responsibility and endurance through hard days of work. The chores I did around the house were bringing in armloads of firewood for warmth and buckets of fresh water from the barrels outside that we used for drinking and cooking. It was a lot of work for me as a little boy because my father was away, but I got things done, even though it may have taken me a while to finish each task.

The year that I was five passed in the wink of an eye, and it was already time to go to school. I was finally six years old, the magic age to begin school in September. I was looking forward to school because of all the stories I had heard from my brothers. I was excited to think that I would have a head start by understanding the letters and drawings my brothers had shown me from their homework. The day came for open enrollment, and my mom registered me at Twin Lakes Boarding School. That same evening, I was packed and ready to be dropped off at the dormitory.

The next day, excitement mixed with a little nervousness and curiosity coursed through my body as I explored the many huge rooms that looked like caverns. The dining room was the biggest of all. I saw that the classrooms were located at the front of the building and the dorm rooms were in the back. The dorm rooms held about eighteen bunk beds, and I realized that the student body was not going to be very big. The population of the students accepted from around the Twin Lakes area was about sixty boys and girls. I was very grateful and excited that my cousin Regina, daughter of my Aunt Caroline—the eldest of my six aunts and uncles—had convinced me to go to school.

Soon, though, I didn't like all the rules and regulations that were a part of boarding school life. We had to be inside the building before the sun went down at night, and seating was arranged boy-girl-boy-girl in the dining room and in the classroom. It seemed to me that I had no choices at all. Several times, I tried to crawl over the fence and run away to my home where I had more freedom, but before I could get over the fence, an attendant grabbed me with a vise-like grip and dragged me back to the dorm. I really fought with the dormitory attendants when they caught me trying to run away, waking the other students with my screaming, dragging my feet, and pelting the attendants with lightning fists.

Because of my attempted escapes, we were all punished by having to stand at attention in a single line for about an hour. This only made me more determined to run away. I would refuse to eat for about two days until I got too hungry to keep it up. By the time I got accustomed to staying in the dormitory, it would be time for me to go home for the weekend. I wished that I could be with my brothers at Coyote Canyon.

I tried to get my cousin Regina to run away with me, but she refused with a flat "No!" She was scared that the authorities would come to pick us up and tow us away to an orphanage. Plus, her mom was very strict. I told her, "They don't know where you live." But after begging her many times, I finally gave up. So I stayed at school and took my anger out on some boys, wrestling and fighting with them. That is how I spent my free time and used my extra energy.

Almost every day, the dorm attendants would send some of us to a little room with a black and white TV. This was my first experience of seeing television shows. I was bug-eyed and enthralled by television! At first, I asked the other students about the shows and the characters, but I soon got to know them, and my favorite show was *The Lone Ranger*. Some of the students were always on the Lone Ranger's side just because he was dressed up like a cowboy. We loved seeing the Indians chase him and try to capture him, and the way he always cleverly escaped. The other students and I would be yelling and rooting for the Lone Ranger to get away. We all argued about which channel to watch because each student seemed to want to see a different channel. If I couldn't see *The Lone Ranger*, I went outside to play.

If I had not been so energetic and used to being outside, I probably would have fallen slave to the television. At my grandparents' house, we never had a television set because we had so much work to do—and because we had no electricity. Today, almost every household in our community has all the modern conveniences. It would be a major culture shock to time-travel from the days of my childhood to today's world. A child who is just beginning to crawl already knows what a television is, and probably has a favorite show. When kids come home from school the first thing they do is turn on the television, then sit on the couch with their snacks, forgetting all about their homework.

At school, we were given chores such as sweeping, dusting, mopping, and cleaning off the dining tables, even at a young age. We usually cut corners on our cleaning, sweeping dirt under the rugs and trash bins. We sometimes got caught, and our punishment would be to stay indoors while the other children played outside. We begged for permission to go out, but were denied except on the rare occasion when there was a kind-hearted attendant who took pity on us. I always rushed through my chores, eager to get outside with my classmates, even if only for a little while.

My mom routinely came to check me out for the weekend and take me home or drive over to Coyote Canyon to see if my brothers wanted to come home for the weekend also. The dormitory attendants always notified my mom that I had tried to run away. She would get after me and lecture me with her hands pointing directly at my face. My mom said, "This is for your own good, going to school every year, because the world is changing." So I made a choice, not that I really had a choice, to go to school whether I liked it or not. Sometimes, my brothers stayed at school on the weekends to attend school-related events. They had the privilege of escaping household chores, so I had to chop the wood, chase the sheep into the corral, and do the other necessary chores without them. I liked going home on the weekends, even though it was only for two days, and even if it meant that I had a lot of work.

A majority of the dorm attendants lived around the area, so they knew where the John boys lived. The head of the school would not let me walk home alone because I was the youngest and the smallest. But the "head honcho" at Coyote Canyon Boarding School would let my brothers walk home from the main highway when the weather was nice.

My first year at Twin Lakes Boarding School, I had an African-American schoolteacher named Mrs. Whiting who was an English language specialist. To me, she was an interesting and amazing individual. Never in my life had I seen anyone whose skin was as dark as charred wood. My dad was tall, but this lady was taller and leaner. She reminded me of the dark brown power line posts that lined the highways. She seemed fantastic and menacing at the same time. I wondered if she had the same functions and feelings that I did. I wondered if she ever laughed at something funny-looking or when someone told a joke, as I never heard her laugh out loud. I wondered if she ever cried when she hurt herself or when someone said something mean or degrading to her. I wondered if she got hungry, went to the potty, and if she could run as fast as I could. I would curiously inspect her every time she wasn't looking at me, trying to find signs of humanity.

She had short, curly black hair that looked like plastic or a wig. She had big white eyes like a wolf I had seen in the *Little Red Riding Hood* book. Looking at her eyes, I saw that she had the longest lashes I had ever seen, and they were curled upward. Around her eyes, she painted a rainbow of colors to accent her eyes and lashes. She wore powder on her face to give it a more even color, and rouge on her cheeks, accenting her high cheekbones. She wore bright and creamy lipstick on her lips. As a whole, the painting of her face reminded me of circus clowns, but in a softer and more pleasant way. I had never seen a woman who painted her face as she did, and she fascinated me.

I noticed that her fingernails were painted also, and sometimes she brought her bottles of fingernail polish to class and polished her nails there during our quiet time. The smell of her fingernail polish always gave me a headache, so when I saw her preparing to paint her nails, I held my nose and breathed through my mouth until she finished. Strangely enough, I could taste the paints from across the room. I wondered why she did this. Was it a ritual that her people had done to ask for a blessing, as we do with medicine men and sand paintings?

She wore a dozen thin plastic bracelets on her wrists, and they jangled when she gestured with her hands. The sound reminded me of the sound of the bells around the necks of my grandparents' sheep. She also wore several necklaces around her neck, which jangled along with her bracelets, sometimes harmonizing with the sound of her curiously heeled shoes—another wonderment! This was the first time I saw bare legs fitted into a shoe. The Navajo women I saw at the trading post wore stockings or socks when they wore dresses. But this one, she was totally different. She wore short dresses that were above the knee, exposing a lot of bare skin on her legs. Along with her short dresses, she wore curious-looking shoes with heels that were four to six inches high, like pencils glued to the bottom of her heels. I would look at her heels when she was walking and wonder how she could balance on those high, thin heels. She had many different shoes of many colors, and she always wore shoes that matched her brightly colored clothes. The colors of her clothing were so bright that they could blind a person for a few seconds! If she were in a crowd, I could spot her easily.

Along with her brightly colored outfits, Mrs. Whiting had the added distraction of smell. She wore strongly-scented perfume, so strong that I sometimes had a hard time breathing when she was a few yards away. My lungs would seem as though they were about to collapse in an instant, not wanting to take the smell in. My nose would twitch when she came near me. I thought that her daily beauty preparations were too much just for teaching little Indians like me, but she entertained me with her customs and appearance.

Every day, I wondered where these ebony-skinned people called Africans came from. I always wanted to ask her, but I was frightened. My imagination created a place that she had come from, where everyone dressed alike, in their Sunday clothes, as I had seen at mass. I imagined this society as very proper, where everyone and everything was perfect and in order. I wondered if I could fit into a society like that.

I would ask my classmates, "Have you ever seen anyone like this before?"

My friends would respond, "No, this is my first time, too. Never in my life have I come across a person like this." The way we inquired of one another reminded me of scientists observing a specimen under a microscope.

The Twin Lakes School Board had hired Mrs. Whiting mainly to teach special students like myself. She taught both regular and special students alike, incorporating exercises that benefited both student types. Before I began kindergarten, we were given an aptitude test to assess where we stood in academics. This test also assessed whether we had learning disabilities. After I took the test, I was considered a special student only because I had a speech impediment: I stuttered. The funny thing was that I only stuttered while I was in the classroom performing tasks such as reading out loud in front of the class. When I was at home or just talking to my friends, I spoke normally.

Usually, after breakfast in the morning, some of the students went to the end of the hall where Mrs. Whiting's classroom was located to wait for class to begin. The girls of our class were the teacher's pets. By the time I got there, they would already be waiting for the teacher. There were only about fifteen students in our class. As it was, two of my buddies and I, the Late Trio as we were known, were late for class every other day. The consequences of our tardiness were warnings and extra work.

At the beginning of class, we waited silently for Mrs. Whiting to prepare our assignments. Then she would say in a booming voice, "Get to your assigned desk and when I call out your name, say 'I'm here' out loud." Then she would walk to the blackboard and say, "Today, we will work on this." But before we began our lessons, we had to stand and pledge allegiance to the flag and sing "God Bless America."

During our reading time, Mrs. Whiting made us stand in front of the class and read a page from a book out loud. This was my least favorite part of the day. When it was my turn, I would drag my feet to the front of the class. I was so nervous that I used to shiver and shake and stomp my feet on the wooden floor. The sound of it was like a carpenter working on the roof of a building, hammering nails into the wooden frame. When I finished, I would be shaking as I returned to my desk. I would be too embarrassed to look at anyone for several minutes after I sat back down. This was one of the main reasons I disliked school. The other main reason was Mrs. Whiting's perfume. My desk was right next to her desk, and the strong smell of the perfume would make me dizzy and drowsy and give me a headache all the time. That was why I would always go to sleep in her classroom, and she would send me to the nurse's office most of the time. Every day, it was agony just to go to class.

Later that year, I overheard some students talking about going to a big brand-new boarding school called Chuska. It was located in Tohatchi, on a mesa about five to seven miles north of Twin Lakes. I did not want to go there because I had grown used to this old school. I knew every inch of Twin Lakes Boarding School. I could have given a tour to a newcomer while I was blindfolded. Oh, the secret places I knew!

There was a secret tree house on the south side of the school grounds where most of our meetings took place. I remember that one of the girls had climbed the tree and ripped her dress on one of the branches. When I found out, the other boys and I laughed at her, and the dormitory attendants came out with a blanket, which they wrapped around her as they took her back inside the building, scolding her for climbing the tree.

We had a rule among the students that when you got into the tree house, you had to count fifty cars going by on the highway before you came down. Sometimes it took a very long time for fifty cars to go by, and the dormitory attendants would wonder where we were. They eventually found out about our tree house and chased us back inside.

Boarding school was the place where I first broke or dislocated any part of my body. A couple of us boys had been told to fold the blankets in our dormitory hall. We were serious at first about performing the chore, but then we began to goof off. I was running from one of my friends, jumping from one top bunk to another, when someone pushed the bed away from my intended landing and I fell about four feet down, hitting my face on a chair as I fell to the floor. I didn't know at the time that I had broken my nose, just that it was bleeding so much that I kept going to the bathroom to rinse the towel that I used to wipe away the blood. I was able to hide my injury for the evening until I was discovered and rushed to the Indian Hospital in Gallup.

Later that year, I dislocated my elbow while hanging from the slide on the playground. I fell to the ground, landing directly on my elbow. Again, I was taken to the Indian Hospital, and I left there with a cast and a sling, which I had to wear for two months so that my elbow could heal.

We also had burrows that my schoolmates had dug. I remember one day, two of the boys got stuck when the burrows collapsed on them after school. They were stuck there until about six or seven o'clock in the evening, when someone discovered them. One of the boys cried until a maintenance man heard him and rescued them. The maintenance man was so angry with the boys because they could have been killed. I remember that we were all looking out the windows of our dormitory like little prairie dogs looking out of our own burrows.

Little things like that were important to me at the time. The school held lots of memories, and it was closer to my home. Chuska was not too far away, but I still did not want to transfer to the new school. However, the school board was going to shut down Twin Lakes School and transfer all of its students to Chuska the following school year, so it seemed that I had no choice.

5
LEARNING NEVER ENDS

When my brothers, cousins and I were growing up on the reservation, there would be Mormons coming by to visit, sometimes by walking or riding bicycles. We would try to hide from them by running behind the hills or crawling under the bed. We wouldn't come out until after they left, poor guys. Sometimes when we weren't aware of them, they would notice that we were around and they would talk to us and teach us about the word of God. One summer a couple of Mormon missionaries came to us and asked if we were interested in going to a Mormon Placement school in Utah. Because life on the reservation was hard, with no running water or electricity, we told them that we were interested.

The missionaries told us that we had to be baptized and go to church twice a week in the evening to learn more about the Mormon bible before we went to the next step. I told my mom that I really wanted to go, but my brother wasn't interested anymore. He wanted to stay around the reservation and go to the local boarding school. Apparently I was eager to go to the Mormon school in Utah. I didn't even know where that place was, maybe I was too little to know, but I was still inquisitive about going to another world.

Every year during our summer break there would be a six-week bible school not too far from where I lived. There was a missionary that would come by to recruit young individuals to go to bible study school and learn about the word of God. I think these people were Pentecostal. I never asked, I just attended and was happy to go, but not when there were a lot of young adolescents around. One of the missionaries would drive around from home to home picking up people that they had recruited. I think they drove about ten miles a day, one way. Most of the kids were our cousins that we grew up with. My brother and I got along with some of them, but there were a few that went along just to cause trouble and bully the younger ones like me. Sometimes, a fight would break out with pushing and shoving.

My mom and dad forced us to go to the bible school even though it was only for a couple of hours. I liked being with my age group. We would do arts and crafts, build all kinds of models like wooden bird cages, or help around the community. We would go to where elderly people lived by themselves, and would clean up around their house. I guess this was part of our summer vacation, to learn something about the word of the bible and charity. I assumed learning never ends, because we went to school nine months a year, and then even during summer breaks. Plus our mom and dad were telling us to bring in water and chop wood, and my grandparents were there telling us to look after the sheep and cattle and take them water. This was all a part of our growing-up tasks living on the reservation.

My cousins who didn't live too far from us were members of the church in Gallup. Their mom forced them to go to church at least three times a week, especially on Sundays. Sometimes they would invite me when I went to visit them. I would always tell them to come by the house and I'd be ready. I was eager to go because the environment was different from the bible school. But then they caught me off guard and asked me, "What do you think about the word of God and do you believe it? What about the word christen?" I didn't know what they were talking about. All they wanted to do was start an argument. I myself did not want to argue about any religion and christen. So I just let them be, quietly got on my horse and rode back home feeling upset because they asked me too many questions. The word christen was running around in my head, so I asked my mom later on in the evening. She told me it might mean something to do with Christianity. But she wasn't too clear with it. So that was the end of my research of christen.

My grandma also did not know about Christianity. She taught us about our traditional beliefs, and so did grandpa, but they did not tell us everything. To this day I still get confused about my Navajo tradition because of all the differences between our elders' stories.

The staff from Chuska Boarding School was recruiting some of the students for enrollment the next year. The new school had a list of students who attended Twin Lakes and Coyote Canyon Schools. They were the top priority and the first ones to be drafted to attend the new school. I had hoped that they would not stop by our house, but eventually they did. They came to my mom's house and asked for my mother, inquiring, "Would you like for all of your school-age boys to go to the new boarding school? They will sure like this brand new school because they will have their own rooms and they will have the opportunity to meet other students from this area and from as far away as Arizona." Since the school at Twin Lakes was closing down, my mom signed the papers for us to go to school at Chuska. They were trying to recruit five to six hundred students.

My brothers and I were curious to see the new school, so we asked our mom to take us there. One day in the middle of summer, we went and checked out the new school to see where it was located and what it looked like. During our visit that summer, the school was still under construction. There were some men working there, and my mom asked them when the school would be finished. One of the guys replied, "In a couple of months the construction is going to be completed and the school will ready for students in the fall." So we were all excited, looking at the new school building, walking around and watching the men building it.

In the fall of 1964, I started school at Chuska. The name Chuska is a transliteration of the Navajo word *choosh'gai*, which means "white-colored spruce trees." My room was inside a big brand-new dormitory. My views changed about the school. I felt fortunate to be there where everything was shiny and new. Everything was painted Navajo white. I imagined as I was walking through the rooms that heavenly light was shining from above and I could hear a heavenly choir singing, "Ah!" At Twin Lakes, the walls were worn and muddled with faded colors, and there was a mess of fliers, posters and student projects everywhere. At Chuska, the walls were pristine, with no thumbtack holes or tape or smudges.

Inside the rooms were brown steel bunk beds, dressers that were built into the walls with two drawers for each student, and a big closet with sliding doors for hanging clothes. Down the hall, there was a big bathroom with multiple sinks and toilets, and right across from them was a big shower room with multiple shower stalls. There was still some heavy machinery on the grounds that had been used to level the ground, and I noticed that the construction workers were slowly moving the equipment off of the school property each day.

When school started, a middle-aged Anglo lady with a Southern accent introduced herself as one of the guidance counselors assigned to the students who were living in my building. She took time to guide us through the dorm. She wanted to make sure that we knew our way around the building so that we would not get lost. She showed us a big TV room that had carpet on the floor. The carpet was really nice. I could imagine sitting on it while watching TV. The next big room she showed us was the rumpus room. It had high ceilings and only two entrances. She said, "This is where you will be playing when the weather outside is bad." The room had a tile floor and no windows, which meant that we could play basketball and dodge ball without worrying about breaking windows.

The Chuska Boarding School campus was arranged as follows: The main administration offices, the gym, and the classrooms were on the west side of the dormitories. The teaching staff and government employee residential housing were on the far west end of the campus. As for housing, the single teachers without families lived in adjacent apartments, and teachers with families lived in single-family houses. Cardinal Lodge, whose residents were male underclassmen, was located on the north side of the campus, and was the closest to the dining hall. The female underclass dorm was called Hummingbird Lodge, and it was located on the south side of the kitchen, with the dorm for adolescent female students, Bluebird Lodge, on the south end of Hummingbird. The adolescent male students named their dormitory Thunderbird Lodge, which was on the far north end of Cardinal Lodge. Five-foot fences with three lines of heavy barbed wire enclosed the entire campus. There was only one entrance, at the west side. It was similar to a cliff dwelling, with a single road leading to the campus, which was situated on top of a mesa.

At Chuska, I was assigned to a room that I would share with three other students. I chose my bed first, as I was the first one to arrive. I chose a top bunk so that I could see everyone walking by, and so that I could jump up to my bed. Another upside of having a top bunk was that I could look out the window. I liked looking out the windows at night to see the stars and the street lights.

Every morning at about 6:00, all the lights would suddenly come on, shining in our eyes like spotlights. That was the moment I hated most, when I was rudely pulled from my dreams. I would cover my head with a pillow and try to get some more sleep, but the lights were so harsh that I would have to get out of bed, even if I was still sleepy, just to escape the room's floodlights.

As at Twin Lakes, at Chuska there were rules to be followed that I did not like but could not dismiss. Every morning we would wake up, fold our blankets and make our beds, wash up, brush our teeth, and get ready for breakfast. The dormitory attendants were vicious in enforcing the rules. I would still be loafing around trying to get myself ready and get things organized after I was dressed, and a dorm aide would blow a whistle so loud that it was really annoying. The aides would yell at the top of their lungs, like roosters crowing in the morning, "Everybody go to the front room and wait there until everyone is present, and stand there in a straight single-file line." So we all would line up, and they would get out a clipboard and say, "When I call your name, say, 'I'm here,' out loud."

When roll call was finished, two of the boys would open the door and we would march in single file, like little army men, to the dining hall. It seemed like we were drafted and now were spending the next few weeks in boot camp, just like I had seen in war movies. I found out that a majority of the male dormitory attendants had experience in the military. A dormitory attendant would walk beside us and she or he would say, "When you boys finish eating breakfast, get back to the dorm and clean your rooms and finish your other assigned cleaning duties." I think I swept and mopped miles and miles of hallways, cleaned rooms, and used millions of gallons of cleaning solution.

Usually, we had to repeat our chores later during the day because we apparently did not do our jobs to their specifications. "If you want a job done right, then do it yourself," I thought while they stood over us, watching us like hawks. Everything about our duties and assignments was done to perfection. I wonder if they ever replaced the floor tiles that I scrubbed over and over. I know that floor tiles wear out!

I was about eight years old in the second grade in this big brand-new school. My new teacher was an old, chunky Anglo woman who made us sit boy-girl-boy-girl. She had us write our names in our favorite color or colors on a piece of paper in four-inch letters and tape them to the front of our desks. I was tempted to write a name other than my own, but I wrote my first name in blue and my last name in purple. I remember that one boy wrote his name in red, white and blue colors of the flag in an alternating fashion. The girls were always the perfect students, angels for all to see and glorify. They had written their names uniformly and with despicable detail!

During the first month of school, we all practiced our writing. We tried to learn how to write our names in print and script. We would take turns going to the chalkboard to write our names. I guess that writing was the most important thing in that teacher's mind. By the end of that year, I had written my name over a thousand times and I do not know how many pencils and crayons I had worn down to their stubby ends. We also did some coloring, trying to stay within the closed drawing lines. Sometimes, we would go for a walk around the school building just to get some fresh air or go to the library to check out a book that we could read aloud to the class. We learned how to say, "Good morning," with a smile, and all the wonderful words associated with good manners. We learned how to introduce ourselves and present our projects to the class. Our teacher read books to us, especially the ones about Spot, Dick, and Jane, which I will never forget because they are imprinted on my brain.

At about ten a.m. each day, the teacher would tell us to go to the back of the room to play. Some of us would get the little wooden ABC blocks and see who could build the highest tower before the blocks came crashing down. In any school, there is always a bully in the classroom, and sure enough, we had one in our class. When we played, he would cause trouble by crashing the blocks down or taking away the toys we were playing with.

After our little spats, the teacher would make us all take naps on a large floor mat. Two of us would use a beanbag to take our naps. Afterwards, our teacher would call us back to our desks and tell everybody to get in line and wash our hands thoroughly before we went to lunch. She would say, "This afternoon, we will work on a little arithmetic and some more reading," which was not my favorite subject at all. About once a week, we would go to the music room and try to play instruments. I did not really focus on learning a particular instrument. I liked to beat the drum just to make a lot of noise, with no hint of a rhythm at all. We tried to learn different songs, but it was difficult for me because I stuttered and I was too embarrassed to stand in front of the class and try to sing or do any kind of presentation.

About every two weeks, my parents would check me out for the weekend and I would go back home. I was usually not in a good mood, as I did not like the school at all. I told my parents that I did not like the school because they had a lot of rules and regulations that we had to follow. I gave them examples, such as the way we had to sit in alternate boy-girl order when we were in the dining hall, eating and looking straight ahead while we did nothing else, and leaving one hand under the table with no elbows placed on top of the table. I told them we had to wait until everybody was finished eating and ask permission from the teacher to be excused. I told them I hated the rules enforced throughout the day and the duties we had to perform and the floodlights that woke us every morning.

My dad told me that it was for my own good. He told me that he did not send me to school to goof off and play, but to learn math and English and to learn good manners and all that the school had to offer. He told me that he wanted me to learn my studies because he only went to grade school and he wished that he had continued with his studies. He wished that he could hold an office job with the railroad, but he couldn't because of his limited education.

At Chuska Boarding School, when somebody got into a fight, all of us were blamed, and then came the dormitory attendants, blowing their whistles at a high pitch. Everybody ran into their rooms like a herd of horses spooked by a predator, and we tried to hide from the aides. We were all called to the front room where we were forced to kneel on the floor for thirty minutes to an hour.

When we were finally allowed to get up, our knees were red and sore and had an imprint of the indentations of tile floor. Another rule at the school was that English was the only language we were allowed to speak. We were told that we were not to speak in our native language, Navajo, because we were there to learn to speak English. But when the staff was not around, we did speak Navajo because we knew it best. When we did so, we always seemed to get caught, and then we were punished. The punishment varied from standing at a wall to doing extra chores to having our hands slapped ten times with a wooden ruler—all because we spoke in our own language.

By the time I became a third-grader at Chuska, I was nine years old. I had attended first grade twice because of my stuttering. I did not like being older and taller than the other kids in my class. The students who were my age called the dorm where I stayed "the baby dorm." When I entered third grade, I moved to the other wing of the dorm because the wing where I had been was for students in kindergarten through second grade. I stayed in that wing for the whole year, but I wanted to run away.

My cousin was in school with me at that time. During recess, we would go to the edge of the playground and look over the fence. We noticed that there were horses roaming the fields, and he asked me, "How would you like to be one of those horses out there in the field, always roaming freely, doing whatever you wanted? They are free." This was the first time that I realized how much I wanted to run away from Chuska. I said to my cousin, "Let's run away! You gave me the idea!"

We planned it for a couple of days, getting extra socks and blankets, figuring that we could get home in a half day. We ran away in the middle of the week, jumping the four-foot wire fence and taking off. We kept running for about a mile. I did not get tired. I kept running like a rabbit down the hill, across the valley, and up another hill. We were dodging the vehicles that came by because we didn't want to be seen and caught. Any time we saw a vehicle or a horse, we hid in the ditch until it went past us.

That was not the last time I ran away from boarding school. The yearning to run away stayed with me until I was a fifth-grader. I ran away from the dormitory constantly, sometimes with a partner, and sometimes on my own. The dormitory attendants would look for me and sometimes I would run toward Chuska Lake and other times toward Hot Springs to the east. I knew the area around Hot Springs because I rode horseback through it when I was checking on my grandpa's cattle when I was younger.

I always made sure that my escape plans were foolproof. I planned my escapes at night, two or three days in advance. I took an extra blanket to wrap around my waist and another blanket to throw on the barbed wire fence so that I wouldn't be scratched and my clothes would not be torn. I usually planned my escapes for the hours between 11:00 p.m. and 2:00 a.m. when everyone at school was asleep. I knew it was time to go when the dormitory hall was silent except for the sounds of snoring coming from the kids who were off in dreamland. I snuck out of my room, down the hallway, and out the back door, which did not have an alarm system. Next, I had to run to the fence at the back of the school property without being detected. I threw the blanket across the fence and climbed over. As soon as I was over, I ran like a bat out of hell until my legs got tired and my lungs burned so that I couldn't draw another breath.

My parents' home was seven miles away, and I made it home without getting caught every time I ran away. My parents would always take me back to school after a couple of days, but not until they had lectured me again and again, waving their hands to emphasize their concern. But running away from school became my favorite activity, always keeping the dorm attendants on their toes.

My third grade teacher at Chuska was a skinny, blue-eyed Anglo lady with long blonde hair that fell to her waist. Her name was Ms. Kilgore. I never cared much about how she looked then, but when I think back, I realize that she was a man's dream woman, blonde and good-looking. Ms. Kilgore was so strict that you could not talk in her classroom while she spoke, even if you were asking a question related to what she was saying. We were told to look straight into her blue eyes when she was explaining things to us, and for that reason, I didn't like Ms. Kilgore. I never liked looking into another person's eyes.

My desk was situated right next to hers, and she was always pointing to me and asking me to do things like reading to the class, which I hated because of my stuttering. I guess that she called on me a lot because I was such a big mouth to the other kids when we were on the playground and I got into things that I shouldn't. She called me the class clown. A lot of the older students made fun of me, but I didn't do anything about it. I was basically ashamed because of my stuttering.

During those times, it seemed that teachers used the power to pass or fail students based on their age and height. At the end of that school year, she passed the students who were older and taller than I was, but I already knew that I would not pass. Even though I was skilled in math, which was my favorite subject, she still flunked me. I believed that she wanted to keep me in her class to terrorize me! I was angry for a while, but I inevitably returned to school the following year to repeat third grade.

Having been retained before, I was determined to make sure that my school work was of excellent quality, which made me one of the top students in the class. In spite of my stuttering, I got along well with my classmates and managed to make a lot of friends. I still stuttered when I read or made presentations in front of the class, but I didn't usually pay attention to the other students' jokes. Sometimes, though, I did get into fights with the boys who made fun of me. With the girls who made fun, I just walked away and let it slide. The remarks about my stuttering did not stop me from doing well in school or prevent my having a good time there. That was the year that I began to like school. I enjoyed the long hours in class. I grew in confidence, especially in fights, because my brothers had taught me how to win!

I noticed that other students thought that the students who ran away from school were cool and that they respected those who ran away. I knew that this was something that I could do with no problem, as I had done it before and never got caught. It was a piece of cake, right? I thought that this would be an easy way for me to get attention and respect, so I began running away from school again.

Today, when I think back to my escapes, I laugh about the way the dorm attendants drove around in military-style dune buggies, only on roads and in residential areas. I laughed at them while I was hiding behind rocks on top of a hill. They looked for me in the homes of people I knew, like my relatives who lived nearby, but they never attempted to look in the less-traveled areas away from the roads and residential areas. I assume they thought that a child would stick to safer areas where there were houses, lights, and more visible landmarks, but I was not afraid to wander in the dark of the hillsides and valleys. Sometimes they would call out, "Come back, and we will give you this!" But I stayed in hiding. Many times, I would go to my grandpa's house way up on the mountain, where they would never believe a small, seemingly unintelligent boy like myself would venture in the rough terrain alone at night. All of the rules, regulations, and punishments were not enough to stifle my longing for freedom.

6
MY TWO WORLDS

One October afternoon when I was ten years old, my grandfather asked me to go deer hunting with him. I thought he was joking, so I chuckled to myself and was shaking my head when he said, "It would be better for you to sleep at my house tonight because your half-uncle will be here very early in the morning."

I was excited then, and a bit nervous, as this would be my first hunt. I wondered what a wimpy ten-year-old boy would do, hunting a huge deer with two older men! I unsaddled my horse, fed him and the other horses, and closed the corral gate. With thoughts of the hunting trip going through my mind, I went for a long walk over the hill and looked around to see where we would be going to hunt. I went back down the hill and chopped some wood for the fire. By that time, the sun was already setting. I went to bed, but I could not fall asleep until late that night, as thoughts about the hunt kept going through my mind.

The next morning, I woke early and dragged myself out of bed at about four o'clock. My grandpa was already dressed, and he asked me if I was ready for the journey. My half-uncle had left earlier in his truck to drive to the northwest part of Cove Mountain. The ground was covered with frost as my grandpa and I saddled our horses, and the wind was cold on my face. I didn't have the kind of warm clothes needed for this trip. When we finished our preparations, we rode out to meet my half-uncle about three miles away, behind the mountain called Banana Ridge. I could hear the coyotes howling in the distance. I asked my grandpa why the coyotes were howling like that, and he said, "They howl because they know someone is hunting, and they want the guts of the deer to be saved for them."

An hour or two later, my half-uncle had already shot and killed two deer. I heard the sound of his gunshots echoing through the valley. My grandpa told me to gather some dry wood and start a large fire. While my half-uncle tended to one of the deer he had killed, my grandpa turned to me and said, "We have to skin the other one and butcher it ourselves."

I didn't know anything about butchering. When my grandfather handed me his brand new buck knife and told me to get started, I said, "Where do I begin?"

He said, "Don't you have any common sense? Haven't you watched your grandma butcher a sheep before?"

"But this isn't a sheep—this is wildlife," I said.

He scowled, "Do not talk back. Just do what I ask you to do!"

We quartered the carcass of the deer and cautiously skinned the hide. "Be very careful when you skin the face of the deer," my grandpa told me. "Never cut around the lips or the opening near the eyelids as it could cause facial disfiguration or blindness in you." I glanced at him and wished that he would do this part of the operation himself!

The butchering of the deer took two long hours of hard work. Then everything was wrapped in Bluebird flour sacks and strapped on top of the horse. I sat atop the wrapped pieces of meat and rode the horse home.

My grandpa owned a green wagon and a half dozen working horses. He traded five cows for the wagon when it was brand new, and he used it to haul water from the community well to our home each day. He used two horses to pull the wagon, and he rotated his six horses so that each pair had two days of rest before they had to pull the wagon again. Everyone recognized his wagon traveling up and down the dirt road to the well. It reminded me of an ant carrying its heavy load from the worksite to its home. My grandpa worked this wagon very hard, and as time went on, the green paint faded from the scorching summer sun and the rain and snow of winter.

Grandpa pumped water from the well with a hose that he attached to the nozzle of the pump. It took time to get this water, but it was necessary. Some of the well water was given to the animals, and the remainder was boiled for our drinking, cooking, and washing.

There was also a social aspect to collecting water. As my grandfather and the other men in our area met at the well to get water for their families, they would catch up on the latest chitchat and talk about upcoming events.

My older brothers liked to ride with my grandpa and help him as much as they could in getting water. Since I was too little to help, I was left behind. I would climb up into a big old cedar tree beside the road and wait patiently for their return, hoping to scare them as they passed beneath the tree. I could usually hear them coming because Grandpa would sing his Navajo Squaw Dance songs and my brothers would awkwardly try to sing with him. The horses always knew that I was there, and when their ears started to point straight up, my Grandpa would be alerted to my presence and would yell, "Hey, you in the tree! Are you a monkey? Get down from that tree before you fall and land on your head and crack it! We know you are up there! Who are you trying to scare?"

My older brother Delbert and my cousin Freeman, who were a lot bigger and stronger than I was, would ask my grandpa if they could take the wagon to the well by themselves. Because they often got into mischief, my grandpa did not like to trust them with his only wagon. One day, my brother and my cousin were playing in the wagon, not paying attention to the horses, and they let the reins drop to the ground. When the reins touched the horses' legs, they were spooked. Believing a predator was at their heels, they bolted with the wagon, trying wildly to escape. My brother and cousin could not calm the horses or control the wagon because they no longer held the reins. In a split second, the wagon careened off the main road and hit a large rock. My brother fell out into a big rabbit brush. My cousin got scared and jumped out, spraining his ankle when his foot landed directly in an old rusty white coffee pot.

The frightened horses kept running into the open field, away from the road. As the wagon bounced over rocks and bumps, the barrels of water fell out and broke apart, spilling the water on the ground. The back wheels fell off of the wagon, but the horses kept running. The wagon was almost completely destroyed before anyone was able to catch the horses. My brother had a headache for a couple of days and my cousin was at home for a couple of weeks, nursing his ankle with the help of my mother and grandmother. He had to stay at home because there were no hospitals nearby where he could see a doctor.

My grandpa did not have the resources to buy a new wagon, so he was determined to repair the damaged one. He needed wood, and since there were no lumber supply stores nearby, he chopped down some trees on a nearby mountain and used his horses to drag them back to our home. He then chopped the wood into pieces identical to the damaged sections of the wagon. After much hard work, he rebuilt the wagon before winter came so that he could use it to haul water and wood. I respected my grandpa's skills and determination even more after this. I believe that if he had acquired the education and training, he could have been a mechanic or an engineer, or maybe a Navajo philosopher.

One day while I was ten years old and living at my

grandmother's home, one of my uncles came with the alarming news that my grandpa had been in an accident. My uncle told us that grandpa was driving his tractor down the side of a steep hill on the shoulder of Highway 491, going north, near J.B. Tanner's store. Later that day, my parents told me that my grandpa had been rushed to the Gallup Indian Medical Center, and a wrecker had towed his tractor to a wreck yard in Gallup.

He was in intensive care for several weeks, until he was able to sit up and begin working with a physical therapist. He relearned how to walk, a little at a time every day, like a small toddler. He needed to build up his endurance so that he could get around. Since there was no one at his home to help him when he was released from the hospital, I was chosen to take this responsibility. My mom took me out of Chuska Boarding School and then to my grandpa's house.

I helped him get in and out of bed, did what little cooking my mom had taught me, took care of the horses, chopped wood, and hauled buckets of water into his house. At first, he was extremely heavy and I was terrified that I might hurt him even more, but I did all of these tasks selflessly because he was my grandfather and I loved him. After he recovered and was able to take care of himself, I went back to live with my parents and returned to boarding school at Chuska. I hated school and was sad when I had to go back.

A few months after my grandpa's accident, during my summer vacation, my grandpa, my half-uncle and I went to Gallup to the Inter-Tribal Indian Ceremonial so that we could watch the events and my grandpa could get reacquainted with some of his old friends. It made me uneasy when he tried to carry on conversations with people from other tribes. Some would ask him what had happened to his leg, because it was curiously bundled up with paper sacks and tree sap, tied with a strip of a Bluebird flour sack. I was somewhat embarrassed and tried to distance myself from him. In retrospect, it was actually funny because from one side his leg looked like a huge elephant leg. He told me, in Navajo, "Come back over here, my little grandson." He told all those people that I was his grandson!

I assumed that my grandpa knew all of these people since before my time, as he just walked into their tent as if he were a member of their family. My half-uncle had a hard time locating us, and when he did find us, he had a harder time getting my grandfather to leave, as he was enjoying talking and drinking with his friends. My half-uncle told my grandpa, "It's time for us to go home. I believe it's going to rain, and it's already getting dark." I fell asleep while waiting for Grandpa, and it was after midnight when my half-uncle finally coaxed Grandpa into going home. When we got there, it was raining heavily.

I was eleven years old when I began the fourth grade. I was still in the same dormitory at Chuska, but in a different wing of the building, the wing called Cardinal Lodge. It was in this year that pictures of the birds for which each of the dormitories were named were painted on the outside windows of the common area of each hall. These paintings of birds were about thirty feet wide and forty feet high.

In the fourth grade, I had a new teacher whom I despised. He was an older Anglo man of medium height and build named Al Buchanan who was retired from the military. His time in the military service dominated his persona. His dress was always sharp and professional, his suits neatly pressed and fitted. He wore khakis, white or pinstriped shirts with ties, and spit-shined shoes that were eye-catching. He always wore either an English driver-style cap or a zoot suit hat that was set atop a clean military crew cut. Over this, he wore a sharp black trench coat. Mr. Buchanan's appearance began to incorporate itself into our dress. In his classroom, a dress code was set. We were pressed and unwrinkled, with clean and shiny shoes, neat haircuts, and shirts tucked in.

Our behavior was also strictly regulated: talking only when spoken to by the teacher, always facing forward, walking in single file while looking straight ahead. At lunchtime, we were expected to concentrate on our food, and only on our food, with no distractions. Even his teaching style was military, simple lessons were always blunt and focused lectures. At times, he would take us back into his past, recollecting his experiences in the armed forces. He stressed the importance of setting and pursuing careers for our futures.

Al was a quiet type of man who held attention and authority. The only time he talked was when he lectured on the day's schoolwork. He did not look at us when he spoke, but he always held our attention as he walked around the classroom. There was no horseplay in his class, as we were afraid of the possible consequences.

It seemed to me that he held an unspoken dislike for Native Americans, or more specifically, a dislike for me. He singled me out to read out loud in front of the class, especially when we were divided into groups for projects. Other groups were allowed to choose their own group speaker or presenter, but he would always select me as the speaker for my group. I would get panicky when the time came for me to present our projects or to read our daily readings. I would begin to shift my weight in a constant, erratic manner. He would tell me to stand still and continue with my presentation or reading. When I came to a word I did not know, I would try my best to pronounce it, but then, with a bit of help coupled with what I saw as ridicule from him, I continued. After my reading, he would ask me to continue standing in front of the class until he permitted me to return to my desk. I could always sense his predatory eyes siphoning courage and freedom from my very being.

Toward the end of the school year, my perception of Al began to change. No longer was he the militant dictator and bully, but someone who had cared about my personal point of view and wanted to help me learn. One day, when I was selected to stand in front of the class, I reluctantly stood up and walked to the front to face my classmates. I began to read an excerpt from a book I had checked out from the library, and then gave a synopsis of the story. At the end of the book report, I returned to my seat and realized that I had not stuttered as much as I had in previous years. I had started to overcome my stutter! This was an exciting development because it meant that I was more comfortable and open to reading in front of the class. I actually looked forward to speaking. I felt drawn to participate in classroom activities and projects. Before, I had to hide behind other students in order to evade notice, as I had not felt confident. At the end of the school year, Al told me, "Wherever you go, don't give up!"

Today, I think about this man and wonder if he knew how I felt about reading aloud in front of the class. He was a great teacher. There are times when I am alone and I think about him and when I lost my stutter. It gives me the courage to keep going and not give up on whatever I am doing. I know now that he incorporated his military experience into teaching to give his students a sense of responsibility and a desire to leave bad habits behind. He was focused on teaching his students self-discipline and the habits that would build their self-esteem along with the academic subjects he taught.

It was time for me to start fifth grade, but my grandfather had asked me to help him round up his cattle and drive them to the biggest corral in the area, which was located near the Tohatchi/Hot Springs area. That is the place where most of the livestock owners came to try to locate their lost cattle and claim their livestock. This was my first cattle drive. My brothers were in school; they had helped my grandpa with previous cattle drives and wanted me to have the experience this time. My grandpa was like my second father. I asked him many questions about cattle and the work involved in owning them. He instructed me in the work that needed to be done and had me practice the tasks that he told me about. There was always something new to learn from him. When my behavior was out of line at times, he would discipline through lectures and giving me extra work to do. He was a man who insisted on reason, responsibility and accountability.

My grandpa always made certain that tasks were done correctly. He was a great teacher about the ways of tending to cattle. I looked up to him for advice in solving problems. Sometimes, when I asked too many questions, he would ignore me. I remember that some of those questions were ones that were not to be asked by a child, such as where babies came from and how to make them and how to get a girlfriend and get married. I remember asking him if he would ever get another wife and family. His response was a glance, after which he avoided eye contact with me for the rest of the day. He did not expect children to ask questions about his private life.

The day before the cattle drive, I checked my horse to be sure that he was in good condition and shined my saddle with coat after coat of saddle wax. I reshaped my straw cowboy hat again and again. I remember that we got up before dawn on the day of the drive. My grandpa and I wanted to get most of our work done before the day became too hot. I got on my horse, Blaze, and met my grandpa about a half-mile west of where we lived. I had no idea what I was about to do. I thought that all I had to do was get on my horse and chase a few cows to another pasture for a couple of days. I didn't know how much hard work was ahead of me.

My horse was fresh and as eager as I was. He was running and jumping at the same time, acting very energetic. My grandpa's horse was not as excited, just trotting along. My grandpa told me to slow my horse down because if he kept up at that pace, he might not be able to keep going for the whole long journey. But Blaze would not settle down. I thought that it was probably because he had been in the corral at home all summer, with no exercise out in the fields.

When we got to Tohatchi, my horse was all sweaty and huffing hard, so I unsaddled him and took him into the corral where my grandfather's camping gear was already in place in the spot where he camped every year. He said, "Look, Gibben, I brought you along because you are going to be my eyes. I can't see the brands as clearly as I once did, as I am getting old." When he said this, I wondered what would become of him and his cattle without his good eyesight. I remember that in earlier times, he had used binoculars that my uncle had given him to spot his brand. Before we had left, I saw him pack them in his gear. Now he used a stick to draw his brand in the sand and told me to remember it. Then he cooked our supper on the open fire: thick slices of pork bacon and canned beans, tortillas that he had prepared at home before we left, and venison jerky.

While we ate, my grandpa talked to me about his strategy for rounding up the cattle. He drew figures in the sand that pointed to the South and then to the East. He told me that the big corral was about two miles North, near the foothills. I was very tired and sore from riding in the saddle all day. The next morning, we woke up early and started out before dawn. I could see the dawn on the horizon, and I told myself that it was too early and too dark to be out. I had goose bumps on my arms from the cold early-morning breeze. My grandpa offered me some coffee to help me to warm up, but it was as thick as syrup and so bitter that, when he was not looking, I went behind the tent and poured it out. I drank some water and took a couple of apples to start my day. Then I used all of my strength to lift the heavy saddle onto my horse's back. Blaze looked tired from the previous day's hard work, but when I mounted him, he was as jumpy and energetic as he had been the morning we left.

I rode about a mile and a half south to my intended landmark, the only watering hole at the windmill. By the time I got there, the day was already heating up. I began driving the cows north for about two hours. The cattle had a tendency to scatter, and it takes skill to keep them all together and moving in the desired direction, so I had to put hard work into the task. At times, the bulls would get into fights and mother cows would separate from their young. I had to make sure that no calf was left behind. The putrid odors of cow manure and animal sweat mixed with the rising dust was almost unbearable. I had dust in my eyes and nose, and my lips were chapped by the time evening came.

I had searched the horizon for signs of my grandpa and the other cattle that he had rounded up, but he did not seem to be anywhere in sight. After about three hours, he finally showed up, and I told him that this was hard work and my horse was giving up on me. My horse seemed to share my sentiments about cattle driving, the odor, and the hard work. My grandpa did not respond to my complaints except to say, "It's going to take two or three more days of this kind of work, so be prepared for it. This work can't be taken lightly. This is serious hard work." I got off my horse and started to walk toward the camp to get a drink of water and have something to eat. I could not walk straight—my legs were bowed and my back muscles were sore, and my body was covered in dust. We still had one more duty to perform before dusk. I helped my grandpa round the cattle up into the corral, which took about an hour and a half. We were finally able to set up camp for the night in the corral that we shared with the cattle.

We continued this work for a couple more days. There were three hundred or more cattle in the herd that I was driving by myself. I was becoming worn out and exhausted from riding horseback all day, and my horse was faltering and becoming stubborn, which made my work even harder and more frustrating. I was ready to give up when finally some of my grandpa's relatives came to help. They took up some of the workload and helped to alleviate the stress I felt. They told me that my horse appeared very tired. I did notice that Blaze was ready to fall over, but I knew that he was willing to keep going for me. I was upset that they had not come to help until we were only a few hundred feet from the destination corral. I was proud that I had accomplished this test of endurance and responsibility.

When we got to the Tohatchi/Hot Springs area, we made a head count of my grandpa's cattle, and I found out that he owned the largest herd of cattle in the area, and that he was a well-known and respected man. I was proud of him. There at the corral, my grandfather would separate the older cattle from the younger ones. He would sell the older cattle at auction and keep the younger ones, which he knew could survive the next year.

A feeling of relief washed over me when we arrived at the corral later that afternoon. I said to myself that my work was over for now, and I found a place to lie down on the highest stack of baled hay, where I hoped no one would notice me so I could enjoy a little rest. Later, one man was nice enough to invite my horse into the corral. I unsaddled Blaze, but he showed no interest in the grain and water that I offered him.

I went back to the hay bales to take a nap, and when I woke, I saw people cooking supper. They were having a cookout, and the aroma of the food they were cooking was delicious. I looked over the top of the bales of hay and saw the cattle in the corral. I could hear the mother cows mooing and looking for their young. There was constant motion there. Cattle owners were negotiating prices and trying to strike deals with the buyers. As I took in the sights, some of the older cowboys caught a glimpse of me and they motioned to my grandfather that I was up on top of the hay bales. They must have been looking for me, wondering where I had gone after our cattle drive. They asked me to come down and have supper with them. The smells tugged at my tremendous appetite. As I climbed down, a column of hay began to tilt and off I went, down to the ground flat on my face, along with the bales of hay.

As I ate my supper, I could feel the grains of sand mixed in with my food, but my grandpa told me to eat as much as I could since we had a few more days to go and I would feel better if I had food in my stomach. My grandpa and some of his relatives discussed how many cattle they would be able to sell at the auction, and I overheard my grandpa say, "I know there are forty cows for me to sell at the auction."

The next day, we headed to the auction on horseback. My father had brought a fresh horse for me. I was happy, but I was also very tired and sore. I was riding on the fresh horse, Bozo, and he made a big difference. Grandpa told me, "This was hard work, but you pulled through. Keep it up. Next year, you will help me again. But when you come down this way during your leisure time, be sure to check on the cattle. If anybody should ask you who you are and where you are from, tell them that you are my grandson." He told me to mention his name, Sam Bowman. After the auction, we both departed for home on horseback. Boy, was I happy and relieved!

I was twelve years old when I started fifth grade. I began the school year late, as I had been on the cattle drive with my grandpa for the first three weeks. I had an African American teacher named Ms. Thorpe that year. She was a very nice lady, about fifty years old. I used to draw a lot when I was in class, usually landscapes and animals. She asked me and another student named Chee, who was from Window Rock, Arizona, to draw the school mascot, a bronco horse. She asked us if we were interested in entering the contest for the best drawing of the mascot. The contest winner would have their rendition of the mascot painted on the gym wall and would also win a free pass to the movie theater in Gallup. The painting would be done on the east side of the gym.

I had brainstormed a pose for the horse and what color the horse would be. I decided that the horse would be sorrel-colored and it would be in an upright stance with its forelegs pawing the air. Over the course of the week, we discussed the details of our drawing. We drew the mascot on a piece of paper that was about two feet by three feet. After a week had passed, we were ready to submit our drawing. Then we waited anxiously for the announcement of the winner.

We were informed that we had won the contest, and they painted our mascot rendition on the gym wall. The painting itself was enormous, about twenty feet by thirty feet. The horse was a brown bronco and not a sorrel as we had anticipated, and it looked wild. Everyone knew of the bronco mascot at Chuska Boarding School, as we used it for all of our sports teams: football, basketball, softball, cross-country and track teams.

In the fifth grade, I felt a new freedom as I had overcome most of my obstacles, especially the stuttering that had made life so hard for me. I noticed that a broad range of new classmates accepted me. I was ecstatic about overcoming my speech impediment, and I wanted to take part in every activity available, even if I was not perfect in the field. I was unafraid of any rejection that might come my way. My self-esteem skyrocketed and I had a new-found confidence. There was a new joy in speaking in front of my class, and I raised my hand to answer every question. I started to read more often and my class participation increased. My reading comprehension improved and this was a jumpstart to my learning ability. My teacher was surprised at my sudden interest and participation in learning. Her interest in me helped me to become a leader in my class. At the end of the year, I, Gilbert John, was named the outstanding student in my fifth grade class. During an awards ceremony, I was given a certificate from the school marking my accomplishments that year.

7

A TURNING POINT

I grew in many different ways during my fifth grade year, some in happiness, and some in sorrow. One evening, about a week before Christmas in 1970, my dad came to Chuska Boarding School to check all of us out to go home. I was surprised to see him, as it was the middle of the week, and it was not time for our Christmas vacation to begin. When I asked him why he was there, he said that he would tell us when we got home. It had snowed all that day, so he kept a watchful eye on the road as he drove toward our house, and soon he pulled over to the side of the highway to put tire chains on his truck so that we wouldn't get stuck in the snow on the road to our house. My brothers and I helped him with the chains.

When we got home, my mom, my grandma, and one of my aunts were sitting down at the kitchen table eating supper and talking. My mom told us to sit down and keep quiet as she had some bad news for us. She said that my grandpa had passed away. When I heard this, I felt like I had been kicked in the stomach by a horse, and something inside me was screaming, "No! No!"

My mom said that early that morning when my grandma was opening the gate to the sheep corral, the dogs were barking up on the hill near the house, and when my grandma looked up, she saw my grandpa's horse. It was saddled, but the reins were dragging on the ground. My grandma knew that something was wrong, so she

68

walked quickly over to my parents' house to tell them that my grandpa's horse was here with no rider. When he heard this, my dad saddled his horse right away to go and look for my grandpa. My grandpa lived about a mile from our house at the base of Cove Mountain. The shortest way to get to his house was by a trail, and the trail could only be used on foot or on horseback. When my dad rode the trail up to my grandpa's house, he could find no tracks or any sign of my grandpa because the snow was a lot deeper there. So he came back to the house and got his truck so he and my mom could take the long way around, on the highway, to my grandpa's.

When my mom and dad left in the truck to search some more, my oldest brother Lawrence and I put on our snow boots and coats and started walking toward my grandpa's place. When we got to the top of the mountain, we saw our parents driving toward my grandpa's house. We could see the two cows that he put in the corral to be butchered like he did every Christmas. We ran to our parents and asked them what had happened and my dad told us he had asked the lady who owned the Sagebrush Bar if she had seen my grandpa. She was a good friend of my grandpa and my dad, as they traded with her. She said that she had seen him only one time recently, about four days ago. My dad said that he had questioned a sheep herder along the way and this person said that he had heard someone yelling a couple of nights ago, but it had been late and it was too cold to go out and try to find out what had happened.

My dad told us to go back home and chop some wood before it got dark, and said that he was going back to the Sagebrush Bar to ask some more questions. After we started toward home, my dad drove in the other direction and spotted the sheepherder again, and the sheepherder was waving him down to say that he'd spotted my grandpa. He said that my grandpa was lying face down in the snow, partially covered by a snowdrift in the middle of the trail. He had noticed him when the sheep were walking around him as he took them to the windmill for water. When my dad heard this, he quickly drove his 4x4 truck toward the windmill and found my grandpa. Then he drove back to the bar and told the lady there that my grandpa had died up by the windmill and asked her to call the ambulance and the police. About thirty minutes later, a bulldozer came to plow a path for the ambulance and the police to investigate and then to take my grandpa to the morgue.

My dad said that he believed that my grandpa's horse was spooked by some kind of animal and he threw my grandpa to the ground, where he had hit his head on a rock.

My mom called all of her brothers and sisters that day to tell them the bad news. My uncle in Phoenix came back home that very night and helped my mom in making funeral arrangements. Despite the bad weather, all the people who knew my grandpa came to my mother's house to offer their condolences and to bring food and money to help with expenses. In keeping with Navajo tradition of burial within four days of passing on, my grandpa's funeral and burial took place a day or two later, and he was buried at the Sunset Memorial Cemetery in Gallup.

This was a great loss to me and I still miss grandpa today. He was my inspiration in my young life. There is not a day that goes by when I don't think about him.

When I was thirteen, I crossed the threshold into sixth grade. When I entered my classroom, I immediately recognized Ms. Kilgore, my third grade teacher. She still looked the same, but her personality was somewhat different from what I had remembered.

She recognized me and asked, "Didn't I have you in third grade?"

At first, I looked at her remembering the anger I had felt when she had flunked me. Then she called my name and said, "Would you please come to my desk?"

When I got to her desk, she repeated her question. I gave her a cold look and said, "Yes, I was in your class, and you flunked me."

She countered, "I flunked you because you were not meeting all of the academic requirements you needed to pass."

After that, I walked quietly away, unperturbed, knowing that I had certainly progressed since my last encounter with her. About a week or two later, she called me up to her desk again and said, "You are very different now. You have lost your stutter and you can read more skillfully now. You are also better at math than you were before." Then she turned her attention to the class and began roll call.

I noticed that her teaching method was not as strict as it had been in third grade, and she seemed to have softened, acting almost considerate. She was now more structured and organized in the way that she taught, and when she announced our different activities, she seemed to be asking, rather than demanding, our participation.

She brought a new concept into the classroom that year. She told us that all of us, boys and girls, were going to learn to cook. She brought in skillets, dishes and utensils as well as an electric burner. She noted that the kitchen hardware, with the exception of the electric burner, had all belonged to her. We started our cooking studies by learning how to fry an egg. Our lessons in the culinary arts usually took place at the end of the day, around two o'clock in the afternoon. We experimented with easy dishes like hot dogs and burgers, and then we moved on to learn how to follow recipes. Our first assignment involving a recipe was baking a cake. Later in the school year, we learned to make doughnuts. The process was hard to comprehend at first. We were divided into three groups with six students in each group. Each group took turns every day in learning the correct methods of preparation, cooking, and cleanup. Ms. Kilgore taught us the uses of cooking utensils and seasoning techniques. She made sure that we all wore aprons to protect our clothes when we cooked. The activity I loved most was eating the foods that we had prepared. Sometimes, I would tell her that I was not hungry, and that I would eat in the kitchen, not in the classroom. She said, "You really have changed, Gilbert. Now you are able to speak up for yourself."

That year, I finally moved from the little boys' dormitory, Cardinal Lodge, to Thunderbird Lodge with the older boys. Our counselor at the dorm was a person we called "Mr. Clean," after the mopping solution we saw advertised on television. His name was actually Mr. Kilgore. I learned that he was married to my teacher, Ms. Kilgore, and that they had actually been married ever since she was my teacher in third grade.

Also in my sixth grade year, the school adopted new policies for Thunderbird and Bluebird Lodges, where the older boys and girls stayed. For each hall, the school appointed two student resident assistants to take on the responsibility for cleaning and appearance detail and student conduct. They had to make sure that each hall was clean and in good condition. So, basically, all of us became Cinderellas! One abominable test to ensure the correctly made bed was to toss a coin on the surface of the bed. If the coin did not bounce, the bed was not correctly made, and had to be stripped and redone. Other military habits we had to follow included spit-shining our shoes, wearing our hair in crew cuts, ironing our clothes and tucking in shirts, marching in single file wherever we went, and going for early-morning runs. Usually, our marching was accompanied by military song and rhyme.

Another regulation brought into our routine was the use of the point system. Actually, it was not an official regulation, but an unofficial one instigated by the dormitory attendants. We could earn either merit or demerit points. To earn merit points, we had to correctly perform our classroom and dormitory assignments. When we cut corners in our duties, we got demerits. I was given a few demerits due to an error in assigning them to me instead of another boy named Wilbert John, who had actually earned them. I protested, but my claim went unheard and the records were not amended. So I resorted to my old habit of running away.

I felt that escape into the cold winter's night might help to bring light to the injustice that had been done to me. So I planned my escape, preparing my clothing by wearing triple layers of clothing to school that day. All day, I waddled around in all these extra clothes. When night finally arrived and everyone was sleeping soundly, I headed out back like I had done many times before. I took a blanket with me, as I knew that it would be very cold. The snow was falling thick and the wind was blowing fiercely. I wondered a few times as I was running into the night if this was a wise thing to do just to try to prove my innocence. But my determination to be heard overcame my rational thoughts. During that night's escapade, I was on alert for those who wished to report me or turn me back to the authorities. I saw the Navajo Police cars, and I knew they had been alerted to my absence by the school when they discovered that I was missing during bed check. I knew they were combing the area, looking for me as if I were a louse. Once again, I managed to get home, only to meet with concern on the part of my parents that I had run away yet another time.

I was returned to school after this winter adventure, and I had to face the principal, my teachers and counselors. They inquired about my reasons for running away from school on such a cold winter night, and I told them, flat out, that I ran away because of the mistreatment I was receiving from the dormitory attendants. I told them of the incidents that tarnished my merit record, and how the attendants were not willing to rescind the demerits wrongly given to me. I informed them of the only means of negating demerits— work and cleaning details. To my shock, I discovered that the principal and the teachers were unaware of the merit system used by the dormitory staff. By the end of the year, the principal abolished the point system and the discipline methods used by the dormitory attendants. So my act of protest was heard. I got what I wanted, and my demerits were expunged. Granted, my actions were complicated, but I guess that sometimes one has to go to extremes in order to get a point across to others.

Today, I occasionally see some of the former attendants from Chuska Boarding School. Usually they shy away from a conversation with me or avoid me altogether. Maybe they are ashamed now because of the times that they used their punitive merit system against us, or all the times they gave harsh punishments to us as kids to keep us from speaking in our native language. Today, it is almost shameful for Navajo children not to know the Navajo language. The usage of our native language is now encouraged, though the parents who were taught not to use it do not usually teach it. Now the children are taught Navajo and English in bilingual classes at our schools.

8
ME AND BIKES

A few weeks after the running-away incident, my parents seriously considered the idea of taking me to Phoenix, Arizona to live for a while. They were worried that I might run away from school again, and they were afraid that something would happen to me, especially during the winter months. They were also unhappy about the treatment that I and the other students at Chuska had received.

My mom and my dad decided to pull me out of school and take me down to Phoenix, where I was to live for about two months with them. My dad worked as a deliveryman at a factory there, packing big semi-trucks with vegetables that were picked from the fields. Some of my mom's cousins also had jobs as field workers there, picking vegetables. They came down during the winter months to earn money, as they were paid daily for field work.

My brothers were still in school at Chuska, and my dad went back to get them to bring them to Phoenix for winter vacation. We spent a strange Christmas there, with no snow or cold weather. During the day I stayed at home in a little apartment, babysitting my second-youngest brother, Terry. On weekends, I sometimes worked in the fields picking carrots, cabbage, and onions to earn some extra spending money for myself.

While in Phoenix, I had a bike accident. I crashed into an irrigation ditch while racing with a few neighborhood boys coming back from the local convenience store. After my bike accident, I had a bad stomach ache, which was a prelude to the following week's illness. It began with the stomach ache and frequent headaches, and then chills and sweating began to take over my body. I thought maybe it was the heat. My temperature began to rise, and I was sweating more and more. My parents decided to take me to the Phoenix Indian Hospital to find out what was wrong. Once there, my temperature was taken, and a doctor examined me. When he applied pressure to my right side near my waist, I yelped in pain. The doctor said that my appendix needed to be removed. I was admitted to the hospital right away, and surgery was performed on me that night to remove my appendix, which I later learned had ruptured.

After the surgery, I woke up during the night to find a needle, tubes, and tape on my arm. There was also a tube going into the side of my stomach. I asked the night nurse what the tube was for, and she explained that my appendix had ruptured and the tube had been placed there to drain the fluid from the area. With all these foreign objects placed in and on my body, and being alone in a strange place, I became frightened. I wondered where my mom and dad were. I found out later that my mom was at home and my dad was at work. I did not receive a visit from them until the following evening. This was my first experience in spending time in a hospital. The nurses there were very nice to me, maybe because I was a young Navajo boy. Anyone who was tiny and young was deemed innocent. Anyone innocent was deemed cute. So, I was cute, tiny, young, and innocent.

I spent Christmas and New Year's Day in Phoenix in the Indian Hospital. I was the youngest patient in the Intensive Care Unit. I stayed in that ward for about four days after the surgery, until I could eat solid foods again. For Christmas Day, all the nurses pitched in and gave me a present so I wouldn't be lonely. The gift box was pretty big, and it was wrapped in Santa Claus wrapping paper. I opened my present eagerly. As all the nurses watched, I ripped the paper off to discover a new mini Hot Wheels in the box behind glossy plastic. One of the nurses was especially nice to me, asking me questions about where I was from and how I liked Phoenix and what I thought of it. I didn't say much to her because I was still somewhat shy.

After New Year's Day, I was admitted to the recovery ward. I did not like it there because it was just one big room with thirty or forty other patients. I had gotten used to having one-on-one care in the ICU, where I didn't have to share a room with others. Here in the new ward, there were young and old male patients. I noticed that the older male patients tried to flirt with the nurses. Some wanted more of the nurses' attention because they felt that the nurses were paying more attention to me. I guess they were jealous of the attention I got. A couple of times, a nurse came with a wheelchair to take me on a joy ride through the hospital, pointing out different spots in the city from the windows. It was pretty fun, especially with the warm winter weather, and knowing that winter was taking its toll on the reservation in Twin Lakes. It never occurred to me at that time that I would be in a wheelchair again later in my life.

During the summer before my seventh grade year at school, my dad took me along with him to run his errands, and we went to White's Auto and Sporting Goods store in Gallup. My dad spent some time visiting with the owner, whom he knew very well. The owner had previously asked my dad to make some jewelry pieces for his wife and daughter. A month earlier, I had also purchased a weight set from his store. I browsed through the store while my dad was talking, and two items caught my eye. I stood transfixed before two mini dirt bikes, one painted bright orange, and the other yellow. I ran my hand over the sleek motorized bodies encased in glossy chrome. I imagined myself straddling the leather-cushioned seat on this flashy piece of hardware.

My father walked over to me as I looked at these bikes with longing eyes, and I noticed that he also seemed to be enthralled by them. He pointed out that the tread of the tires was knobby, making it good for all types of terrain. I wanted it, and so did he! He reasoned that I would be able to track down the cattle and horses throughout the back roads and fields of home on it. My father felt it would be an excellent and handy piece of machinery to possess. At that moment, a salesman came up and said that it would be ideal for fun and work, and he suggested that I take it out in the back alley and try it out.

We took the bike out the back door and I straddled it. The dirt bike's motor had a recoil starter, so the salesman pulled the cord to start the motor. He told me to hold the bike upright while he pulled so that it wouldn't fall. I was holding the handlebars, and without knowing, I turned the bike to full throttle. When the motor sprang to life, I was thrown against the salesman at the recoil of the dirt bike as it sped down the alley, without a rider. It crashed into a garbage can near where two drunks were sitting, and I saw them scramble to their feet in fear and run for their lives as the bike sped toward them. The owner came running from the store, wondering what all of the noise was about, and my father was laughing hysterically at the salesman and me as we lay on the asphalt, stunned.

When his hysteria subsided, my father decided to purchase the bright yellow mini dirt bike. While loading it into the back of the truck, I imagined the speed at which I would ride over hills and trails. As I moved in a daydream, my father was telling me that the bike was not only for pleasure and entertainment, but foremost to be used for work-related chores around home. I would be able to track and drive the cattle and horses without having my horse run out of steam. Also, having the dirt bike would bring ease to the horses if we ever needed to go out on tough terrain. Sometimes they were injured as we rode them in areas where there were a lot of prairie dog holes. My dad said the responsibility of keeping the bike in good condition was up to me, and that I must keep it well maintained.

It took me about a week to learn to operate the bike well. Besides using it for work, in my free time I would take it through high rough terrain, challenging it to go through the back hills where we had never gone before. My brothers caught on to the entertainment aspect of the dirt bike. One of my brothers and I built ramps for the bike out of old lumber. We were playing carpenters, trying to build variations of ramps, usually rising to three to four feet high. My grandma had asked us what we were building and we jokingly replied that we were constructing a shed house to store hay during the winter months. My brothers and I would laugh at my grandma's gullibility. It took us several days to complete the ramps. We tossed a coin to decide who would be first to test them, and I won the toss. My first jump was exhilarating, though frightening. In midair, I felt a rush of adrenaline, but fear crept into my consciousness as I wondered what would happen when I landed. I crashed and ended up covered with dirt from head to toe. Apparently, one of the boards that we used to build the ramp had broken, causing the crash. We replaced the board and repaired the ramp. Then it was my brother's turn to test it. Off he went, and to his surprise, he made a good solid landing.

I had the dirt bike for about a year before it finally gave out, but during that time, we tested it to its limits. We were only amateurs trying to act like professional daredevils, but we did not consider our feats amateur. We argued about who had made the longest and highest jump from a straight ramp that was raised only three to four feet above the ground, which was hardly difficult. We tried to make jumps over little ditches, but never succeeded. Usually, someone would take a tumble with minor injuries resulting.

I guess that we were influenced by television shows we saw at boarding school. There was always news about dirt bike riders doing all kinds of stunts and tricks. I had seen television shows about Evel Knievel and a movie called *Hell's Angels On Wheels*, and I imagined myself someday riding a big Sting Chopper or Harley Davidson, with sunglasses, leather clothing, and long hair. Of course, that was not going to happen while I was living at Twin Lakes. I had a dirt bike, and my dad wouldn't let our hair get long enough to cover our ears, as he believed young boys should have crew cuts. We challenged every possible little bump and turn to satisfy our adolescent whims. A two-mile course was trailed into rugged terrain. It consisted of steep hills, sharp turns, pretty high jumps, and rocks everywhere. The course was located in the back hills behind my grandma's home. Each rider was timed on the course. When there was an extension in a rider's time, we knew that something might have happened out on the course, a possible accident with an injury. We would go see what had transpired. Usually, it was a minor accident where the handlebars or a good fall knocked the wind out of the rider. My grandma would investigate where we spent our time during the day. She would track us, following the dirt bike trails and scolding us about the tire marks and ruts and the depletion of grazing grass caused by spinning the rear tire in place.

A few times we tried to rope some wild horses that were roaming around the hills behind my grandmother's residence. One of us would sit behind the other with rope in hand and would try to lasso a horse. At times we succeeded, but most times we did not. My brother wanted to capture a horse that he had seen a couple of times before on our outings. He said that the horse was beautiful and he wanted it for a prize. Never before could he capture it while on horseback and this was his chance to do so on the bike. There were a few moments of laughter as we discussed how we would capture his dream horse.

Right before our success in the capture of this horse, we hit a prairie dog burrow and up we flew into the air, twisting and tumbling around each other. Our prize for the moment was dust in our mouths and hair, bruises and scrapes here and there, and afterwards difficulty in starting the motor bike.

I sure made that piece of machinery work hard! I even rode the dirt bike when the spokes began to break. First there were a few and then more began to break in sequence. The bike's frame finally broke. We welded it back together and it held for a while. But the second time around, we just left it like that and didn't bother to repair it. That was the end of the little yellow bike. All that was left were broken parts. My dad and brother removed the motor and utilized it as a makeshift buffing machine for our silversmith work because we did not have electricity running into our residence.

In the early fall of 1972, I purchased my first true motorcycle, a Honda CB100 street bike. When I first saw it, my dad, my brother and I were just looking around at this store called Tony's Honda, where they sold motorcycles and chain saws. Prior to this, my dad had purchased a chain saw and we had gone back to the store so my dad could have some maintenance work done on it. That is when my eyes caught sight of the yellowish-gold motorcycle that was parked in the "used" section. The bike cost only $350.

I wanted this bike so badly that after I saw it, I asked my oldest brother to lend me part of the purchase price. He agreed to loan me the money on the condition that I would pay him back in full within two weeks. I sat on the bike and checked it out to see if it was the right size for me. It was kind of small, but I wanted to take the bike the same day.

One of the salesmen approached me and asked if I wanted to try the bike outside. I agreed, so the salesman wheeled it outside without starting it. Then my dad, my brother and I followed him and watched as he demonstrated how to operate it, and showed us how many gears it had. This was the first time I had ever heard about bikes having gears. The salesman seemed anxious to sell the bike and I really wanted it. We finalized the sale, and I asked my brother to back up the truck so we could put the bike in. The salesman seemed very happy to get rid of this used yellowish-gold motorcycle.

On the way home, my dad turned off of the main highway and onto a dirt road so that I could ride the bike the rest of the way home. He wanted to see if I knew how to operate the motorcycle as the salesman had demonstrated at the shop. This was the first time that I had seen a motorcycle which used a key to turn it on and an electric starter button to start the engine. I turned it on, grasped the clutch with my hand on the handlebars, and looked down at my foot to see where the gear was. All I had to do was push up the gear with my foot and slowly release the clutch, and off I went!

After I had learned all the details on how to operate this little machine I rode it all over to places where I had actually wanted to go all the time on the days when I was not working on silversmithing. I even drove it at nighttime because it had headlights. I was amazed that it had headlights and taillights that would brighten my pathway so I would know where I was going. I drove this bike through all extremes, in mud and snow as well as hot weather. Unfortunately, I didn't realize that it was using a lot of oil during all of the hard work I put it through, and the engine finally blew. That was the end of my little yellow-gold motorcycle.

9

SCHOOL GETS BETTER

At fourteen years old, I entered into the seventh grade. Being older than most of my classmates didn't bother me. Also, there were a few other students older than me who were still in the seventh grade. That year I had a good teacher with whom I recall having an excellent relationship. I called him Mr. Pea. His real name was Mr. Palmer. The reason we called him Mr. Pea was because he liked to cook black-eyed peas and cornbread in class. He was an African American man from South Carolina. After learning our names and becoming familiar with us, he seemed to favor me. I was called to Mr. Pea's desk and he informed me that I had a quick learning ability. He asked me if I would like to assist him in the daily classroom activities and studies. I was appointed a classroom leader although I had no inclination or desire for leadership. I did not want to carry the burden of extra classroom responsibilities. He always depended on me when he left the classroom to run his errands. Usually, things would go haywire and the class would be in an uproar upon his return.

My desk was located in the front of the classroom and Mr. Pea's desk was directly in front of mine. I always seemed to sit right next to a teacher, whether I disliked or liked the teacher. Mr. Pea always picked on me and in return I always picked on him. I could tell when he was bored because I would be working hard on my activities, thoughtfully quiet, and he would interrupt me from my work to do unimportant duties. Some days he would ask me to dust the blackboard erasers by pounding them into the concrete steps outside the classroom. Or at times, he would ask me to straighten his books on top of his desk. I was always called upon first when there was something to be done. Sometimes, I would counter him by telling him to ask someone else. When he lectured, I would make fun of him at times and he would be content with it. My classmates referred to him as my father because they knew he favored me, which was hilarious. But sometimes on his bad days in class, he would have a temper and he would say to some of the students, "I'll throw this book through you." He would get in a bad mood especially when the boys of my class would mess with his hair. His hair was always clean cut and styled, but as soon as one finger touched a single strand, his temper would flare.

Toward the end of the school year, Mr. Pea pulled me aside from the rest of the class and told me news concerning his health. It turned out that Mr. Pea was suffering from high blood pressure and heart complications. I was completely unaware of his medical history and did not think that he showed any symptoms, aside from his occasional temper tantrum. Because I had not known, I was a real hardball of a student, giving him a hard time during class hours. When I had the inside scoop on his health problems, I gave him an easier time, easing up on my jokes and attitude. When his temper exploded, I gave him enough time to cool off. During those times, I kept to myself and did my work. When he yelled, "I will throw this book through you," I would look at him as if to dare him to do such a thing. He never did—he was all talk and threats, but no action. He gave me a nickname. He called me Ghee. To this day, I still do not know what he meant by that.

Mr. Pea was a person who cared for the education of his students. He encouraged learning. He really wanted the whole class to learn more about arithmetic and reading. I was interested in algebra and going on to learn more about math. He taught me how to do algebra and I admired him for that. I know Mr. Pea was a teacher who really cared about his students, and that was rare in a teacher at that boarding school.

Every classroom at Chuska had two electric burners for cooking on occasions when home economics were being taught. Mr. Pea was an avid cook. Twice a month, we would hear the clanking of his metal cooking utensils coming down the hallway. This reminded me of the times I had gone camping with my grandpa. Enter Mr. Pea. He carried many different sizes of pots and pans and a few students would usually assist him.

He declared that he was going to introduce to us the culinary art of cooking foods from the South. Mr. Pea told us that he was going to bewitch our taste buds and have us wanting more of his own blend of soul food. He gave us a history of the cuisine of his ancestors. Mr. Pea prepared enough food for the class to sample a common dinner, which consisted of black-eyed peas, white pork, and home made cornbread. There was an absence of an oven and not enough time to prepare cornbread in class, so he baked his cornbread the evening before at his apartment. I used to hate eating beans and cornbread from the cafeteria once a week when it was served. The cornbread made in the school cafeteria was dry and I did not like the sensation of dry and dull food absorbing all the moisture from my mouth.

Although beans and cornbread is a good combination, it was an overdose to have it every week. Mr. Pea's favorite dish of black-eyed peas was bland and tasteless. On the other hand, his cornbread was a lot softer and fluffier than that from the school cafeteria, almost spongy, and tastier with added seasoning. I thought it looked funny that Mr. Pea was in an apron and serving platters of food to his students in class. He only needed to add a tall white chef's hat, a twirled mustache, and a camera crew to complete a 'Cooking with Mr. Pea: A Day of Southern Cuisine' episode!

During the long days in Mr. Pea's class, there was not one day where boredom got the best of any student. Our teacher was a go-getter! Whatever resources were available, whether academic or extracurricular, he made sure that they were integrated into our daily activities. He would enter our class or an individual student into school competitions or school contests being held at other schools. If we entered into a competition and won, Mr. Pea would arrange an incentive trip to the movie theater. At one time, he nominated me for an award of "Outstanding Student" from our class. I rejected the award, thinking that I was not an outstanding student. At that time, I thought of myself as a regular student who did not have any special qualities, talents or gifts. There were other students from other classes who were far brighter and more talented than me and I knew it. Mr. Pea also took us on field trips to see educational movies in Gallup. The whole class went on field trips twice a year to Albuquerque, Farmington and other places. Mr. Pea was always nice to his students and we tried never to take him for granted. He always put our educational interests first in planning school activities for us.

It was in early spring when Mr. Pea announced to us that he had entered the whole class in a school contest. This was a speech contest that was to be held about two months later in Many Farms, Arizona. Almost every boarding school on the Navajo reservation had entered the contest. Our class entry was to be presentation of a poem that he liked. He set aside classroom time for the next two months to practice our poem.

The first few weeks, we sounded like a traffic jam in New York City—a garbled, discordant ruckus. My classmates were shy and incoherent in our classroom while trying to practice as a group. A leader was needed, an extrovert who was gregarious and willing to jump to the front of the line and take action to lead our class. We needed someone to keep time and cue, to establish a rhythm and pace in which we were to recite our poem. After about a month, our class finally began to recite in unison.

On contest day, we were all nervous and excited. Three girls complained of being ill and wimped out of our performance. Upon our arrival at Many Farms Boarding School, we saw that the parking lot was way beyond packed with yellow school buses from many different regions across the reservation. Buses were parked outside the lots and along the highway. Inside the gym, there were many students. I could not comprehend the number of hustling and bustling people who were present for the contest. All I saw was a blur of faces and a loud commotion in the dark gym. The sounds consisted of clapping, murmurs and yells of conversations, cheering and jeering. The only sound that was coherent was the lady on the microphone announcing schools and what was to be recited by a single student or a group of students. The contest stage was the only illuminated area. My classmates had quickly become terrified of the swarm of students from other schools, and some began to doubt that we would be able to place. Mr. Pea just told us to relax and have confidence in ourselves, to focus and give the best performance we could.

As soon as our school was called upon, my nerves were dulled and my mind was set on the speech and the end of our performance. Standing on the stage as a group was exhilarating. I felt that our nerves settled because we were part of a group that supported one another. We performed our recitation in unison, sounding like a choral group. The two months that had been exhausted in practice was funneled into a five-minute performance. At the conclusion of our performance, I literally saw relief run through the bodies and minds of my classmates. Most of their worries had finally been relieved. But anxiety kicked in when we had to wait for the judges to decide on the performance of each school and where each school placed. Our class earned the first place blue ribbon and a plaque for our group performance!

I returned late for my eighth grade year at Chuska Boarding School because I was distracted by the idea of wanting to go to public school. My younger brother Hilbert was attending a public school already. I did not want to spend another year waking up in a bed that did not belong to me. I did not want to go through another year filled with dormitory hall detail, curfew and strict regulations. I had a long, taxing discussion with my parents about my hope of not going back to school at Chuska, but going to public school instead. My parents disagreed with this idea.

This debate had been ongoing in my mind since the beginning of summer vacation. My parents commented that my choice was probably made in haste and they were afraid that I was not motivated to learn. My dad asked what my main reason for not wanting to return to the boarding school at Chuska was. I said that I could be doing something at home after school every day if I went to a public school. I told him it was just too hard going back and forth every two weeks, and coming home only for weekends. I would get used to staying at the boarding school after a week or two, then the time would come when my parents would check me out for the weekend. The adaptation to boarding school life would fade and disappear as I spent a whole weekend at home, and when it was time to return to school, I did not want to go. The transition between school and home, accompanied by feelings of attachment, occurred every other weekend. I did not want to continue with the conflict through another year.

My dad told me, "You only have one more year of school left there. After this year, you can go to Tohatchi High."

I tried to counter, "But, dad, who's going to take care of all the cattle we brought back and the new horse that we got in the corral?"

He replied with a hint of sharpness, "Don't worry about that. I'll take care of that and I'm sure your grandma will look after it too. When you come back on the weekends you can look after the cattle and ride your horse around. I'm not too worried about that. The only thing that bothers me is that you are not going to school now. The reason why I'm saying this to you is when I was your age I didn't have the opportunity to go to school. The only thing there was for me to do was go to work on the Santa Fe Railroad with my father. I was the only skinny boy among all the big men." No matter how much I resisted, my parents still had the say-so, and I reluctantly returned to Chuska for another year.

Boarding school was already in session when I returned after my heated debate with my father. I noticed several new faces. These were new students from different schools, but the majority of the eighth-grade crowd were my old classmates who had been with me from the beginning of my school career. The moment I saw my old friends, I felt that I had an obligation to finish out the year with them. My memories of their friendship and our collaboration on school projects and games took hold of me, and I felt amazed at the close ties I felt toward some of my friends. I wondered if I would have these kinds of feelings when I went to the public school. In the end, I felt happy that I had decided to stay and complete another year with my friends at Chuska Boarding School.

I was fifteen years old and the eighth grade was my last year at Chuska. Many of my classmates who were my age had already graduated. I was glad that many of them had decided to continue into high school, but there were those who ended their education, believing that the eighth grade year was the highest and last grade to accomplish. Many of those who had that belief went to work, earning minimum wage. Some of those jobs began in apprenticeship and the students tried to work their way up the ladder. A lot of these graduates were seventeen to twenty years old and already had families of their own. They needed to provide for them.

That was a life that my parents did not want for me. They expected me to continue into high school after Chuska. After my high school years, my parents wanted me to go to college or the military because my uncles and aunts had done so. Schooling and higher education were concepts that my grandpa promoted when he was still living. So, eighth-grade was my last year at Chuska, but not the end of my education. It was also a time I could live to the fullest and leave an impression on the school and myself. There were many things to look forward to that year.

10

JUST TAKE A CHANCE

During my final year at Chuska, my mind was set on athletics and academics, but mostly athletics. I tried out for the basketball team, along with one of my cousins named Lester and one of his friends. Lester had already made the team the previous year. He had received the "All Tourney" award for that school year. His friend and I practiced hard for weeks with Lester as our coach before the tryouts started. He coached us in the loops and techniques of basketball. We felt confident enough of our skills and potential when tryouts for the team finally arrived.

We began the tryouts by practicing among sixty students for the next two weeks. By the end of the second week, the coach knew which of us had made the team and which did not. The sixty students listened to the coach and we waited nervously for his recruitment list. The coach had talked to us for a while and said to us, "Not all of you made the team, but I cannot pick all of you boys. I only need twelve of you to be on the basketball team." Then the coach called the players for the starting team. My cousin Lester, his friend and I were the first three to be chosen. Lester was the only player left over from the prior basketball season.

What appealed to us was that the three of us were all in the eighth grade and in the same classes. We all hung around together like there were no wedges between us. We all went everywhere together and did things together except for the times when one or more of us was checked out for the weekend by our parents. When I went home for the weekend I did not want to come back to school when Sunday arrived. I loved my dirt bike and riding around up in the hills, chasing away all the animals that came near to where my parents and grandma lived. What brought me back to school was the team. I did not want to let the team down.

We had practice on Saturdays, too. Being in the starting five was very hard work because our coach was very demanding and expected a 200-percent effort from us. He wanted us to play the way he said, according to his play list. I was the starting point guard and my cousin was the center. From time to time, I became discouraged during a play and Lester would tell me to focus on my technique, rather than on scoring points. All throughout the fall, I ate, slept, and drank basketball. During the playoffs for the NBA, I would be up half the night watching the game, cheering on my favorite team, the Los Angeles Lakers. I dreamt about basketball and how many points I wanted to score for my team with the crowd cheering me on in the background. I even slept with a basketball beside me on my bed almost every night!

The Chuska Boarding School basketball team was considered an average team; although we won many games, we also lost some. Actually, we probably won about half the games and lost about half. Every year, the school held a big tournament at the end of the basketball season. The school would invite a variety of different teams from other schools across the reservation to come and participate. Representing our school in the championship round, we shot for the basket but the basketball never went into the goal. The ball seemed only to hit the rim or miss, never giving us a score. Everyone on the team was getting irritated with one another. I could feel the tension and frustration of every teammate. We lost by a margin of twenty points to our rival, Tohatchi Boarding School, which was just down the hill, not too far from Chuska. They were known as the Tohatchi Pirates. By the end of the game, I despised them because it seemed like fortune was in their favor with every basket attempt giving them points.

We placed second in the tournament, which was good enough for my first year on the team, though I would have loved for our team to place first. We took the trophy and placed it in our school's showcase. A lot of memories are behind that second-place trophy. I have been meaning to visit the showcase to try and recall the smell in the air, the cheer of the crowd, the squeaking of our rubber soles on the gym floor, and the moment when we received our trophy. I have not seen the trophy since I graduated from Chuska. I had been obsessed with basketball during that season, but a new obsession was about to take hold of me.

It was time for softball season when spring came to tickle the frost off my nose, and there was still a chilly breeze coming from Chuska Mountain. This would be the second season that Chuska Boarding School was going to participate in softball tournaments. My friends and I decided to try out for the softball team to see if we had hidden talent. The day was slightly windy and cool when we tried out. I did not have a particular position in mind that I wanted to play, but I did like the sensation of catching a hard-thrown ball followed by the tingling in my catching hand. I could hear the whoosh of the batted fly ball, the whiz of a straight path of the ball, and the thud of the calculated bounce off a ground ball when I played with my brothers. I have always liked the padded thud of a softball hitting the leather glove.

The coach and school provided all of the necessary equipment for our tryout. The softball gloves given for the tryouts were tiny, with thin padding, sometimes inappropriate for particular positions. I had a nice glove of my own, purchased from the local sporting goods store. I remember the storekeeper who had sold me the glove saying that players in the professional league used gloves like this. He demonstrated the proper way to find a first-class glove. He said that gloves are as different as our own hands. The storekeeper said there are gloves for people who are right handed and for those who are left handed. There are gloves for small hands with long fingers and some with short fingers and so on. The storekeeper noted that there were different types of gloves for the different positions on the field. He fitted a glove on his hand and pounded his fist into the palm of the glove. The one he held had a shallow pocket—the area of leather on the palm of the glove. He said that this glove was excellent for infield positions because the player would be able to feel the ball and quickly launch it elsewhere. An outfielder would want to have a deep pocket with more padding, to absorb the heavy impact from fast incoming fly balls and ground balls, especially when the player is on the move. He then noted the webbing style between the forefinger and the thumb. In his case, the glove was openly webbed, which he said would be excellent for middle infielders because of quicker release. Depending on the webbing, it could be an excellent support for outfielders and second and third basemen. I know now that professional players wore thinner fitted gloves inside along with the catching gloves over them.

The softball coach continued the tryouts for about two weeks, assessing the strengths and weaknesses of all the players. During that time I kept notes on the coaches' mannerisms and teaching styles. I found out that these coaches were strict perfectionists when it came to choosing players for the softball team. They wanted the players to toss the softball with precise technique. For instance, a straight fastball was thrown with a side swing with a step forward into the direct path of the ball. The coaches were adamant about using proper technique, be it batting or pitching.

I had noticed the coaches kept a close eye on my performance, especially at my skill in stopping a ground ball. They would pull me aside asking if I had ever played softball before. I told them of my games played with my brothers using a solid homemade bat from a tree branch and without gloves. Whenever a batting opportunity came up for me, I did not do very well. I knew I was not a batter. Throughout the tryouts, the coaches placed us in various positions on the field. They tested our teamwork abilities and how we complimented each other in rotating positions. They wanted appropriate players in appropriate positions to gain the optimal softball team. One of the coaches decided who was going to play in different positions for the team. Then they announced our playing positions and who was going to occupy the starting positions. My friend was positioned at first base and I was to play second baseman as well as a catcher. The coach ended the announcement with, "I want a winning team."

Our softball season went very well. We were undefeated throughout the season, mostly due to our long, hard practices. The coach said that practice after practice would pay off, and it did. One of his quotes was, "If you play as a team, you win as a team. If you play like one, you win like one." We traveled across the reservation to different boarding schools, challenging schools on their home turfs. All of the schools we challenged were from Arizona and New Mexico. The schools in Arizona were Holbrook, Many Farms, Toyei, and Greasewood. In New Mexico the schools were Crownpoint, Wingate, Tohatchi, Ramah, Naschitti, and Navajo. I enjoyed that softball season and our winning year, especially when there was a trophy to bring home. Softball was the school's most popular sport besides basketball, especially after our winning year. Teachers and students attended a lot of the games and there was always something to chat about. I remember that Tohatchi High recruited many of the students from Chuska because of the number of skilled players at the school.

Another sport I really enjoyed was flag football. Football was a lot of fun. In this version of football, the rules were different and tackling was not part of the game. My position on the team was cornerback. I had pretty good catching skills, and in my first year on the flag football team we were undefeated. I really enjoyed the thrill of the games and the reward of winning many trophies.

When springtime arrived, the school always held an arts and craft show for students to enter their creations. Some of the items entered included drawings and paintings, sculptures, beadwork, leatherwork, sewing, and weaving. This was a good opportunity for the students to show their artistic skills and sell some of their own arts and crafts. The students began to brainstorm on their projects from the beginning of the school year. Each dormitory hall received a large amount of funding, and a portion of that went to arts and crafts materials.

For my project, I drew up plans and a list of possible materials to produce a poncho. Actually, I did not know what kind of material I needed for the poncho. I browsed through all the materials, wondering what would be best for my project. A dormitory aide assisted me. She suggested a material that was thin enough to allow me to stitch yarn through it. I decided on that material and fetched six different colors of yarn. I used the yarn stitching to produce a traditional design on the borders of the poncho. The end product was a beautiful beige poncho with earth-toned traditional designs on the borders, which sold right away during the show for sixty dollars. The poncho that I created took me about two months of frustrating work. This is where I learned how to sew for myself.

Throughout the school year, most of the students would work on their projects when they felt bored. Certain project rooms were assigned throughout each dormitory hall for a specific craft. The reason for this was that there were a lot of noises coming from the banging of hammers, drilling, and especially laughter and commotion made by students while working on their projects. Teachers and skilled school employees aided us in our projects.

In my dormitory hall, leatherwork was done in a closed area in the rear of the hall. Drawing and painting were also done in a single room. Sewing took place in the front of the dormitory hall and occurred about three times a week. Every student from the boarding school was given a chance to learn how to sew. Cooking also took place in the same room used for sewing. All these projects were done throughout the year, up to the day of the arts and craft show.

The arts and crafts show took place in the school gym and went on for about a week. Visitors came to the school, browsing through the finished crafts of the students. Several dormitory attendants sat throughout the school gym, keeping a watchful eye on the displays.

One evening after the excitement of our successful softball season and arts and craft show, I sat quietly working on another project and thought back to my last practice with the softball team. We had a cookout at the coach's residence and we listened to his last words of advice for us. "I am glad to have been your coach. It has been an honor to coach such talented young athletes. You all have set a high target for next season's team. I know that many of you will be continuing on, 'graduating' I should say, from Chuska. I will have only a few of you coming back next fall and I hope we continue the winning streak. But I say to those continuing, you should make an effort to be all that you can be. Be it softball or baseball that you play in high school, I hope you will not spend all your talent on athletics. Education is sometimes taken for granted. Take the opportunity and it will certainly take you far. There is enough talent for everyone. If you find yourself wondering what to do next, just take a chance at something that seems out of the ordinary. You will probably find another hidden talent. Good Luck. Now go eat!" His lovely wife smiled at our hungry faces staring at her in their backyard, and we began serving ourselves hot dogs, burgers, potato salad, chips, sodas, and juice, everything worthy for a cookout.

The coach's comment, "If you find yourself wondering what to do next, just take a chance," echoed in my mind. I remembered seeing an announcement on the bulletin boards for a leatherwork class. This was an opportunity to learn something new, especially when I did not have anything to do during arts and craft hours. The class was open to anyone with an interest, and the school seemed to have leftover materials that had been set aside for the arts and craft show. So I jumped up and hunted for the instructor. I found him in the main office.

As I was signing up, he asked me what I wanted to make. There were boys who wanted to make wallets. I said I wanted to make a belt. He smiled and joked that I already had one.

I countered with sincerity, "I want something that is mine, something that I can hold and have on me. I want my own mark."

He smiled and motioned me to follow him. We went to the leather shop in the rear of the building. The instructor asked me to select the width and thickness I wanted for my belt from the available leather straps. Then he asked me what designs I was interested in. There were various types of designs: flowers, leaves, and line and brand designs. He pointed out the types of tools that I would use to cut, design, and buff my belt.

I brushed aside the designs he was showing me. I said, "I want to dye the belt dark brown and engrave my clan with burgundy into the back of the belt. The rest of it will be plain. The buckle will have the silver ranger set with the silver ranger tip. I am going to make the buckle at home and it will be extra-heavy-duty." He chuckled and commented that I had already brainstormed and designed my buckle. Little did he know that this little Navajo boy thought of it as he walked away from the bulletin board, glancing back at the announcement, and headed to the main office.

I worked diligently on this article that meant the world to me, a piece that engulfed my heart and mind. It was my own and it belonged to no other. My instructor taught me the ins and outs of working with leather and the tools needed to make my project. We were told we had three months to finish our projects. After the three months of project work, there were the final two weeks of school, and those graduating had to prepare for the ceremonies. It took about two months to finish my project and I found that leather craftwork was an easy thing for me. Before I finished my project, I spent several days on polishing with burgundy leather dye. I engraved my Navajo clan, *Naakai dine'é* on the belt. My final product was glossy brown leather with burgundy engraved letters, an authentically made belt. The buckle was of heavy silver with stamp designs that I forged and soldered at home. This tangible strap of leather consumed my indigenous creativity, breaking barriers to the core of raw composition.

The new accessory was ready to be worn. I knew that the belt was going to go through processes of daily polish and shine. I believed that it would last for a long time. I wore this belt in high school, and it became an eye opener and a conversation piece.

I learned to sand paint from the same instructor who had taught me the skills in leatherwork. The room where I learned the leather craftwork had displays of sand painting. While I was working on my designs for my belt and buckle, I had noticed the intricate designs on the sand paintings. Many of the paintings told the stories of our ancestry and myths of the *Diné*. I noticed that the designs were circular and symmetrical, a distinct characteristic and configuration usually seen in jewelry made by silversmiths. I had an eye for detail in any piece of work, whether belonging to another or myself.

I asked the instructor if anyone could learn the art of sand painting. He knew I was interested in learning, and he asked if I was able to set aside time before the end of the school year. As the days rolled by, he taught me the basics of sand painting and what materials were needed. Wafer boards were the ideal piece of foundation and the most basic of glues to use was Elmer's Glue mixed with water. I wanted to know more about the sand used for the painting. I remember that he told me that the sand was taken from various riverbeds or sandstone from various locations throughout the reservation. I wanted to know how the sand was colored. I knew there was a process, but also that some of the sand colors were natural. The instructor even invited me to his home, where he had a shop built for his private use, to learn more about leatherwork and sand painting.

It saddened me to find out later that the person who taught me how to do leather craft and sand painting had passed away a year after I graduated from Chuska Boarding School. I heard of his passing on the local radio station.

Graduation was creeping along and I had plenty of free time since the athletic season was over. I decided to make use of my free time by debuting as a member of the Indian Club, my first and last year as a member. A classmate of mine had encouraged me to join earlier in the school year, but at that time I was really focused on my sports and arts and crafts. I noticed him again in my class and I thought back to his offer. I approached him that morning and asked him if it was not too late to join the club, and asked what the club was about. He informed me it was a Native American dance club, a club for learning traditional dance. I wondered why they had named the club, "Indian Club," when it was purely for dance. He informed me that Native American tradition and costume making were part of the dance. I told him that I did not have a costume, but he told me not to fear, as there were extra wardrobe items available. Choice of costumes was open to personal preference, so I could make my own.

There was not enough time to design and produce my own costume before graduation. The club member told me that the club was holding tryouts later that day for a position that was occupied by a dancer who lacked devotion. He mentioned that I would be an excellent candidate for the position because I was the right height for the particular dance position and I was athletic, which was an important point of consideration for recommendation to the club. He was pretty sure that I would be able to snatch the position away from the other dancer, even if I did not know how to dance traditionally, just as long as I was devoted to learning. I tried out and

I got the position. I was in for an extreme test of physical fitness!

When I won the position, I joined the Apache Crown Dancers, as we were called. The costumes these dancers wore were very intricate in detail and authentically made from genuine materials. There were three main pieces of each dancer's costume: dresses, crowns, and painted masks.

The dresses were made from synthetic leather. The dormitory attendants contributed their help in making these dresses. They were cut and sewn in about three weeks. The dresses also had pieces of conical-shaped tin attached to the fringes. With those pieces attached, one would recognize the dress as a jingle dress, commonly seen, worn, and heard today at powwow events. The tin pieces would make a jingling noise when you walked or danced. Sometimes, the dress sounded like rain hitting the tops of tin cans in a basket. The more the dancers moved, the more sound the dresses made—the more rain, the louder the noise.

The crowns were the most detailed and time-consuming to design and produce. We made the crowns with papier-mache. Usually, the crowns were painted black and offset in white with intricate traditional designs that were called storytellers. Each design told a certain story taken from the Apache myths and legends. The mask was very simple. The mask was just a black cloth with holes for the eyes. Our moccasins were made of gunnysack material with a thin leather strap with bells attached to it. We wore socks underneath the moccasins. We painted our bodies with black powder watercolors, mixed like mud, from our waists to our necks and down our arms. The paint sometimes became itchy and uncomfortable. The uncomfortable feeling usually occurred while we were dancing and sweating. Then the paint cracked and started to run.

The Indian Club would perform at powwow gatherings alongside the other dance groups. Our dance instructor and two other students were the singers for the Apache Crown Dancers. I was a little nervous the first time I danced in a field with other similar dancers. But soon the fear began to blend in with the excitement of the crowd and the dancers. Also, other students and the crowd could not have spotted me out of the dancers because of the black cloth that covered my face. I took comfort in that.

There were different groups of dancers from various boarding schools from around the reservation. When we were announced and came out onto the grounds, a lot of people from different areas were waiting for us to perform, encouraging us with screams and whistles. They were constantly taking pictures and wanting us to dance more in the center of the space. We all danced as a group for about twenty minutes and we waited for the judging and the distribution of the trophies. To my surprise, we captured first place in that powwow event. We were one of the best groups in the region, and the crowd loved us. They cheered for more of the Apache Crown Dancers performance.

That same year, I volunteered to work in the kitchen. I volunteered for two reasons, and I do not think that anyone would blame me for them. One, I had access to a supply of food and a variety of beverages. It is common knowledge that all boarding schools' cafeteria servings are almost minimal serving sizes, so usually everyone is still hungry after breakfast, lunch and dinner. The bullies were especially hungry. They took food from younger and feebler students to satisfy their hunger. This was an opportunity to benefit from free, abundant sustenance. Secondly, it exempted me from dormitory work details, as it brought to me students willing to work off my punishments in exchange for a few pieces of delicious leftovers. My kitchen privileges gave me a child's view of fame and fortune, a view where a pair of new shoes or boots, along with a new shirt and a pair of pants, and a nice haircut made me feel like a whole new person. I must say that my participation in arts and crafts, the kitchen, and athletic activities transformed me into an individual who looked forward to opportunities and the future.

In 1973, the day came when graduation from the eighth grade at Chuska was a reality, and I did not find any enthusiasm in leaving Chuska. I even wished on that day that Chuska had a high school. I wanted to stay at the school one more year because I had learned to take chances and believe in myself. I graduated from Chuska Boarding School in late May with about sixty other students. I did not consider myself intelligent, just average. But I graduated within the top five of my graduating class, which was a surprise.

I had noticed that there were several students who were not able to graduate because they did not have the required credits or grades. I wondered what was so difficult about getting a decent grade. Most of the work is done just by listening patiently to the lectures and paying close attention. I thought that you could get a decent average grade by doing that. If you really wanted to be a brain or an egghead, you would have to study hard and complete your homework.

It was amazing that I graduated from this school. There were many memories and sentiments attached to Chuska. I thought back to the days I ran away, hating the school and the teachers. There were many teachers and school employees that I had despised, but in my final year, I had really grown into an open-minded person who had allowed instructors and coaches to become acquaintances, and even true friends.

My parents had offered to purchase a suit for my graduation, but I didn't think that it was important to be so dressed up for the event. I thought that the more important concept here was that I was growing into a more mature person who was continuing his mission into high school. That day I decided to wear regular blue jeans with my cowboy boots that I polished the night before. Somebody from the previous year had donated a blazer coat to the school. It was light blue with dark pin stripes. The coat fit me fairly well. Oh boy, it sure did make me look like a theater usher! It did not bother me at all.

I entered the gym with the feeling of just wanting to get through the next few hours without any hardships. I wanted a nice, smooth and easy day. We lined up for our graduation places and took our seats. Finally, my name was called and I went up to the podium where I received a certificate. I returned to my chair and that was that. I had survived my years at a rough Bureau of Indian Affairs boarding school.

11

SILVERSMITHING, SCHOOL AND MOTORCYCLES

The summer weather was sneaking up on us when my dad and I sat down and began talking about expanding our silversmith business with a comprehensive plan. I was displeased with the thought of starting a bigger business because it would require a lot of my time and responsibility, and workers who could be counted on for consistent quality work were scarce. My dad did not worry about these things as I did. He had taught me how to work with silver when I was around ten years of age. The first pieces of jewelry I made were a ring and a bracelet. I learned to make them on my own. A few years later my father asked my brothers and I if we wanted to start our own silversmith business from home. We had been at this two years, and now my dad asked me to be the boss.

When we discussed the family business, I was terrified to voice my opinions and ideas to my father. He had a short temper, and I had to be careful of what I said about the business. In our business conversations, when I would suggest an idea that was not to his liking, he would become upset and I would remain silent for the remainder of our conversation. I found that the best avenue of action for me was to simply listen and take his orders. He was not someone most people dared to argue with; only my mom dared to disagree with him. These arguments pertained mostly to his use of finances, like lending money to his brothers, sisters, and other relatives. My brothers and I grew up making jewelry with him and his demeanor was not surprising to us, but we were mostly doing individual work to make profit for ourselves.

I would have felt better about my father's plan if two of my brothers could have contributed to building our business, but they had responsibilities of their own. One was helping my grandma, herding the sheep and working around her home. My oldest brother had a family, and he therefore attended to their needs. My dad informed me that he would be our salesman and market the jewelry in all corners of the reservation and outside of reservation land as well. I was not too happy with my dad holding on to our profits, because he would lend the money to relatives all the time. Usually, the workers shared the profit that was made and it would be split equally among them, but mine would be spent before my father returned home from his sales trips.

When dad asked me to be the person in charge of our silversmith work, I really didn't want to because I was uncomfortable with this duty. I was not an organized person and did not know how to take charge and tell other workers what to do. This was the reason why I had been doing individual work. To me, my dad sometimes seemed similar to a prison warden, cautious and strict, so I was not comfortable hiring a few of my able friends, even though they knew the ins and outs of silversmith work. I had second thoughts about his request for me to be the boss and I informed him that I would give him a definite answer the next day.

He turned around and looked me straight in the eye and said, "You are going to be the person in charge. You're always working on your jewelry here on this work table in this shop. And I know you're the last person who leaves because you don't stop until you finish your work."

That was true, but I knew it was because I had a hard time concentrating on my work, especially when I got interrupted by a visitor and didn't know how to control how long to visit. For this reason, I felt that I could not be in control of others, let alone supervise them and instruct them on how to do silversmithing. I didn't have any confidence in my ability to be a supervisor. I left the task of hiring to my father, so that he could use his own judgment in finding reliable and skilled workers. He hired two of his nephews and the husband of one of his nieces.

I was aware that these three individuals had never worked on silver jewelry a day in their lives. They were a lot older than I was and I didn't believe that they were good choices for the business that we wanted to develop. I didn't want to instruct somebody who was older than me because I felt that they would not take instructions from a younger person. I had learned my silversmithing at a very young age, how to solder and do buffing, but they had never done anything like this. I told them that they could learn by observing me for one week, and that they could start learning how to do the work themselves the following week. I knew we were going to get behind and lose some time by my working alone while the three observed how I did everything. They asked me many questions which I felt were unnecessary, and I did not like answering them.

I asked my next-younger brother to help me with the silversmith work. He was very close to my grandma, as she raised him from the age of twelve. Sometimes I had a hard time asking him to help me out because he was inflexible. He would only agree to be the buffer and to saw out little items. It was very hard for about one month after my dad hired the infamous trio. They reminded me of that saying, "You can lead the horse to the water but you can't make him drink." They didn't know how to work or take advice from a younger person, but my dad left me with no choice. So I just went ahead and advised them on what their duties were and I finally found confidence in myself. My dad directly told them that they had to learn and work with me as the supervisor and that they would have to keep up the pace because he had too many orders that needed to be filled.

My dad would be gone for days at a time so I was left alone with the lazy trio that just wanted to eat all the time. They always came to work late, then just sat around waiting for me to advise or direct them on when to start working. All we worked on were small projects like rings, earrings, bracelets, and pendants. However, we turned out a huge quantity of jewelry. We would make three hundred sets of earrings, five hundred rings, and at least two hundred pendants. This was the only way that we were able to get a large sum of cash to pay these worthless, lazy employees. I reminded them of this when we got behind on our orders!

At that time, my mom was working every day at a local Chapter house for the Navajo Nation as a social worker. She departed early in the morning for work and came back around six in the evening. She wouldn't approach me when the infamous trio was working, but she pulled me aside and talked with me alone.

My mom asked me how the business was operating and how far along we were with the orders. In reply, I told her the employees were lazy and taking too much time. I informed her that I hoped that by the next week they would start working faster and coming to work on time. My mom asked me to bring several pieces of the jewelry to the house so she could help out putting the stones in the finished products. And after listening to my concerns, she said she would notify my father to advise his nephews to come to work on time and not to be loafing around. My mom worried that I was doing most of the jewelry work. She asked if I had eaten yet.

I said, "No, I'm too busy to take a break." My mom advised me that I should take a lunch break and have a sandwich or something to eat, and not try to work all day without a break.

After a while, I felt more comfortable working with my cousins. When we finally began to get along with one another, one of the things that made work fun was telling jokes about what we were making. I used to tell them what my dad would say to me when I first started: "This soldering is like a little boxing match with one opponent trying to knock the other down." I never disagreed with my father because he knew more and was the most experienced welder for the Navajo Nation Water Development Department, working all over the Navajo reservation.

We all worked from 8 a.m. to 5 p.m. during the week. We took the weekends off, but sometimes my cousin and I would work through the night and had very little sleep. We tried to sleep in the next day, but my dad was always around and would tell us to get up and get to work despite the fact that we only had a few hours of sleep. Sometimes it felt like I didn't have any free time for myself.

It was much easier and a respite for me when the infamous trio learned the task of silversmithing. They began to actually collaborate with me and say, "OK, boss." We would tell jokes to one another, and laugh while we all listened to the radio station KGAK, which was the only one in the surrounding area that broadcast in the Navajo language most of the day.

As our pace quickened, we began running out of silver supplies more frequently than we anticipated. When this happened, we had to wait for more supplies, so we didn't work that entire day or sometimes for a couple of days. Then we would just sit around and converse about our upcoming assignments, or we would help my dad's nephew work around the place, fixing corrals and doing general maintenance, taking care of the cattle and horses. Sometimes when we finished the silversmith projects and had time to play around, we would have a roping contest to see who could rope the dummy the most, or we would get on the bucking barrel to see who could last the longest time on the bucking barrel ride. Although we were supposed to be working, my dad's niece's husband had an old used car and would say to us, "Let's go for a cruise to town to get something to eat," and we would go.

After all the long months of jewelry making, I decided to put aside a quantity of funds each time I sold some of my individual jewelry work. I was determined to save up an adequate amount of money to purchase a full-sized motorcycle that I had dreamed of owning. My main initiative was to get the biggest and the most monstrous motorcycle ever to be owned on the Navajo reservation. In high school, I had always admired and checked out some of the other students who had come to school on their monstrous motorcycles. I was curious and asked all the students who owned motorcycles questions as to how fast their bikes ran and how to operate them. One of these students became my close friend, and he demonstrated to me how to operate it and gave me the opportunity to drive it alone. That is when I built up my interest in someday purchasing and owning my very own huge motorcycle.

Finally the day came when I was able to save enough money to purchase a used 554cc Honda 4-stroke. It was a street bike that was very economical on gas but had a powerful engine. It was brown with an assortment of chrome on it, and in the middle of the gas tank it had a logo that said "Honda." My dad co-signed for me since I was not of age. I treated this motorcycle like it was a little baby. I spent most of my time washing and polishing it to enhance the shine of the chrome. I valued this huge motorcycle so much that I moved my twin bed into the shack house right next to my motorcycle just to sleep by it.

My family, especially my dad, informed me that I spent too much time with my motorcycle. He thought that I should be more mindful of responsibilities at home, in our jewelry business, and to our livestock, especially the horses. Taking care of the cattle was a task I was not too worried about because I could herd them with my bike.

Later on, I made a few additions to my bike. I installed a fiberglass windjammer shield protector, which kept the wind and cold rainwater away from my face. I liked this because I never liked wearing a helmet with a face shield. It seemed to me that I was suffocating inside that helmet, and I felt like an astronaut ready to go to the moon or outer space when I wore it. I also purchased a padded "sissy bar" that I had spotted in one of the local motorcycle shops while visiting in Albuquerque. I used the sissy bar to rest my back when it got tired on long road trips.

I made a journey to Albuquerque at least twice a month to rummage around for parts that I needed for my motorcycle which were not available in Gallup. When I went to Albuquerque alone on these trips, I also talked to jewelry retailers there to ask them questions without hesitation and in greater detail regarding what they wanted me to create, and I discussed my own ideas with them. On those trips when I went alone, I was more comfortable and could concentrate better than when I was with my father.

In September of 1973, it was early fall and warm, which some people call Indian Summer, or just simply "hot" in this region. It was time to go back to school, and it was my first time going to a public school and using public transportation. I had finally struggled past the 8th step at boarding school. It had been tough, trying to learn the white man's way. What was I doing to myself? Was I learning something, or forgetting who I was—or did I want to be somebody I couldn't be? At any rate I was overcome with enthusiasm. This was another new beginning.

The high school was called Tohatchi High School, and it was located only about ten miles away from my parents' residence. When I went to registration, I saw that I already knew some of the students, some of whom I used to rodeo with, and some of them were my cousins. I had a nickname, Spyder, which some of my high school friends called me because of the way I presented myself. I also made new friends. It wasn't hard making friends at school, because everybody seemed to know one another and where they were from, but I was a new student there as a freshman.

My fascination with motorcycles grew. Soon, I had set aside a sufficient amount of funds to purchase a brand new blue motorcycle. I saw it in the showcase window of a shop in Gallup. It was a 1974 Honda, with a 360cc engine with a two-stroke manifold. For my sixteenth birthday my father gave me part of the purchase price for my new motorcycle, with an agreement that I was to pay the remainder. Prior to coming up with my portion of the cash, I went back occasionally during the week to see if the motorcycle was still in the showcase window. I didn't want to lose out on the special deal that the owner had made with me.

After I purchased the motorcycle, I took it for a test drive for the very first time. The owner advised me about the number of gears the bike had, the front and rear brakes on each handlebar, and the clutch. It was a bit confusing because it was the first time I had heard about such placement of brakes and gears. I couldn't remember where the brakes were the first time I rode it home, and my alternative solution for stopping the motorcycle was to jump off and wreck it into a sand dune not too far from where I lived. This caused a medium size dent in the middle of the gas tank. After this incident I learned quickly how to operate the gears and how to control my brakes.

So my freshman year in high school started off unbelievably well. Every day I was eager to get up early in the morning and head for school with no one reminding me. I drove my motorcycle to school regularly on nice days and left it parked at home during the winter season.

My dad reminded me every day that I had chores to do. "Don't come home late, you have a lot of chores to do. Feed your horses, and check to see where the cows are before you begin on your jewelry work. I also need your help around the house." My younger brother, Hilbert, also had a lot of work that he needed to attend to around our grandma's house. My older brother, Delbert, just drove around and we didn't know where he was most of the time. He always wanted to be by himself and did not want to be bothered by anyone else or help around the house. Delbert's head was constantly under the hood after school, working on his car engine. My dad didn't hassle me because the majority of the time I tended to do what he wanted done around the house. I did some of my jewelry work, along with my other chores.

In early October 1973, it rained constantly, and eventually started to snow. My dad, his brother, his nephew, and I planned a hunting expedition to Quemado one weekend, in hopes of bringing back a deer. During our long day of tough walking in the mud, snow, and freezing temperatures, we didn't spot any deer. My dad had given me a 30-30 automatic Winchester rifle that I took along with me during our expedition. We spent two nights all bundled up around the fire trying to keep warm as much as we could. Finally, Sunday came, and I was glad! We just got out of that location as quickly as possible, because none of us spotted or shot any deer.

When we returned home, it had already gotten dark and we were all exhausted. I know that my dad was sore and cold from the freezing night temperature, and he went straight into the house. Hilbert greeted us in front of the house, and helped me unload and store the camping gear into another truck just for the night.

We were disappointed that we had not brought back a deer from this hunting trip as we had planned. My mom had also expected that we would bring back a deer or two. She said to my dad, "You always bring a deer home. What happened this time?"

All he said was, "There were too many hunters, but no deer. We are going to try again this weekend in the back of Cove Mountain.

I said, "I'm sure the other day when I was feeding the horse I spotted a couple of deer going up toward the mountain. They just come down the mountain to get a drink of water because they know I always chop a hole in the ice in the earthen dam over that way."

One day in the middle of the week, I was exercising one of my horses, riding out in the mountains. Late in the evening I saw traces of deer tracks. The weather was good; there was a slight cool breeze. As I was checking out the scenery from on top of Cove Mountain, I sighted some deer below. There were two bucks, at least eight- or ten-pointers.

As I was on my way back home, the thought of seeing the deer kept going through my mind, and I had a strong desire to get one of them. Upon my return home, I asked my dad if there were any extra 30-30 bullets left from our hunting expedition. First, he just looked at me with a negative look in his eye. It took him a minute or two to think about it. He asked me, "What are you going to do with these bullets?"

Then I explained to him that I had seen two big bucks around Cove Mountain, and that I really wanted to get one. He looked at me with a smirk on his face, and handed me a leather belt that held bullets. This leather belt didn't hold the whole cartridge of the bullets, and it also didn't fit me around the waist. It was too big, so I just hung it from my shoulder, down to my waist, and the rest of the bullets I placed in my jacket pocket. In my other hand, I had a 30-30 automatic Winchester rifle.

I went to bed that night thinking of those two bucks. I had a hard time going to sleep, and I kept waking up. So instead of sleeping all night, I got up around 4:00 a.m. My dad was already getting up, too. In the early morning hours the deer are not afraid to come out. I explained to my dad that I would be using my horse to go way in the back of Cove Mountain. The deer are afraid of the scent of a human, but they will not be afraid of the smell of a horse. So I walked outside and headed for the horse corral. I saddled my horse, and started off. I was so excited that I didn't even eat breakfast, I only had a drink of water.

I began toward the hill on the top of the mountain. I saw all kinds of animals, like wild horses, coyotes, and bobcats. There were no deer in sight along the way. A little further alongside the mountain, I stopped my horse and got off. I was looking around and

I sighted the same two deer that I saw the evening before. I wanted to get closer so I could get a clearer aim at one of them. Before I could get too close, I heard a loud noise, like a gunshot. There were four or five deer racing across the ridge at a place called Banana Ridge. I just got back on my horse and kept on going northwest at least a half a mile.

I spotted six deer down below in the valley, at the edge of the meadow. However, I never saw the two bucks again. As a result I decided to shoot one of these six deer. It was a young four-point buck, but I was satisfied with that. By this time the sun was already up, and the day was already getting too hot. It was nine or ten o'clock in the morning, so instead of riding the horse, I placed the deer on top of the horse in the saddle and tied it down with a rope, and headed straight home. I led the horse by its reins, and held my rifle in my other hand.

I got home around noontime, and my dad came out with a surprised look on his face and said, "You got one!"

I said, "Yeah, but this is a four pointer, I sought after the ten pointer."

He asked me, "How many bullets did you use?"

I told him that I used six bullets.

Then he said, "If you were a good hunter, you would only use one bullet."

But I told him, "No, I tried to shoot at the other two bucks, even though they were running, that's where I wasted the other five bullets."

Then he told me to never aim at a running deer.

I just said, "OK." My dad and I butchered and skinned that deer.

We had a lot of snow that year. It was a foot or more deep. We had a tough time with the cattle and the sheep because there was too much mud from the melting snow, which kept them from grazing. Due to the extreme weather, the roads were impassable.

Even though the roads were bad, my dad always managed to get to the feed store to get a large amount of hay and grain for the animals. After my dad and a couple of my brothers brought back the hay and grain, my brothers and I shoveled the snow out of the sheep and horse corral so the animals would have some clearance to eat. After all this labor was done, my grandma was happy and satisfied to see her flocks nibbling on some hay and know that her flocks were fed for another day.

My brothers and I would walk to the road to catch the school bus. It was almost two miles to the bus stop and it was tough walking back and forth, but we had the endurance to walk lengthy distances. We would start early in the morning. After I got home from school, my responsibility was to chop a lot of wood because it would get extremely cold during the frigid winter nights. Since there was no light source of any kind to enable us to distinguish what we were doing in the dark, everything had to be done before nightfall.

As the sun came out during the day, it got warm and the snow started to melt. It got awfully muddy and water was rushing everywhere, it was dreadful for everybody, especially the livestock. I already knew that I couldn't ride my motorcycle to school as it was extremely cold and the roads were icy and slippery, so all I could do was to shine, polish, and start my bike. Around mid-November, I only kept two horses in the corral to feed and look after, Roper and Baby. The other horses I put out to pasture, as the cost of feeding them was too much and we could not afford to feed them all at one time. They were always close by in the nearby hills. Every day after school I chopped a hole in the ice with an axe so they were able to have drinking water, and I fed them hay and grain every other day so they could be physically strong for the winter and would not wander so far away. My grandma reminded me constantly by saying, "Don't let the horses drink in the late evening, the winter nights are long, cold and bitter!"

When spring came, there were days that I would get lost in the hills while exploring the mountains on my motorcycle, where there were only old roads with deep ruts where nobody had been in a long time. The only trails I could see were those made by wild animals such as deer, bobcats, and wild horses. There were no porch lights or streetlights to be seen at night since there were no electrical lines running to my parents' residence.

Sometimes I went camping for two or three days at my late grandfather's residence, the place where he lived permanently for the remainder of his years after my grandparents separated. Before their separation they used to share this particular camp for the summer to graze their flock. My grandpa worked on his cornfield frequently as he planted his crops in the springtime in anticipation of an abundant harvest in the fall.

During my camping retreats, I utilized this time to think about what I wanted to do with my future. I could almost hear my grandfather speaking to me in the cool swish of the fall wind, giving me a sense of guidance and direction over my young life. Riding in the fresh cool air and enjoying the scenery put my mind at ease and allowed me to enjoy my freedom. Generally when I didn't return on time, my dad and my brothers would wonder why I was gone so long on my retreat and would search for me on horseback to see if I was in a difficult situation. When I would spot them at a distance coming towards me, I would wave at them and be astonished because they had taken time out of their busy schedules just to check on me to see how I was doing.

A couple of my trustworthy buddies from high school lived nearby and had decent dependable motorcycles, too. We were like teenage motorcycle ruffians who got together and caused all kinds of trouble and did crazy things. Sometimes, we would raise Cain at concerts held in the surrounding areas such as Gallup and Window Rock. We would first come up with a plan to meet at a certain spot, knowing that things go awry. The local law enforcement officers quickly found out we were troublemakers, and they were constantly on the lookout for us at these events. They knew we were driving our motorcycles without driver's licenses and they would make every effort to catch us. Sometimes they would succeed and other times they would only catch or question one of us before anything had happened. We looked and acted innocent and sometimes were lucky enough for all of us to get away. After our getaway we would use residential roads and try not to disturb others where we were not supposed to go on our motorcycles.

During the summer months we had basketball tournaments outside with other local boys at recreation centers in the surrounding area. When we defeated the other teams they would attempt to start a fight that would begin with name-calling, shoving and pushing us around on our way out of the recreation center, and then all hell would break loose. The other teams would start to argue, saying they had won the game. We tried our best to avoid getting into all of these altercations.

Before we headed home after the games, we would sit on our bikes cooling off, discussing which route to take to get back home. There would be a posse of girls surrounding our motorcycles wanting us to give them rides back home or just to cruise to the store and back. Most times I would only take my favorite girl, someone I already knew from before; but there was always a new one who would approach me and introduce herself with a smile and I could not refuse to accept her little heart. I would agree to take this new girl to wherever she wanted to go. This is how we accumulated girls. Before it got too late at night, I knew that I had to get back home and tend to my jewelry business, horses, and cattle. I also had other girlfriends at the rodeos that I attended. I knew my two worlds would never come together, meaning that my girlfriends would never see each other, let alone know anything about one another.

There were many times when I used to challenge my new motorcycle to the top speed of ninety-five miles per hour. I felt like

I was flying in the air, and the motorcycle would vibrate from side-to-side with the acceleration from the excessive speed. This vibration caught my attention as I realized when it happened that I had to take my motorcycle to the shop to have my wheels balanced while it was still under warranty. Even though I had adequate protection, in the back of my mind I still feared that I was an accident waiting to happen.

I liked cruising my motorcycle every day to the nearby convenience store and back, especially on my lunch breaks, just so I could see who was out and about and to get some munchies. It was easy for me to do this because my motorcycle was economical on gas. There was no one to interfere or stop me from jumping on my motorcycle so I could get away to run an errand at any time. I liked to feel the cool breeze hitting my face and body and blowing my hair back on those hot summer days. Even though my bike was a street bike, I challenged it to go in the deserted areas that a street bike wasn't made for. I drove my bike to its limits.

12

ROPING AND RIDING

Early in September 1974, I returned to school and began my sophomore year. I was looking forward to going back to school and excited about the upcoming school year. I knew most of the students by then, but I also noticed that there were a few new faces at school, and that most of them were freshmen. I went to school early on my first day to register, but there was already a line of students picking out classes and comparing with their friends so their class schedules would be similar.

One thing I wanted to do was to try out for sports, but my dad always disagreed with high school sports and said, "What? The only students who try out for sports are the ones who have no livestock or other chores to do at home. You have a lot of things here to do instead of messing around out there with a ball or such other school activities." I didn't appreciate what he said, but I already expected him to say something like that, so I respected his decision and didn't try out. I just decided to let go of sports and concentrate on my academic studies. Rodeo was the only sport that I did while in high school, but that was not a school activity.

I had to pay attention to my dad and be of assistance at home. My father was very strict and sometimes I hesitated to go back home when I had spent some extra time at school. Sandwiched between the chores at home and homework from school it seemed impossible to participate in anything. Without his knowledge, I did sneak away a number of times, typically at night because he would go to sleep early before anyone else and be up the next day by dawn. I would go to high school basketball games and to movies in town. Sometimes I would just drive around and go hang out with some friends from local surrounding areas. When I got home from school I would do all my chores first, before going horseback riding in the mountains. Most of the time I would only try to go if there was enough daylight left. My horses always looked forward to exercise, because an excessive amount of time in a corral can cause a horse to become restless.

When the days were pleasantly warm and the roads were nice, I rode my motorcycle back and forth to school so I would get there first, and after school I would race back home right away before it got dark and cold. At the end of November, I stored my bike inside the shack house until the next year at the end of March when it turned nice and warm again.

During Christmas break my brothers and I would enter the rodeos in Window Rock, Arizona, and Farmington, New Mexico, so we would have some extra money to feed our horses. If we won in the event that we entered, we would get prize money. I really took pleasure in going to these rodeos in the winter because they were always indoors. I could feel the chill, but it was alright for the animals, since there was no snow on the ground inside.

After the New Year in January 1975, I continued with my school and registered for new classes again. January and February were the two months that I despised because the days were just as cold as the nighttime. These months were tough on the livestock, so my brothers and I had to keep a watchful eye on the cattle. This freezing weather kept me inside the house attending to my jewelry work in addition to my homework.

Then came March roaring like a lion in the jungle. Although the wind blew everywhere, left and right in different directions, it didn't inconvenience the animals. Then it was time to take my bike out and go for a short spin, which I was looking forward to during all those wintry months.

During April, it started to get a little warmer and the days were longer. The longer and warmer days gave me more time outside to ride my motorcycle and do other activities. My brothers and I would help out my grandma with her flock because of the lambing season; it took her a long time to separate the mothers from the newborns, and that's why she needed our help all the time.

I always looked forward to May because school was let out for the summer. Then I could pay more attention to my horse and practice roping on him. He was happy to get out because he was in the stable all winter long. I also had jewelry work that required my direct attention because this was my only source of extra spending money.

At the beginning of the summer of 1975, I began to feel restless. I began losing interest in the rodeo, roping practices, and the daily exercises that my horses required. I even lost my motivation to do my silversmith work. It seemed as if complications would suddenly appear out of thin air, even in the simplest chore or task that needed doing. I wondered if the world had started to spin backwards and if I was caught in a cosmic imbalance. I wanted to be by myself all the time; freedom and a vacation was what I needed desperately. I needed to take a break from home and the endless work involved in being there.

I felt I needed to ride my motorcycle on a daily basis and wanted to be with my friends. I had one close friend whom I always wanted to hang out with. Like me, he had a motorcycle, and we would get together and fill up our tanks with gas and go riding around the back hills and explore the indigenous landscape. Nobody would ever attempt to bother us. We would stay away from the main roads just to avoid seeing police officers who were patrolling the main highways. During that time the local community didn't like motorcyclists because of the loud rumbling of the engine, especially when a group of motorcyclists came cruising around. There was a general fear of anyone on a motorcycle and a common misconception that a motorcyclist was bad news, especially because of news reports seen on TV. Generally when an officer of the law saw cyclists, he would chase them and then try to hunt them down until they were cited with a ticket or a trip to the jailhouse. If I were caught I definitely would have been cited for not having a valid license to operate a motor vehicle. I'd had a number of motorcycles during that time, but never found the time to get a license. There were a number of times when I was chased by local law enforcement officers, but I never was caught or cited. I knew the back roads like the back of my hand. To me, the back roads were the safest roads that I cruised on.

During summer vacation of 1975, when I was seventeen, my brothers and I ate and slept rodeo. We took turns inquiring of other local cowboy partners where the next rodeo event was going to take place. We would go to the nearby gas stations to see if we could come across some flyers, posters, and up-to-date newspapers with rodeo information. We also listened to the local radio station in hopes that the disc jockey would announce a rodeo event in the surrounding area. We were among the youngest members of the All Indian Rodeo Cowboy Association (AIRCA), which was the only sanctioned rodeo at that time on the Navajo reservation, aside from the local amateur and junior rodeos. During that year it appeared that the only way to participate in a rodeo on or off the reservation was to be a member and have a current membership card to prove that we were affiliated with the AIRCA, and two of my brothers and I were pleased to be members of that association.

We typically did team roping together, and I put some money aside from my jewelry making to participate in a calf-roping event. We regularly attended rodeos all across the Navajo reservation, which included Tuba City, Dilkon, Shiprock, and Ramah. We arrived with anticipation and determination to be successful in our rodeo competitions. We were among the first competitors to arrive at the rodeo grounds so we could choose a good spot to set up our camp for the weekend. My oldest brother was always the one pulling our white two-horse trailer with a brand new sandy brown GMC pickup truck while I comfortably slept in the back on our lengthy drive. This brand new truck was constantly packed with rodeo gear and camping equipment. The truck bed was our only option for sleeping and resting while waiting for competition to begin. There were times we would go in a maroon, two-door Chevy Impala, which gave us added comfort and had air conditioning to give us relief from the hot summer heat. There were times when we spent a couple of days and nights sleeping at the rodeo grounds in the back of the truck and using camping gear and utensils to prepare our own meals on an open fire. Our two rodeo horses nibbled on the hay that we brought along from home with us, and we had two buckets so we could get water from the nearby well.

I only traveled to the rodeos with my brothers when I could take time from my other work and activities. Taking care of my horses wasn't an easy task because I was the only one looking out for these horses and I also was running the family business. It was quite an obligation to water, feed, groom, and keep inventory of all riding equipment required for our rodeo competitions. I would converse with my horses and keep them company at all times so they would not get lonely or feel left out. Even animals have feelings, just like us human beings.

It is a great challenge and transition from riding a ram or wether sheep to riding a big beast like a bull. I never expected this beast to have this tremendous strength until I experienced it myself in a rodeo event with people cheering me on, although at the time I was not hearing their cheers or yells as my total concentration and nervousness was focused on the ride and the next moves the beast might make. In preparation for my bull ride, which was the last event of the long restless day, I stretched and limbered up as much as I could and tried to calm myself down from the adrenaline rush of nervous excitement. From time to time, I won or placed and earned some pocket money. Other times I fell off and threw my hard-earned money away giving it my best shot trying to stay on for the full eight seconds. One jump, two jumps, left or right spin and I would fly off like I was a piece of paper or a rag doll and the bull would attempt to plow over me. In fear I would take off quickly in a different direction to avoid getting gored by its horns or being trampled by the raging beast's hooves. There was always a rodeo clown trying his best to protect the riders.

Most of the time I would succeed at riding the full eight seconds. It was a great experience and a great feeling, with the rush of excitement, and the tremendous power of a bull and the cheers of the crowd. I was proud of myself. I rode a 1500-pound beast and it was an extraordinary challenge for me, but scary at the same moment and worrisome for my siblings. One of the reasons why my mom never attended any of the rodeos was because she was afraid of an unwanted outcome.

The origin of all this interesting entertainment goes back to when my brothers and I were just young and innocent kids herding my grandmother's flocks up in the hills where she would not see us. One of us took a rope, twirling it up into the air and trying to make it sound like a whistle. This was just to keep our grandma from becoming suspicious of our intentions. My two older brothers would be planning this all along while my younger brother and I shooed the flock out of the corral by ourselves. My older brothers would pick on my younger brother and me by challenging us to get on top of one of the biggest, strongest and meanest rams and ride it as long as we possibly could hang on. The majority of the time when we only wanted to tag along to get away from the chores around the house, my older brothers would force us in a mean tone of voice to try this even though we did not desire to. All we could do was whimper and think about falling off and landing on the soft ground. If we did not ride long enough to satisfy them, they would get a lasso and rope another wether sheep and tell us to get on top again. Again and again we would whimper and be forced to get onto a wether sheep. The struggle of trying to stay on top of the sheep would take most of the morning, which hindered the other sheep from grazing in the pasture.

Despite all the whimpering as a young child, this action paid off when we grew to adolescence, and it gave us courage to get on top of an enormous beast like a bull at a rodeo event. The result of all these activities at home along with extensive practice with bucking barrels helped me train to stay on top of a bull for a full eight seconds.

I think most of the cowboys who we competed against in the rodeo did not have the resources or the head start or the endurance that we did, riding rams or wether sheep. All these events in the rodeo took a long, hard time and endless exhausting practice. One of the cowboys would ask us, "How did you get a good roping horse and where did you learn how to rope?" All I did was smirk and walk away thinking to myself that preparing for these competitions is not done overnight. I learned all these things when I was a child as I helped my grandparents.

Most of the time when my bull-riding event came up and I made a successful ride, the other riders would ask me, "Where did you learn how to ride? Did you go to a rodeo riding school?"

My reply would be, "Is there any such thing as rodeo riding school? I learned how to ride at home."

They would say, "Do you have your own stock that you practice on?"

I would say, "Yes, but I learned this as a young boy while herding sheep and wether sheep and riding bucking barrels. There were plenty of brothers for me to compete against. This would take all afternoon and sometimes throughout the nighttime or until we got real tired. This is all I did with my brothers for entertainment as we were growing up as young boys at our parents' and grandparents' residence. My grandpa is the one who gave me the excellent advice as to what kind of horses are good to ride on the range and which ones are good to compete in different rodeos on the reservation."

The good advice that my grandpa gave me when I was a young boy came back to me later when I was searching for a quality horse to buy. My dad and I went to several ranches where they sold horses. At one particular ranch, my eyes caught sight of a sorrel gelding that was just barely being broken in. I bought the horse, took him back home and started working with him constantly every day to train him to be a good roping horse. It didn't take him too long to catch on. This gelding had excellent speed and I made him a first-class roping horse for my roping events.

When I was done working on my jewelry for the day, I used the remainder of the afternoon and evening to practice on bucking barrels that my brother and I made with empty 55-gallon water barrels, and real bucking bulls that I kept inside the corral for practice only. I had at least five bulls that I raised from the time they were calves. Sometimes my cousins and I would compete with one another for money. One ride would be ten dollars. If there were more than three then the winner would take the entire jackpot.

I thought it would be fun and beneficial to have other practice partners, so I arranged a practice group that consisted of my dad's nephew, Lorenzo, and my younger brother, Hilbert. We would practice almost every day, usually in the afternoon when it cooled down. My brother Hilbert and my cousin Lorenzo started around mid-morning rounding up the cows from their grazing so they could rest in the corral. This way they would be ready in the evening for us to practice our roping. Our practices took the rest of the evening and we would stop when it got dark. At the time, Navajo Nation

Rodeo Cowboy Association was barely emerging as an organization. A number of the older cowboys from around the Crownpoint area were organizing this group, but I never inquired about being a member because of my busy schedule with the family business at home and my other affiliation with the AIRCA. I never foresaw that in the future these two would collaborate with one another and become sister associations.

During the July 4th celebration, rodeo and fair in 1975 at the Dean Jackson Rodeo Arena at Window Rock, Arizona, I spent a tremendous amount of time practicing my roping techniques on my roping horse, calves and steers, alone and also with the help of my brothers. When I arrived at the rodeo grounds with my dad and my horses, I looked around everywhere, but my brothers were nowhere in sight. It seemed like they had vanished into thin air, so I had to take on the huge responsibility all alone with nobody to assist me in team roping. My mom and younger brothers and sisters went to the fair in a different vehicle. Their main interest at the fair really wasn't the rodeo, but the carnival, the fireworks show, and the other events that were taking place at the same time.

I decided to search around for somebody to help me in this team-roping event, to do the heeling. Finally, I came across Tony, one of my cousins who knew how to do team roping, as we had practiced and rodeo'd together in the past. I asked Tony to team up with me in the team-roping event because I knew he had true skills, and he agreed. The pressure and anxiety that I felt and carried for a few hours about not having a teammate disappeared after Tony agreed to team up with me. We felt we had the ability and confidence in ourselves to take the team-roping title.

My events were calf roping and team roping. During my calf-roping event, I was so nervous about the huge, overwhelming crowd that I missed the calf and struggled to tie it to no avail, forfeiting any chance in placing. In our team roping event, I did the heading and Tony did the heeling. Since our turn was toward the beginning of the event, we made a good time, but toward the end there were two teams that made faster times. We ended the event in third place.

At that time, I didn't know, and never gave a thought to the idea that this might be the last rodeo that I would ever participate in, the last time I would ever have a rope in my hand. I'm glad that Tony and I almost took the team roping championship title that year.

After July 4th, I finally decided to finish my silversmith project alone. This project was already half-finished and it took no more than two days to finish. Then, my dad and I traveled to Durango, Colorado, to sell the finished jewelry. My dad and I succeeded in selling the jewelry for an excellent price. When we got home there were no more silver supplies to work with, so I asked my parents for permission to take off from work for a week's vacation.

I went to the place of one of my friends close by and asked for permission to stay there for at least a week. All we did was ride our motorcycles all over the back hills behind where he lived. I guess my mom and dad were worried about me, wondering where I was and how I was doing. They wanted me to come back home so I could do some more work. They had purchased some more silver supplies. However, I stayed away from home, having a lot of fun riding my motorcycle and sleeping late in the morning. We had a cookout with delicious foods that we prepared ourselves and we camped in the back yard. Basketball was part of our daily activities.

13

THE DAY I CAN NEVER FORGET

It was July in the summer of 1975. I had stayed overnight with my oldest brother Lawrence, his wife and their son at his place near Twin Lakes. About five o'clock the next morning, my brother woke me from a pleasant sleep to notify me that they were all leaving for Albuquerque to sell jewelry they had made. After they left, I went back to sleep.

I woke up around noon and took a long, hot shower. My brother had left me responsible for making sure that the house was locked up and everything was secured before I decided to go anywhere. I decided to make the long walk back home in the scorching sun to get some lunch. It was approximately two miles from my brother's house back to my house. As I was walking along the country dirt road, I could see a cloud of dust in the distance, and I knew that a vehicle was coming towards me. It was my family. My mom, dad, and sister were on their way to do business and run errands in Gallup and Window Rock. They asked me if I wanted to go with them, but I said no because I knew that their business would be time-consuming. As I continued my walk, I kept thinking about what I was going to do that day. When I arrived back home, I prepared some lunch, ate, and lounged around for a while. Finally, I made up my mind to rev up my motorcycle and go for a ride.

I spent the afternoon cruising over the local dirt roads. As I came down towards the main highway, a shimmer in the distance caught my eye. I squinted and saw a gray car that looked familiar. It was parked on the side of the road, and I assumed it was broken down or out of gas. As I came closer, the picture came into focus. I saw three people standing and looking at the car. One of them turned and started waving me down. I realized that it was my cousin Ray, who lived nearby. Ray was about twenty-two at the time, and he worked at a body and fender shop in Gallup. He was a short man, about five-four. He had a dark complexion and dark brown hair, which he wore in a crew cut. He was kind of chubby, and usually wore jeans and working boots. He was shy when he wasn't drinking, but when he was drinking it was a different matter. I pulled over. Ray was with his buddy Will, who owned the gray car, and Ed, another buddy of his. Ed worked with Ray at the body and fender shop. He had a dark complexion and short hair. He dressed more in the style of a cowboy, and he even wore a cowboy hat. I did not know Ed very well. All I knew was that I didn't like him very much. To me, he seemed like a show-off because of the way he presented himself.

Ray said that they had run out of gas, and he asked me to give him a ride to the gas station. I agreed to give him a ride, although I noticed that he didn't have a gas container. I realized that all three of the men were intoxicated, but I felt sorry for them standing by the road in the hot sun with their car out of gas.

When we got to the gas station, Ray said, "Let's go to the gas station on top of the hill. There are some guys waiting for me there. I refused and took him back to the car where his buddies were waiting. He was mad at me for not taking him to the other gas station, and while I was still sitting on my bike with the motor running, he started to push me around. I turned off my motorcycle.

"What's wrong with you?" I asked.

All of a sudden, I saw a fist rushing toward my face and with an instantaneous reflex, I dodged his attempted blow. I knew that a serious fight was about to erupt. I returned his punch, which landed in the middle of his face. From his nose blood squirted everywhere. He tried to tackle me, but like a cat I jumped back quickly, and he missed and landed on the ground. I was preparing myself for another round, but his two buddies jumped in between us. At that point a blue Ford Maverick drove up. It was another cousin of mine. He saw that we were pushing each other around. He jumped from his car and plowed between us yelling, "Stop what you are doing! Don't fight!" I took this moment of distraction to get on my motorcycle, spin it around, and get out of there.

I headed in the direction that would take me back home, but as soon as I was out of sight, I took another route to the Thrifty Way gas station. When I got there, I put in two dollars worth of gas, which was almost enough to fill the tank. I went into the convenience store to pay for the gas and to buy some goodies for my brother to munch on. I took them back to the hogan where my brother Terry was and gave him a bag of potato chips, a can of Coke, and a hoagie sandwich. He wanted another soda, and since I wasn't doing anything except trying to cool down after my altercation with my cousin, I made another trip to the gas station. I bought each of us of a Coke, and I bought myself a sandwich, too.

After spending a short time talking to my brother, I decided to check on the horses and cattle. My brother told me that the horses might be over the hill, so I drove on the path to the top of the hill, but there was no sign of horses anywhere. There were only a few cattle grazing across the big arroyo. I looked up toward the mountain. The sun was glaring in my eyes, but I could see one horse. When I looked at him closely, I was confident that the horse was not mine. I drove along a narrow path alongside the arroyo, and as I looked closer to the foot of the hills and the valley, I saw one of my horses under a big cedar tree trying to cool off. As I got closer, I could see that all the horses that belonged to my brother and me were there. I whistled to them because I knew that every time I whistled or waved an empty coffee canister at them, their automatic response was to come home for their daily serving of oats. I whistled again, and they started to come toward me. I turned my motorcycle around, and they started trotting after me. I sped up on my motorcycle, because I didn't want them to catch up to me. I got all the way back to the corral, and when the horses reached the corral, I put them into their feeding pen. I gave them oats and threw in some hay so they could nibble on it. I left the corral gate open so they could make their way to the windmill to get fresh water, which was about a half-mile down the main dirt road.

I left the horses and went to the Chevron gas station that was located on top of the hill just north of Gallup. To my surprise Ray the troublemaker was there. He was sitting in his sister's truck, trying to look innocent, but I knew that he had probably just taken off with his sister's truck without asking, because it was the truck she used for work every day to support her kids. He was with that guy Ed. He asked me to go for a ride with them, but I told him that I didn't want to leave my motorcycle alone.

My older brother Delbert and his friends were at the gas station, too. I knew my brother would back me up if anything erupted. However, I didn't want to start anything, out of respect for him. Delbert and his friends were in the garage fixing his clutch, which he had burned out the night before racing with other cars on a gravel road. I didn't want anything to interrupt or disturb their concentration as they worked. Ray asked me to go for a ride again, but I refused his invitation and left the gas station.

Around four or five o'clock in the evening, when the air had cooled off, I had an urge to cruise around Gallup, and then go to Rico's Ranch, which is south of Gallup. I wanted to meet up with my Anglo cowboy buddies, so that I could catch up on the latest rodeo news. On my way to Gallup, I stopped at the Chevron gas station and garage. Delbert and his buddies were still working on his clutch. After watching them working for a couple of minutes, I left to go to my friend's place, and got all the rodeo news updates.

On my way home I decided to stop at the Chevron gas station again. I saw that my brother and his buddies were still working on his vehicle. I also saw that Ray was still there. He approached me and said, "Let's go for a ride. We'll be back in five minutes or less." Not thinking about the altercation we had been through earlier, I thought about where five minutes would take us. Hopefully, we would just go down the road and come back. For some reason I decided to go with him. I parked my motorcycle in a safer spot near the front of the garage and came back to his truck. I didn't ask him where we were going. I just got into the truck. I sat between Ray and Ed in the front seat. Ray drove away from the garage and down Highway 264, westbound toward Window Rock. We were traveling on a two-lane highway, and as I looked over at the speedometer, I could see that we were going nearly 80. I was terrified, and I regretted taking a ride with these two older guys. I wondered where Ray was going in such a rush.

A few minutes after we left the gas station, we approached the Sagebrush Bar, which was located on that side of the road. This bar sold beer and liquor, and I decided that this was Ray's planned destination. I wasn't old enough to possess liquor or have it sold to me. Ray and his buddy were much older and could purchase the liquor they craved. Before going inside they asked me what I wanted to drink. I told them they could buy me a can of soda, and then I watched them walk unsteadily into the bar. In a few minutes they came out with my soda. They offered me a can of beer, too, but I refused it.

There were some guys in a truck that was parked beside us, and Ray decided to stir up some more trouble. Ray started by insisting that his sister's truck was faster than their truck. The guy who was driving the other truck took the bait and began to argue about which truck was faster. They decided to settle it with a truck race. The winner of the race would be rewarded with a case of beer purchased by the loser. But there was a passenger inside the other truck who realized that both guys were too intoxicated to be racing. The passenger, who may have been the driver's wife or girlfriend, said that it wasn't a good night to be racing. There were too many Navajo and state cops patrolling the highway. Also, there was a Navajo traditional ceremony called a squaw dance taking place close by, and there were too many vehicles on the road. The passenger convinced the driver of the other truck not to race.

We got back in the truck and left the bar and headed back onto Highway 264. I knew without a doubt that Ray was incredibly intoxicated. Why had I gotten myself into this situation? Why had I gotten into the truck with them? This thought kept running through my mind. Fear of the unknown paralyzed me.

Ray had turned east when we left the bar, and we were headed back toward the Chevron gas station and garage. Ray was still ticked about the argument he'd had with the other guys outside the bar. He said that we should've raced those guys to show who was boss and whose truck was faster. Then he started directing his anger toward me and telling me that my brother's car wasn't fast enough, but I tried not to pay attention to him. I sat terrified in the middle of the truck just looking straight ahead, watching the oncoming traffic as we sped down the narrow highway.

When I glanced sideways at Ray, I saw that his head was nodding toward the steering wheel like a chicken pecking the ground for worms, and my heart started to pump faster with fear. I turned and looked to my right at the other passenger who was leaning against the door and appeared to be unconscious. The truck was veering on and off the right shoulder of the road, and when I looked at the speedometer, I saw that the truck was going about 95 miles an hour. I kicked Ray's foot off the gas pedal and tried to get hold of the steering wheel. I yelled to try to wake him up, but he was passed out.

I grabbed the steering wheel, the truck veered to the right side of the road, where it hit a pothole, and the tire on the front passenger side blew out, making it difficult to maneuver. I saw little pieces of tire flying in the air. Again, I tried to take control of the truck, but Ray suddenly woke up in a rage, and as if possessed by the devil he started fighting with me. Without any concern about the oncoming traffic or the direction we were traveling in the truck, he swung at me, making contact a couple of times, which caught me off guard. I didn't return any of his hits, my total concentration was in trying to guide the truck.

At that moment the truck was going about 70. I was at least happy it had slowed down. There was a Rainbo Bread truck ahead of us. We hit the Rainbo truck twice from behind. The second time we made impact, the back of the Rainbo truck swung open. Boxes of bread flew out onto the road. Then the truck we were in started going off the right side of the road. I saw that there was an arroyo in our path, and I knew that the truck was going to hit it at an intense speed.

Some witnesses said that the truck started flipping over from the front to the back, as many as four times. I slightly remember tensing my body during multiple impacts, grasping the seat and anything that I could get a hold of. I remember flying towards the windshield and seeing bright flashes of light upon impact. I believe that when you are intoxicated, you don't know what is happening, but when you are sober, as I was, you are terrified of what is going to happen to you. As the truck was flipping over the doors flew open, Ray and Ed were thrown out of the truck. When the truck came to a stop, it landed straight up. I was the only one stuck inside the truck, and I was the only one severely injured. The day had been very hot, and although it was late in the evening when the accident occurred, I could still feel the heat from the transmission. Dust and little pieces of glass from the windshield were everywhere. I don't remember feeling any pain at the time. Everything happened so quickly, it was like the wink of an eye.

The top half of my body was hanging out the rear window of the truck. I could hear many voices. One lady asked me, "Are you okay? Are you doing all right? Can you move your arms and legs?"

I couldn't answer her. I couldn't focus on anything. I faintly remember what was happening, but I was starting to lose consciousness. My nose was bleeding, and I was bleeding from cuts on my face and behind my ears. A girl was trying desperately to help me, but there was nothing she could do. I was hanging out through the broken rear window of the truck. My right leg was wedged between the door and the seat on the driver's side.

I heard sirens in the distance, and then these sounds came closer and closer. I could hear all kinds of noises. Police from different agencies arrived at the scene and started to direct traffic. People driving by were curious, and the policemen were trying to direct them to get out of the way.

The Rainbo Bread truck was on the side of the road, and bread was scattered all over. A bunch of guys surrounded the truck I was in. My older brother was among them. Someone who had passed by the accident scene had notified a state policeman who had been parked at the Chevron gas station where my brother and his friends were working. As soon as my brother heard the alarming news about the accident that had happened over the hill, he and his friends wanted to know who was involved, and they drove to the accident scene and saw that someone was hanging out the broken back window of the truck. He was shocked and terrified when he realized who it was. He asked me to try to get out, but I couldn't move.

I wondered how I could get myself free of this accident. I wanted someone to help me, so that I could just walk away from this scene. Many months later, when I was recuperating at the hospital, I recalled that this was the longest five-minute drive of my life, and I wished that I could take back those five minutes. In reality, those five minutes are endless and shall continue for the rest of my life. I sometimes wake up in the middle of the night sweating and wondering where I am. Am I in a dream? Why can't I move my limbs? I had few encounters like this before while riding bulls and motorcycles.

The cops told my brother to get away. Ray and Ed had both been thrown from the truck. Ray had sustained no outward injuries. Ed had lost consciousness, and the medical personnel had placed him on a stretcher. When he regained consciousness, he was in great pain and later found out that he had suffered a broken pelvis.

The firemen and rescue personnel went to work to get me out of the truck. They had to use the Jaws of Life, a tool designed to open and cut metal in accidents where individuals are trapped inside their vehicles. They cut an opening and removed the jammed door on the driver's side so they could release me from the mangled truck. Most or all of the windows were broken. Two or three tires were flat. I don't remember how they got me out or how long it took because I lost consciousness.

When I regained consciousness, I was in an ambulance with an oxygen mask over my face, and I was in excruciating pain. I noticed that Ray the troublemaker was strapped down on a stretcher secured in the ambulance with a paramedic beside him. Apparently, he wasn't experiencing any pain, and he didn't want to go to the hospital, but the medical personnel knew that he might have some injuries that were not visible.

The ambulance started, the siren screamed, and I could feel the bumpy road at first and then the smoothness of the main highway. I don't remember much of the ride except being aware of a bright light shining directly in my eyes inside the ambulance. We were transported to the Gallup Indian Medical Center for evaluation and treatment.

Since it seemed that I was conscious enough to answer some questions, a state policeman approached me and began asking me questions about the accident. I told him every detail that I could recall. I watched him as he scribbled the information down in his report on a clipboard. He asked me, "How many miles an hour were you guys traveling? Who was driving?"

I told him that the guy lying across the room on a stretcher was the driver. Ray could hear all the questions and my answers. When he saw the police officer, he quieted down and just lay there. I guess he was afraid they were going to put him in jail. Later he attempted to escape from the emergency room. The medical staff wouldn't tolerate it. They tried to keep him under control, but he caused a lot of disturbance. The officers helped the doctors and nurses by strapping him down on a gurney. They finally quieted the troublemaker with some kind of medication and stabilized him and admitted him to the hospital for further examination.

A neurosurgeon and an orthopedic doctor had to be called in to assess my situation. I didn't know what was going on. All I knew was that I was frightened and drifting in and out of consciousness. Later that evening one of the nurses informed me that I was the only one critically injured, and I was afraid of what they would tell me. I hadn't been in this hospital for a number of years, and I detested hospitals. The medical staff didn't know how severe my injuries were. One of the doctors put a collar on my neck to prevent any further damage. It was very uncomfortable, and I was in a lot of pain. I mean excruciating pain! From time to time I would pass out.

At one point the doctor said, "You're hurt badly. You injured your neck. That is the reason why we put the neck collar on you. We are going to take x-rays to see if any of your vertebrae are damaged." A doctor started asking me questions, but I passed out again. I was trying to stay conscious, but I couldn't because there was too much fear and too much pain to ignore.

I heard another doctor direct a nurse to take my blood pressure and to call the laboratory technician to take a blood sample. The doctor said, "Get his clothes and his boots off." Two of the nurses cut my clothes off with a pair of surgical scissors. The doctor said,

"We'll need x-rays of his whole body." I asked the doctor to give me something for the pain, but he didn't want to give me any medication because he didn't know what was going on with me yet. They took me to the room to get the x-rays done and after they were finished I went into a deep sleep.

After what seemed like hours, I woke up on a cold, hard table. I could hear the sound of machinery, and bright lights were shining into my eyes, as bright as the spotlight on my dad's truck. A thought ran through my mind at this moment that I was at home. The only things that alerted me to the fact that I was in the hospital were the excruciating pain and the smells of the hospital. I asked a nurse where I was, and she told me that I was on an operating table in the operating room. One of the doctors instructed a nurse to shave off all my hair. I remember the buzzing sound and vibrations of the clippers as my hair fell off. Then the anesthesiologist approached and told me that she was going to put me to sleep by injecting me with some kind of medication through an intravenous line.

At this time, my mind was not focusing on what was happening around me. I could hear clear voices of different tones and see medical staff approaching me in white lab coats. They looked like white angels hovering around me. I wondered if I were still alive or if I had been transported to another world.

The doctor's voice brought me back to reality when he said they were going to drill into my skull and place screws at four points to hold a device called a "halo" in place. I asked, "What is that?" I was terrified, just thinking about them drilling into my head! The doctor explained that the halo was an oval shaped metal "crown" that would help to stabilize my neck. Metal rods extended from the halo to a chest frame that extended from my chest to my shoulder to prevent further damage that could occur if I moved my neck. At this point, I fell back into unconsciousness.

I woke up sometime during the middle of the night and all I felt was a lot of pain. Most of the time after that operation, constant, excruciating pain was the only feeling I had from my neck to the top of my head. When the pain was so bad I couldn't stand it, I went unconscious. Pain became a constant, everyday thing for me. The doctors still refused to give me medication for the pain. They said that it was because of the severity of my injury.

I was on a weird bed, actually a Stryker frame, which held me like a sandwich between two canvas panels and flipped me from front to back every two hours to prevent pressure sores. After a few minutes of trying to figure out where I was, I saw a young Anglo female nurse approaching me with a flashlight. Right away, I asked her, "What is this contraption that I am laying on?" She told me that it was a Stryker frame and that it was used mainly by patients with spinal cord injuries. Then she told me that I had injured my cervical vertebrae numbers 4 and 5, and that I would be lying in the Stryker frame for the rest of my stay at Gallup Indian Medical Center.

I asked her how I could move or stand up. She said that I couldn't. I asked her "Why?" and she wouldn't give me a direct answer. She got a puzzled look on her face, then she looked away and said she had to go and answer some calls.

The nurses came in every two hours and secured a white canvas to the top side of my body and to the Stryker frame. Then my body was flipped over like a pancake. After a while, I felt a little bit like a shish kebab turning over a fire, but I was too cold to imagine a fire beneath me. It reminded me of making sandwiches—I felt like the filling between the two pieces of bread!

The unit where I stayed in the hospital was closed off from the other wards because it had to be environmentally safe and secure. While I was drifting in and out of consciousness, one of the doctors came by my room where I was dreaming that everything was okay and I was in no pain at all. When I woke, he brought a plastic model of a spinal cord to my bedside and used it to demonstrate to me as he said, "You are paralyzed from the neck down. You are severely injured—you have fractured vertebrae on the fourth and fifth cervical level and there is also a pinched nerve in your spinal cord. We will not operate on you because you are not totally conscious and alert. At times, you pass in and out of consciousness. We can't operate on you while you are in that state. We have to get you stabilized before we can perform any kind of surgery, so we will just keep your neck stable and aligned with your spinal cord with the halo."

Most of the time while I was conscious all I could see were the ceiling and the floor, and all I heard were the echoes of voices and the squeaking sounds of the nurses' shoes on the waxed floors as they approached. When I was facing up, I could see their faces and the bright lights on the ceiling. When I was facing down, I could see the white tips of the nurses' shoes and the black shiny shoes of the doctors.

When the nurses turned me in the Stryker frame, I could see a guy lying on a regular hospital bed on the other side of the room. I recognized him as Ray, the troublemaker who had been driving the truck at the time of the accident. He tried to talk to me, saying all kinds of weird things. I couldn't comprehend what he was trying to get across to me, especially since I was in so much pain and spent most of my time sleeping. He told me that he was going to lose his driver's license and his job, his friends were turning against him, and he would have to go to jail for sixty days.

I told him to look at me, that I wouldn't be able to walk for the rest of my whole life.

His response was that he didn't care, and that I had caused a lot of trouble for him. A lady who had come to visit me told me not to listen to him, and she drew a curtain between our beds.

Many days passed, and I was still in the hospital. I didn't have the slightest idea about what would happen to me. The doctors wanted to operate to relieve the pressure on my neck that was causing the pain I was experiencing. My dad absolutely refused to sign the release for the surgery because he was afraid that the operation might cause me to take a turn for the worse. If the operation had been successful, I might have been able to use my upper limbs; but I've always been thankful that I didn't have the surgery. I have met people with the same level of spinal cord injuries who have pain in their necks and shoulders from the metal plate that was inserted to fuse their vertebrae. They say it is like a sharp, hot pin pinching your neck muscle and is too severe to ignore, and that prescribed pain medication does not help except for a short period of time.

The doctors used another technique to relieve the pinched nerve. Attached to the halo, I had weights that were hung off the head of the stretcher by a durable rope and rollers that held them in place, and I had more ropes and rollers going from my waist to the foot of the stretcher. It felt as though I was being pulled apart. Most of the nurses, especially the young nursing assistants, didn't know how to handle me or how to turn the Stryker frame alone. The pain I felt when a nurse released the weights one time was so great that I passed out instantly. The doctors and nurses came running to revive me. That nurse was not allowed to work with me alone again! In general, the nurses at the Gallup Indian Medical Center didn't have the patience or knowledge to care for patients with spinal cord injuries such as mine. The majority of them seemed to be afraid to handle a severely injured patient. In my case, the nurses negotiated silently among one another, just staring at me until one took the lead and the rest walked out of the room as fast as they could like it was the end of my life. The Navajo nurses might have been thinking about the taboos that their grandparents had taught them. It is said that if you come into contact with any kind of abnormality or disfigurement, or anything that was used by an individual with such a condition, the consequence is a casting of a similar affliction. This concept of "guilty by association" was taught by the ancestors.

The doctor advised me of the purpose for the weights: they were there to separate my damaged vertebrae to relieve pressure on the damaged area of my neck. To me it seemed like the nurses, doctors and experts were having a tug of war trying to answer their own questions—a very uncomfortable position and feeling.

After the doctor explained my condition to me, the medical staff told me that I needed to move to a specialized hospital where they were better equipped to treat spinal cord injuries. My doctor called around, and a few days later two doctors and a social worker came to my room and stood beside my bed. They asked me what I wanted to do. I didn't know what they meant. They said that perhaps I should go to the Craig Institute in Denver. One of the doctors said that I was too young to go there, as I was only seventeen years old at the time. The other doctor remarked that there was a good hospital in southern New Mexico called Carrie Tingley Hospital and Rehabilitation Center for Crippled Children. He said that I could finish my high school education there. The doctor asked the social worker to find out where Carrie Tingley was and see if I could be admitted.

14

CARRIE TINGLEY HOSPITAL

I lived an independent, able-bodied life for seventeen years. Then I was conveyed to another world. Suddenly, I awoke to the horrible realization of living the rest of my life with a serious physical challenge. I encountered many experts: medical personnel, counselors, and clinical social workers giving advice and guidance to me on how to accept my disability. I felt like I was trying to put a puzzle together with all the pieces of information I got from these experts. I stared at them with a stone face, and many times I wondered to myself why these medical experts were constantly lecturing me; they were not physically challenged, and I didn't feel they fully understood my situation.

Before my departure from Gallup Indian Medical Center, a lot of my close friends, family, and acquaintances came to visit me when I was conscious, especially on my very last day at that hospital, before I departed for Carrie Tingley Hospital. They couldn't comprehend the complexity and severity of my paralysis or how to talk to me about it. They would make comments like: "You are going to be okay. You are going to walk again. You are going to be with us once more, so don't be too concerned. Have intense feelings of faith in yourself." My mom, dad, aunt, brothers, some of my cousins, and my rodeo buddies came to visit me. Many relatives and friends had gathered in the hospital lobby when they heard the shocking news of my terrible accident and they were very concerned about me. That's what my mom informed me later on when I was conscious, but at the hospital I didn't know what was happening.

One summer morning, early, the chief surgeon who was also my primary doctor, and two of the nursing staff came into my room and said, "Surprise!" I looked up at them with astonishment and asked, "What is the surprise about? Did you finally discover a way for me to walk again?" Apparently, I was finally conscious enough for about ten or fifteen minutes to realize who they were when they came into my room. I had been going in and out of consciousness throughout my stay at the hospital. When I was conscious, I felt drained and my vision was blurred. The only thing I was able to see was the intense bright light shining directly into my eyes from the ceiling.

They informed me that I was going to be transferred to a crippled children's hospital; after a short meeting, I would be transported to the Gallup Airport by ambulance and then flown to Truth or Consequences, New Mexico. The facility was Carrie Tingley Hospital, the only rehabilitation center for crippled children in New Mexico. The professional staff at this facility offered specialized one-on-one treatment. They also provided information and resources to help patients cope with their disabilities.

To prepare me for the rough trip, the Gallup Indian Medical Center doctors stabilized my neck by putting a frame on my chest and attaching it to the halo around my head with four stainless steel rods; two rods were placed on my forehead, and two rods were placed on the back of my head. I couldn't feel where the back of my head was. I couldn't even see my feet. After the rods were placed on me, I was so stiff that I felt like a log. They strapped me down to a stretcher that was so inflexible that I couldn't even move an inch if I wanted to. My eyes were the only parts of my body that I could move. When I was conscious, every time I thought about moving any other part of my body a little bit, a sharp pain shot like a bolt of lightning from my pinched nerve that was located around the fourth and fifth cervical vertebrae. The pain was beyond excruciating, and I became unconscious from time to time, to escape my misery.

Before I was put into the ambulance, I breathed the fresh outdoor air and listened to the noise of traffic in Gallup. Once again, I saw a clear blue sky. In the ambulance, the Emergency Medical Technician asked me questions like, "Are you comfortable or do you have any pain?" He also asked me, "How come you never yell in pain?"

"What's there to yell about?" I asked him.

Then he asked again, "Are you experiencing any pain?" I just stared at him while they were taking my blood pressure and putting an oxygen mask on my face. Silently, I felt the pain that continued, but in my mind I was strong and determined not to show my emotions. Strapped and harnessed, I was unaware of the movement of the ambulance.

In the ambulance, the light from the ceiling was disturbing, shining down into my naked eyes. The EMT informed me that I was going in a chartered airplane to the hospital for crippled children. It was going to be a rough three-hour flight. My mom came along with me because I was a minor; an adult had to accompany me at all times. I had flown before in a helicopter, but never in an airplane in my young life. Before my terrible accident, I enjoyed riding my favorite horse at my grandparents' beloved back land. I would hear a buzzing noise overhead like a bumblebee; I would glance up and I would recognize that it was a small airplane. I always wondered where it was going and what was keeping it up in the air, not realizing that one day I would be inside a similar airplane taking me away from my native land to an unknown destination.

At the Gallup Municipal Airport, a pilot was already waiting for us. The pilot told us we had to make a quick stop at the airport in Albuquerque so we could pick up another patient on our way to Truth or Consequences. It was a very hot, sizzling day in the last weeks of July, 1975.

The EMT transferred me onto the plane with the help of the pilot. Because I was close to the floor of the plane I could immediately smell the oil from the engine and the gas fumes from the exhaust pipes. The smell reminded me of the gas station near where I live, where I took my motorcycle to fill it up.

At that moment, the pilot turned to me and he said, "I'm used to this. I have been an air medical pilot for five years, with experience in flying charter planes and transferring all kinds of patients in the Southwest region."

Regardless of whether he was a nice person and had five years experience as he claimed, I thought that five years was not enough experience to transport medical patients with severe injuries like mine! After he finished clamping and securing the frame of the stretcher that I was lying on, he turned to us and asked, "Are you guys comfortable and ready?"

When all of the pre-flight assessments were completed, the plane started, moved slowly until it got on the runway, and then accelerated in speed. All of a sudden, we were hundreds of feet up in the sky! From time to time, the plane hit small air pockets and bounced, seeming to draw the air from my lungs. I was conscious off and on during my short flight to the Albuquerque International Airport. At one point, I woke up and wondered where I was. It became clear to me that I was inside the plane when I saw the two dirty little windows on each side of me.

I was fearful on my first flight because I didn't know what would keep the plane in the air for such a distance. Finally, I heard the sound of the pilot's hoarse voice saying, "We are landing at the Albuquerque airport. We are going to make a brief stop to pick up a patient and then depart for our final destination, Truth or Consequences." We waited a while for the pilot to return with the other patient. However, when he returned, he said the patient was unable to fly with us because he had multiple bone fractures, and he was going to be taken by ground medical transportation. The pilot turned around and he asked me, "Are you okay?" I didn't respond to him because I couldn't see him. Next the pilot announced, "We are on our way to the Truth or Consequences airport. Is everybody comfortable?" That was the last thing I heard, and we were off on our long flight down south.

Because of my accident, my physical endurance was diminished along with so much of my normal physical capacity. On the last part of our flight, I was napping off and on. I had fallen asleep again listening to the humming of the airplane engine. I didn't have the slightest idea how long the flight was, but the rough landing instantly awakened me. I could feel the plane bounce on the rough landing surface and hear the rat-tat-tat of gravel stones on the underside of the plane. The pilot's voice sounded again, "Everybody wake up! We have arrived at the Truth or Consequences airport!"

The pilot told my mom and me that he believed our transportation to Carrie Tingley Hospital was waiting for us. After this announcement, he approached me to release the clamps from the stretcher frame located on the floor of the plane. The pilot and the driver carefully removed me from the plane. I was finally able to breathe fresh, cool air again! As difficult as it was to look around, I could observe from the corner of my eyes what the small airport was like. The building was a bright yellow charter airplane hangar. Apparently, the bright yellow color of the building helped the pilots to locate the airport from above before landing. I saw a second hangar that held four small charter planes. The pilot's recollection was that only two planes were operational because there were no airplane mechanics on duty most of the time.

The driver of Carrie Tingley Hospital's state-owned station wagon was a tall, middle-aged Anglo male with salt-and-pepper hair who came to meet me first and then greeted my mother and the pilot. He was overjoyed at the anticipated arrival of a new Indian patient and visitor to Carrie Tingley Hospital. The driver had already opened the back door of the vehicle before he greeted us. As the pilot and driver wheeled me on the stretcher toward the white station wagon, I noticed the red Zia in the yellow New Mexico state seal on the door. I assumed that this was a state hospital and when I asked the driver, he confirmed that it was indeed a state hospital and rehabilitation center for crippled children.

The pilot and the driver transferred me with much care and stabilized the stretcher by securing clamps installed on the floor in the back of the medical station wagon. Instantly, I knew it was a hot day because a hot draft rushed over me, and I could feel the heat from the pavement. From inside the car, I could hear the vents on full blast, the air conditioner sending out blasts of freezing air. The driver turned his head around to ask, "Is everybody ready to go for a short ride?" I hesitated in my mind; I wanted to go to a different hospital because "crippled" was not the word I wanted to hear from anybody, but the pilot replied, "Everybody is enthusiastic, eager and prepared for the trip!"

I appreciated that in every stage of my careful transportation to Carrie Tingley, my driver and pilot were very conscious of my mental and physical comfort. I had never experienced this intensity of concern from strangers before in my young life, and I felt secure with them. Despite all the pain I had, I ignored it. I didn't want the driver or the pilot to know how much pain I was having.

The words "crippled" and "paralyzed" scared the living hell out of me any time anyone said them. I never once in my life thought I would end up in a crippled hospital or become crippled. I testified to myself that I was not crippled. My mind was already set on walking again, right out of this hospital.

The pilot and the driver were engaged in pleasant and continuous conversation all the way from the airport to the hospital. I could hear them talk about their experiences in their medically related fields, the length of their service and descriptions of their adventures. I overheard the pilot say that I was his third patient on the medical flight out to Truth or Consequences during the past year. Observing from the corners of my eyes en route to the hospital, I saw from time to time the sporadic tall standing green tree and the street light poles along the roadside, but there wasn't anything really interesting for me to see along the way. I remember feeling anxious, afraid, and unsure of what my stay at the hospital would be like because this was my first longtime confinement in any institution. Feelings of wanting to escape started to take form in the back of my mind. I was confident that I could jump out of the vehicle at the next stoplight and sprint away to my home or another secure location. I laughed silently in my mind as I thought of where the safest place would be besides the hospital. Then the medical station wagon started to slow down, and I overheard the pilot's hoarse voice say, "We have arrived safely at our destination."

The driver and pilot started to unclamp me from the medical station wagon. Despite the very hot day, a fresh cool mist was evident in the air because the water sprinklers were on. I didn't observe too much of the outside of the hospital. However, it appeared to me it had only one floor, and it was an antique white building. At the main entrance, I saw two young, smiling Hispanic nurses aides holding the heavy white outer double doors. They introduced themselves to me pleasantly as if I were a child. One of the young nurses aides informed me that this was the Intensive Care Unit, and this is where I would be staying for the duration of my rehabilitation.

Once inside the hospital, the two cheerful aides opened the next set of heavy white double doors; I felt a sudden cool breeze rush over me, along with a strong odor of rubbing alcohol or some type of cleaning solution that gives a hospital its unique smell. The strong cool smell made me recall the hospital I had just left in Gallup.

I was admitted immediately to the Intensive Care Unit where my medical records had been sent from Gallup. I did not know anyone there at that moment. My mom was directed to a different room while the nurses were evaluating me. It was difficult for me to voice my opinion in this new environment where I saw different races of strange people speaking their own languages. I just kept silent, because nobody at home spoke as much as these people did. They sounded like a moving radio. One of the Anglo nurses was really conversational and she asked me without hesitation, "What Indian tribe are you from?" I stared at her uncomfortably without saying a word. I was tired from the long hard flight and ready to go to sleep, but I was in a lot of pain, which kept me awake. I asked the nurse if I could get anything for pain.

Meanwhile, the nurse supervisor was reviewing my medical records, and the other nurse informed me that she was going to be the main nurse to care for me at this specialized facility. She guided the gurney, with me on board, to my room. Once I was settled in my room, one of the unit medical clerks came to tell me that she had ordered my dinner. I didn't have an appetite due to the painkillers making me drowsy. I just wanted to sleep for the rest of the day and not be bothered. I was feeling numb and sleepy after the Demerol took affect.

At that moment, a young Anglo male came into my room wearing a long white lab coat, and the nurse supervisor mentioned my name to him. He quickly retrieved my chart without saying anything and he sat down to review a few pages. I noticed he didn't really read my chart, but just flipped through some of my medical records. He turned around and asked me my name and introduced himself to me. "I will be your primary doctor while you are here for your rehabilitation. My name is Dr. Lehman. I've heard a lot about you from Gallup Indian Medical Center. Do you have any questions?"

I told him, "No, I don't have any questions. But the nurse gave me a shot of Demerol, the one you ordered for me." I told him that the medication made me drowsy and nauseous. I didn't verbalize anything else to him because I was still in shock, and still in a state of denial as to where I was and what had happened to my body. I didn't want to tell everybody about the extreme pain I had, because I was one stubborn Indian! I just wanted to be left alone to sleep in my white claustrophobic room.

One of the nurses was nice enough to ask my mom if she was tired and if there was anything she needed or they could get for her. She replied in a low tone of voice, "I am exhausted from the long bumpy flight and dehydrated from the dry heat." Right away, the nurse brought a refreshing cold drink. After my mom had rested, the young woman volunteered to guide her to the dining hall where she could get something to eat if she was famished.

Later on in the afternoon, my mom returned from the hospital cafeteria where she had been having lunch with the lady who was to be my social worker. This lady had the loudest voice of anyone I knew, and she couldn't be ignored! She reminded me of one of my dogs named Bullet, I could hear her coming down the hall when she came to see me. She became my mom's true friend, inviting her to her home every time she came out to visit.

The social worker introduced herself as Dotty. She had invited my mom to stay at the hospital in one of the visitors' rooms for a week or two so she could learn how to help me. They would evaluate her ability to care for me and help me to adjust to my new condition as a physically challenged individual living on a rural Navajo Indian reservation. The medical staff would give my mom detailed information about my injuries and train her to provide care for me when I was able to return home. Thereafter, my mom would become my primary caregiver for the remainder of my life, and she would train other members of my family to provide care for me as well.

I do not remember how long my mom stayed for her training. Most of the time I was unconscious, sleeping with my neck tilted back in a halo stabilizer frame. I was very uncomfortable with all the gadgets and devices attached to the crown of my head. Also, I was in the isolation room right across from the nurses station so they were able to keep a close eye on me all the time.

My recollection of the hospital isolation-room stay is that it was like a horror movie. I remember seeing the bare beige ceiling, the images from the bright lights in the hallway like angels that were dressed in clear plastic walking towards me, floating on air when I was on high doses of Demerol and valium. I was not saying a word. I just froze in fright. I had never seen something like that in my young life. The echo of the intercom speaker down the hallway would bring back the memory of the echoes of the canyon walls where I used to live. After a few days of heavy sedation, I developed what is called ICU psychosis. When sleep patterns are disrupted long enough, you can become disoriented, and because you're in an isolated area, slightly psychotic. This is temporary, and has something to do with dark and light, with sleeping in the dark but sensing that you're in the light, almost like daydreaming. I did not know where I was, I did not know what day of the week it was or if it was night or day. Sometimes I didn't even remember my own name. When the nurses turned me over side to side, I was scared until one spoke to me, telling me, "My name is this, and this is so-and-so." There were so many nurses that took care of me, I cannot recall all of the names.

And yet emotionally I felt as if I was in the desert all by myself with nobody to help me. Today I recall all the difficult and lonely times that I spent at the hospital. I was cognitively aware of my surroundings. The dazzling bright lights replaced the bright stars at night in the desert and made me think about when I was able to walk about by myself at night. I tried hard not to think about being paralyzed and not able to walk again. When somebody tells me that I cannot do a lot of things on my own, that really bothers me. This was not going to help me at all in being healthy and living a gratified life.

I became more conscious of my surroundings, the condition of being paralyzed, and the process of the nurses constantly changing my position to relieve pressure and avoid any kind of pressure sores on my body. If they found any kind of pressure area they'd rub it down with lotion to circulate the blood. I had never used the word "paralyzed" until I got myself into this situation, and didn't know what it really meant. I wondered all the time I was in bed trying to heal my damaged vertebrae if I would ever walk again. I would debate with the nurses that someday I would be able to walk on my own without the help of anybody and go where I wished.

I could only see the bare walls, the sink, and the floor during the process of changing my position every two hours, the process I hated most. After it was completed, I was left by myself in the room, wondering why I was alone. One day when I was conscious, I realized that I was by my lonesome in my room again with only a small black-and-white TV that was on 24/7. I hated this TV because sometimes it really made me agitated and annoyed. The reservation I came from had no electricity or running water. I loved the quiet environment that surrounded me at home.

While observing my surroundings, I noticed that the walls were constructed from adobe bricks plastered and painted with light baby-blue paint. The inconsistent layering of paint and visible thin running cracks here and there established in my mind that this hospital was old. I could hear the rumble of the air conditioning motor and voices echoing from the intercom down the hallway and lobby. As time went by, the hospital environment became more familiar to me, and I realized that I was only a few feet away from the nurses station. Now I could hear their chit-chatting and loud, constant laughing. These noises kept me awake in the daytime, and made it difficult to sleep at night.

During my first two months at Carrie Tingley, when I was unconscious most of the time, I was kept away from everybody. The nurses were the only ones allowed in my room. Coming from a sovereign Indian Nation where I only saw non-Indians from a distance—tourists who were passing through the reservation on the highways—it was rare and difficult for me to engage in a conversation with anyone at Carrie Tingley. In a world where English was the dominant spoken language, I didn't try to initiate conversation even if I needed help or wanted questions answered about my condition.

The hospital staff was diverse, mainly Mexican and Anglo, but I never saw a Native American employee. I had never been exposed to this diversity of nationalities or this type of environment before. When my dad came to visit me he always conversed with the Hispanic nurses because he knew how to speak Spanish. When my dad would leave, the nurses asked me why I didn't speak Spanish fluently like he did. I'd tell them I was a real Indian, I spoke my first language Navajo and some English which was my second language. I could pronounce some words in Spanish. It was not that complicated, only a bit of a tongue twister.

Two experienced nursing assistants were assigned to turn me over every two hours to relieve pressure and promote blood circulation. I was astonished that they really knew how to handle me and care for me. I asked them, "How did you learn the method?"

One of them laughed and said, "You're not the only patient with a spinal cord injury that we have treated and cared for at this hospital. We are highly specialized in caring for spinal cord injury patients at Carrie Tingley Hospital."

One morning after breakfast, a new nurses aide entered my room and said with a smiling face, "Surprise! I have been assigned to work with you! I want to get to know you. This is my very first time working in the ICU at Carrie Tingley Hospital. In the hospital where I worked near the East coast, I cared for individuals with spinal cord injuries. Now, I am going to start off by giving you a sponge bath. I will do this every morning."

I had never heard of this kind of bathing procedure before. After looking at her for a while, I asked her, "How are you going to do that?"

She said, "Very simple, it's just like washing your hands. I'm going to get some water and wipe you clean in different parts of your body." She asked me, "Do you use soap on your face?"

I responded, "No! Don't touch any part of my face or body! Get the hell out of here!" My personal feeling about soap on my face is that I dislike it. I presume they were doing this task on me before when I was unconscious, but now that I was cognitively aware of the situation, I did not want anybody performing that kind of task on me. I did not realize the duties that the nurses had to perform daily for disabled individuals who were dependent on them. She had a washcloth in her hand and was eager to clean my face and body. Again, I told her, "No! Don't touch me! Stay away from me! I can do it myself later but not now."

"How much later?" she asked.

I looked at her and replied, "I'm going to take a nap first."

"This is all in your mind," she told me. "You can't move on your own. Let me see you move your arms. If you can move on your own, then you can bathe yourself."

I tried to move my arms, hands and my fingers in my mind. But they just seemed to lie there hopelessly attached to my body with no responses to my commands. I recollected various times before when I was able to pour water into a basin or turn on a faucet to wash my own hands and body with soap. She appeared disappointed, then she left my room, telling me, "I'll be right back."

Apparently, the nurse sought assistance from the nurse in charge of that ward; they both entered my room later. The head nurse started explaining the details of the sponge-bathing task. She continued explaining to me about my condition, that I was totally paralyzed from my chest on down, and that my spinal cord was severely damaged. With an injury as severe as mine, whether the spinal cord is permanently damaged or if it would heal was unknown. She said, "So in the meantime, you need to cooperate with the nurses. They are doing their best to help you. They are your angels here."

I told her again I was not paralyzed, I only needed a few days to recover from my injuries.

She reminded me again, "You are paralyzed and you will not walk again."

Again, I debated with her, "You are wrong! I am determined to walk again because I dream about it every night!" I argued with those two for a while, and after that I gave up to go to sleep. I refused to eat or drink anything that day.

Later on during the day, my doctor came in to examine me. He told me that they might have to put me on an IV to feed me if I refused to eat or drink. He was sticking a needle in different parts of my body and then asking me, "Do you feel that?" He told me that I had a couple of tubes inserted in me. One was an IV to give me fluids to avoid dehydration, and the other one was a catheter. I was not drinking enough fluids, but drinking a lot of fluids caused my stomach to bloat and made me uncomfortable. I asked the doctor, "What is a catheter?"

"It helps you go to the bathroom, to urinate," he replied.

"I do not want to use that catheter so take it out. I'm uncomfortable with the catheter. I want to use the bathroom on my own!"

My doctor pulled a chair up beside my bed to have a one-to-one talk with me. He said, "Listen, Gilbert, your spinal cord is severely damaged. We can only hope for the best, that week after week you will get some of your feeling back. For that reason, we must use all these techniques and attachments to make you more comfortable during your recovery."

In other words, I was expected to put up with the hospital routine. To my dismay, the nursing assistants would log-roll me from side to side on the bed so that they could sponge bathe me and change the bed linens daily. At this point I was still not comfortable with all the procedures that were done on me pertaining to my care. My doctor had ordered the physical therapist to do range-of-motion exercises twice a day with me, which I despised. When I heard her voice crackling down the hallway, I would pretend I was asleep. But I was informed that the range-of-motion exercises would be done for the duration of my stay at Carrie Tingley.

There was another Navajo patient at this facility, and one young Hispanic nurse was considerate enough to ask me if I felt like visiting with him. She continued conversing with me about him, telling me that he was just about my age and she thought we would get along well. He was also diagnosed with spinal cord injury and was transferred here four months earlier from the same hospital that I had left. After a while, she asked me if I wanted to room with him since we were in the same situation and we shared the same culture and language. I replied that we could make our own little reservation here. She laughed hysterically at that and then asked me, "What is a reservation?" The time passed quickly for me when I had conversations with other patients and nurses.

Finally, I was introduced to Kevin from Pine Hill, New Mexico, the first person I had met since my accident who had a spinal cord injury similar to mine. He had been at this rehabilitation center several months prior to my arrival and he was already cruising in his power wheelchair. One day, he visited me to encourage me to get out of bed, but I still had my chest frame and rods that were supporting the halo. He stated to me, in mixed English and Navajo language, "You will soon be riding in a chair just like mine." He would drive his electric wheelchair around the hospital ward using the sip-and-puff control switch that permitted him to move in any direction that he desired. From what little I could see from the corners of my eyes, he would blow air into a tube that made the wheelchair go forward, and when he inhaled into the tube, the wheelchair would go backward; when he moved his head side-to-side, the wheelchair would move right or left. The more air he blew into the tube, the faster it would go. Oh boy, he must've had extra strong lungs like a race horse, to ride all over the hospital.

My physical therapist, who worked with me in exercising my limbs to reduce stiffness, talked to me about this chair when she was ordering my wheelchair. As she spoke of the "wheelchair" I became disturbed. She spoke like the wheelchair was magical. I never imagined myself being in a wheelchair. I didn't give a hell whether it was powered or a standard wheelchair. In my mind I was going to walk again, and not have to depend on a chair that had wheels. I argued with the therapist most of the time, whenever she mentioned wheelchairs.

I questioned Kevin about what it was like to be in a wheelchair. He didn't say too much, just gave me a smirk. He was reserved and distant at first. After I got to know him better, I asked him if he had the same gadgets on his chest and on his head when he first arrived at the hospital. He responded that he had the same thing, but it was taken off three months before my arrival. I told him I was going to walk out of this rehabilitation hospital. I had dreams about my great desire to walk again. He had a habit of just grinning all the time and minding his own business, cursing at the nurses and cruising all around the center in his chair. I determined that he wasn't much of a conversationalist. He was just a long-haired, shy Indian grinner and curser with a luxury Cadillac wheelchair.

There were times when I didn't like to be bothered by anyone; I just wanted to sleep the whole day or stay in the room all by myself. One of the nurses always reported on me to my social worker about not cooperating with the hospital staff, and said that I was giving them a hard time. My social worker would come to my room and she would tell me, "I heard you're having a bad day!"

I would say, "No, I just want to walk out of this hospital. That's the only thing I want to do."

After listening to me, she would reply, "I will not argue with you about your wishes. If I could foresee the future, I would know if your spinal cord system would heal completely. I'm just an ordinary loud-mouth human being dedicated to being a hospital social worker; I am not God, but I have worked with a lot of patients like you."

I know I was one of the most difficult patients to get along with sometimes because I did not like any kind of hospital anywhere. But none of the nurses gave up on me. I guess it was their job and duty to tend to my needs. A few of them got upset with me, which made me really uncomfortable, so when those individuals came in I stayed quiet. I couldn't tell them what to do because they already knew how to handle somebody in my severe condition, and the nursing tasks they were doing were unbelievable, like a piece of cake to them. Especially when it was on the dark side of my day when I would try to shut everyone out of my life. I guess it takes a lot of patience, strength and courage to be a nurse.

15
MISSION IMPOSSIBLE

Several months passed. It was an early morning in October 1975. A team of physicians and my primary doctor had decided to remove the chest frame and halo including the pins from my upper body and the crown on my head. My primary doctor said, "You will feel a lot more comfortable without the device on your head and chest after the halo is removed." Shortly after our conversation, two ER nurses wheeled in a gurney, transferred me, and wheeled me over to the surgical unit where I was transferred onto the surgical table. An anesthesiologist walked in and gave me a shot of anesthetic that put me to sleep, and the surgeons began the process of removing all the equipment.

A couple of hours later I woke up to one of the ER nurses sitting beside me. She asked how it felt without all the gadgets. I didn't realize they were off until she told me. Then I answered, "I am no longer an angel since my halo is off," and she laughed hysterically. Later my primary doctor came in and ordered me to flex my neck muscles for at least fifteen minutes at least four times a day, so that my neck could regain its strength. I had gotten used to the gadgets that were attached to me. I felt weird to be without the halo, rods and chest frame. Some of my skin was peeling off on my chest like a snake crawling out of its skin. One of the nurses came in with cleaning solution to clean my forehead where the pins had been.

I asked her if the pins had gone all the way through my head. She said, "No, just through skin to the skull bone. I am doing this procedure where the pins went through your skin so your skin will heal, and there will be no sore." After this procedure I teased her, "Was I trying to grow horns?" She told me that lately my attitude had changed a lot.

The occupational therapist had measured me for a neck collar to be made there at the shop at Carrie Tingley. The neck collar was used every time the nurses moved me: when they log-rolled me or sat me up in the bed. After a few weeks of neck exercises, I felt a lot more comfortable with my neck being stable and strong enough to hold up my head by itself.

One night when I was positioned flat on my back with my head placed on top of a pillow, I woke up in excruciating pain. The pain was too unbearable to be ignored so I started yelling, "Nurse! Nurse!" I broke into a puddle of sweat while yelling for a nurse for thirty minutes before anyone came to my rescue. My voice was hoarse from yelling. One nurse that I most disliked appeared to assist me. Unfortunately, we'd had no pleasant encounters with one another. Immediately, her unfriendly tone of voice made it worse.

I said, "My neck hurts so bad I cannot stand it!"

"Go to sleep," she replied.

I was unable to ignore the excruciating pain that interrupted my sleep. Actually, in spite of the immense pain, I did not shed a single tear. This nurse's attitude provoked me to hide my emotions when she abruptly stated, "If you have that much pain, then how come you are not crying?"

I told her. "You ask me why I am not crying. This pain is so bad that I feel like screaming and crying but I did not want to disturb other people when they are sleeping. For others crying is a way of releasing painful emotions, I have always kept my emotions to myself."

After this hostile conversation, the head nurse finally entered and said, "I will call your doctor to see what kind of pain medication he can order for you. I reviewed your chart; I know there was some pain medication prescribed for you." She assured me that she would return with some medication so I could go to sleep comfortably.

Dr. Lehman was the primary doctor in charge of my care while I was in the ICU. Early on, he was attentive to my questions and comments. I always told him that I was going to walk out of that institution. I rejected the word "paralyzed." He didn't dispute my beliefs, and stated that anything is possible.

One afternoon after lunch, Dr. Lehman came into my room. He approached me with a gloomy look and said, "Listen, Gilbert, we need to have a serious talk about your situation." He continued to tell me that the seriousness and extent of damage that I sustained to my spinal cord was immense. "It will take time and a lot of hard work for you to get any kind of feeling or movement in your body." Then Dr. Lehman described the severity of my injuries and told me that I had a severely pinched nerve in my spinal cord that was causing the excruciating pain I felt at regular intervals. To perform surgery now to relieve the pressure on the spinal cord was not possible. He stated it was too late for that. The healing process had taken place already in my spinal cord.

I totally shut him out when he started talking about wheelchairs and lecturing me. I closed my eyes real tight like a spoiled little brat trying to get his way. He became frustrated when I wouldn't pay attention to him. To demonstrate his point, he used a plastic model of a skeleton to show me the vertebrae where my specific injuries were. Next, he talked to me about the possibility of implanting artificial vertebrae, but I told him, "You are not going to put a knife to my neck!"

Every day, he tried to explain to me how close I came to dying and that I was a quadriplegic. "You cannot ever walk again because your injuries are too high and too severe!" He illustrated on a chalkboard and showed me pictures daily to help me understand what had happened to me when the accident occurred.

Weeks passed, and when my neck got stronger, I was subjected to another ordeal. I was outraged, with so many fearful emotions that I started arguing with the nursing staff. They wanted to put me in an old wooden wheelchair. The front wheels were big and the back wheels were small, an antique. I told them to get that piece of junk out of my room.

I was even more horrified to think that this was now the only avenue to moving about. I had been in a wheelchair once before when I was ten years old and had my appendix removed at a hospital in Phoenix, Arizona. Every time I got in it while I was recovering from that surgery, I had the feeling that I would fall out on the steps there. Now I said, "Please, please, never put me in a wheelchair! What are you guys going to do to me next? First, it was the sponge bath, then the doctor showing me the plastic vertebrae, now this old wooden wheelchair! Is this what rehabilitation is all about?"

I guess the odds were against me. I still refused to accept being paralyzed and hated the word "handicap," so the idea of being transferred to a wheelchair for everyday activities for the rest of my life was a hopeless torture for me.

Dr. Lehman had ordered the nursing staff to sit me up in bed for about thirty minutes a day for at least one week. Then gradually they were to get me into the wheelchair for one hour a day, depending on my ability to tolerate sitting upright. His orders were to slowly increase the length of time that I could tolerate the sitting position without getting too tired. Doctor Lehman explained to me again that being paralyzed is not what you decide or choose for yourself, it is just a situation that some people have to live through and accept; I'd been in an unforeseeable accident.

It was overwhelming for me to digest all of the information that was given to me. I had been in and out of consciousness repeatedly, escaping from the pain and the hard truth. Then reality would hit me once again that I was just trying to recover from a severe spinal cord injury that had been inflicted on me some months ago.

This antique wooden wheelchair that the nurses wheeled into my bedroom for me to see and use was called a Colson Wheelchair. It looked like a wheelchair that was built in the colonial period, and I thought it might have been used in the Civil War back east. The chair was not stable, causing it to bounce like gelatin. It was a very simple contraption like my grandpa's old wooden rocking chair that he used to sit in underneath the big pine tree. He would doze off while sitting in the rocking chair in the daytime after smoking his favorite handmade corn-husk tobacco pipe. The wheelchair was made from raw lumber: two-by-four boards, finished and varnished into a bouncing, rocking wheelchair. Even the footrest was built from finished lumber and had a manual knob to make it recline. In order to recline the chair, I needed help to unscrew the black knob.

Reluctantly, I forced myself to use the old wooden wheelchair so I could see the outside world once again. I was then sitting up for the majority of the day, as I would from that point on. The wheelchair routine interrupted my quiet time and visitations with others, and the two nurses would also come in to shift my weight frequently so that I would not get pressure sores. This daily activity for me was their hospital policy. I had no choice but to go along with it, and I had to acknowledge that what they were doing was for the best whether I liked it or not. I became accustomed to being wheeled and escorted around in an old wooden wheelchair to different parts of the hospital. I enjoyed going outside to observe the surroundings, but the outing never lasted long enough for my satisfaction.

In my room, my only connection to the outside world was an antique nineteen-inch color TV that was on all day long. I hated the TV, I hated the news, and I hated soap operas. I hated myself sometimes, too, as I resented having to depend on other people to do almost everything for me except breathe, think, and talk. I would express my discontent by saying, "Turn that TV off! Take that damn TV out! I am sick and tired of it! If it is not too much to ask, can I be alone here in silence?" In the meantime, my mom had sent me a clock radio to entertain me when I got bored, when I had finished with my physical therapy, or just to keep me company. After I expressed my frustration to the nurse, she turned on the radio next.

I was completely lost for that day, wondering to myself, "Where in the world am I?" "Where is that station?" I asked. What kind of entertainment could I get from a station where the disc jockeys spoke only in Spanish and played only Spanish music? I honestly did not understand the programs that were broadcast in Spanish. The nurse explained: "It's the local radio station here in town, a little radio station where only Spanish-speaking people are employed." I asked the nurses to change it to a different station that I could understand or get it away from me.

The nurses asked me what my favorite music was. I replied that country music is the only form of music I listened to back home on the reservation. One of the nurses had a smart mouth and she said, "How about entertaining us with your Navajo songs?" Arrogantly, I told her I didn't know how to sing any songs in Navajo. She asked me what kind of Navajo I was. "One that doesn't sing in Navajo," I said.

I was too stubborn to take any type of jokes from the nurses and I was angry at the whole world. I took out my frustration on those nurses even though it was not their fault that I was in such a solemn and complicated situation.

To resolve the turmoil over the radio and television, the nurses decided to move me to a different room in the same ward of the hospital where they could keep a close eye on me in case of an emergency. After I was moved, I was more comfortable with my new surroundings. The room was adequate, but despite the fact that a curtain was placed to obstruct the lighting, it did not completely block out the intensely bright lights from the nurses station. I could hear the nurses chit-chatting and carrying on long-winded conversations about their families and their lives throughout the long nights. That is why I would sleep during the day, but one of the head nurses informed me that she was going to speak to my primary doctor about the medication that I was on.

When I was located across from the nurses station, a lot of visitors would come to ask questions about my condition and they would try to carry on a conversation with me. Also, they would come into my room and approach me just to say, "Hi," as though I knew these people before I got to this hospital. Never in my life had I seen these people! Some visitors would come in without hesitation and ask me how I was doing. Most of them would come in and encourage me by saying things like: "You'll come out of this condition and you'll get better. You will be in good health again. Hang in there, keep your strong spirits up."

I asked some of these people, "Do you think I will ever walk again in my life?" They never responded to the question, but said, "Have a good day."

One day, Dr. Lehman approached me in my room and said, "One of the head nurses was complaining that you're sleeping the majority of the day and you're awake all night." He said that the nurse had complained to him that she thought I was taking a large amount of medication.

I disputed the nurse's theory about the medication and my sleep pattern. I told my doctor, "It is the bright lights from the nurses station shining directly in my eyes all night and their chit-chatting, their loud conversations, and their laughter that is keeping me awake. That's why I sleep most of the day."

After listening to me, Dr. Lehman was apparently convinced, and he told me that he would move me to a different area again. Apparently, a quiet room where I could sleep like a cat was located down the hallway away from the loud nurses station.

I was always in an isolated room by myself because that's what I had chosen when I was transferred. I was more at ease being in a room by myself with all the privacy that I could get. Being in a private room gave me a lot more freedom and confidence in myself. I had many questions and concerns regarding my care, and conversing with my doctor and nurses individually about my injuries in private was better for me. Dr. Lehman usually came daily to see me and check on how I was getting along with the nursing staff and the other hospital staff and patients. He asked me many questions such as, "How are you feeling today? How are the nurses treating you? Are you getting plenty of fluids and nourishment in your body?" I would always respond, "I don't have an appetite most of the time." Afterwards, the doctor told me clearly that I needed to eat to keep up my strength. Secretly, my main focus was still on wanting to walk.

The Mission Impossible in my mind was the desire to walk out of that hospital! Once I got acquainted with the hospital staff and their assessment of my situation, I became bold enough to dispute them and debate on my behalf about the possibility of walking again. My constant thought, over and over, was, "I am going to walk out of this hospital, no matter what lies ahead!" I said that nobody in the world was going to take away my dream. If I could only accomplish the physical act of standing, I reasoned, then in a few weeks I could walk across my room or down the hallway. These were my waking dreams, seeing myself running through the fields toward the hills and climbing the rocks once more as I did in my able-bodied life.

Later on I realized that some dreams do not come true. I was just visualizing and believing in a hopeless wish that I would walk again; maybe someday a miracle might happen. This really upset me and I distanced myself from the nurses and doctors. I refused to do anything I was told, I even refused to eat and drink water. I was very uncooperative and all I wanted to do was just lay in bed closing out the whole world. I hated myself and I hated the world. I had been unresponsive for three days when my doctor informed Dotty of this situation. From then on she came storming in on a daily basis like an unstoppable tornado with a loud voice. Her visits annoyed me. She talked to me about how to accept the reality of being paralyzed, and how to cope. She was very helpful and had a way of getting me out of dark moments. She encouraged me to move on with my life and accept the severe changes in my condition. But even today I will not accept the word paralyzed.

After some months had gone slowly by, my doctor asked me, "Are you getting bored? Are you ready to go to school here?"

I responded, "What school? Where is it located? I thought this was only a hospital for crippled children to be rehabilitated."

He replied, "The school is in the back, adjacent to the hospital. It is for patients who are bedridden or in wheelchairs. The janitors and the maintenance men push the beds with patients in them back and forth. Another option is a van that goes back and forth to Hot Springs High School once or twice a week, if you are accepted there." He said that when I could tolerate sitting in an upright position and was able to operate my own electric motorized wheelchair, it might be of interest to me to check into that school.

At that point, I said, "No, I don't want to go to school there! I want to go back to the reservation where I belong and finish the remainder of my high school years."

"Apparently, you are almost finished with your schooling," my doctor said to me. "You should complete your high school here and get it over with."

I asked him the repetitious key question that was always on my mind: "Will I ever be able to walk again?"

The doctor shook his head and rubbed his palms together and said, "It takes time, but we'll have to see how you are healing in another month and how you are coping with your situation."

At that moment he took out a sharp pin, then he said, "Close your eyes or look the other way. I'm going to stick this sharp pin in different parts of your body to see if you have gained some of your sensation back. What part of your body am I poking with this sharp needle?"

He asked me over and over again and then he poked my foot with the needle while I was looking at him from the corner of my eyes.

"Yes I feel that!" I said.

"Let's not play around. Tell me the truth: do you really feel this needle poking you?"

"No, I don't feel that."

He then responded, "It's going to take time for some of your feeling to come back. Only time will tell." Then he walked out of my room with a look of frustration on his face.

One early morning, a couple of nursing assistants entered my room. To my surprise I saw the same old wooden chair that I had used before when I was doing my sitting tolerance routine. There was no cushion but the nurses placed a couple of pillows on the chair to prevent any pressure sores on my lower part of my body. One nurses aide told me, "You have to get used to getting up every day to attend school." I was not enthusiastic about getting up early to get prepared. Nevertheless, she said that it was time for me to get into the chair so she could take me outside to get some fresh air.

I didn't want to get into that old chair again. I told her abruptly, "Take the chair back out. I don't ever want to be in a wheelchair. I know how to walk out of this room any time I please!"

She did not pay attention to what I was saying. She told me once again that they were putting me in the chair because it was my doctor's order. Then they brought in a different medical apparatus. She said, "We need to crank you slowly up using this Hoyer lifter. Afterwards, we will swing you gently into the wheelchair. If you are getting lightheaded tell us right away."

Because of my disadvantage I was forced into the wheelchair even though I didn't want to be. The two nurses informed me that this was the only method used to get me outside so I could get some fresh air; otherwise, they would have to carry me or use a prone cart to wheel me outside. Those were the only options I had.

"You've been in this room too long! It seems like you're part of the furniture! Aren't you getting claustrophobia in this small room? You need to get out and enjoy the view outside. It will be a great change of scenery for you and a good therapy," one nurse said to me.

I had no choice; there was no one to speak up for me. I argued with the nurse demanding for me to go outside, and finally I decided to let them transfer me into the old wooden wheelchair. I came to realize that I had no choice but to try using the wheelchair if I wanted to finish the remainder of my high school education.

16

COMING TO TERMS WITH MY NEW LIFE

"Let's take a stroll around outside and see what we can get ourselves into. It is a very nice day outside." One of the nurses aides wheeled me outside to get some fresh air. In my room, it was cold because of the air conditioner constantly running. When we got outside I was suddenly blinded by the intense dazzling sunlight.

Later on during the day, while I was sitting under the shade of a tree, some student nurses introduced themselves to me and said they were from New Mexico State University. They were on an internship study program held at this hospital every summer. Most of the students appeared to me like they were over twenty years of age. I saw that they were a lot older than I was. They questioned and worked with the patients individually under the supervision of their instructor. The student nurses asked many questions regarding how we were being treated at the hospital. "How are the nurses caring for you?" "Do you have enough to eat so you can stay healthy?" "Are there enough activities to keep you busy so you won't get bored?" and all the other general questions that medical personnel would ask a patient.

The NMSU interns did their practicum work together with my physical therapist, Lisa; they worked with all the patients in the hospital. Lisa would demonstrate how to do range-of-motion exercises in front of the interns. She also demonstrated the techniques of how to transfer me into the old wooden wheelchair. Most of the time, I was lying flat on my back in bed. The process was to crank up the bed and sit me up gradually on the side of the bed first. This would prevent me from getting lightheaded. Then they wrapped a gait belt tightly around my waist. After that, one of the interns transferred me by holding on tight to the belt, then slowly swivelled me in the air and positioned me in my wheelchair. It seemed to me that I was the guinea pig of the hospital; I was puzzled about why they didn't work more with patients other than me. Despite my concerns, I joked with the interns to make my day go by quickly. I was their only Native American spinal cord patient during their internship. They also had to work with all the other non-Native patients who were hospitalized there with all different types of injuries. Most of the interns learned the daily routine right away. Their young minds must have been eager to learn.

Because they had such a long drive to this isolated area in the desert, the physical therapy students stayed in the same location upstairs where the other medical staff such as doctors, nurses, and visitors were accommodated. At times, when some students were finished with their homework, they would come and visit with the patients in the evenings.

My favorite place to be was in the back of the hospital where I could focus clearly to the north and see Elephant Butte Reservoir. I could see a lot of activity going on around the reservoir, like boat-riding on the lake and constant traffic near there, which also amused me. Toward the evening, a nurses aide would accompany me outside, and she would converse with me about how beautiful Elephant Butte and its surroundings were. I was curious about the reservoir and I asked a lot of the nurses if they had ever been to the reservoir.

Some of the nurses would answer quickly with a surprised look, "Yes, I've been to Elephant Butte many times."

One of the nurses that I got to know at the hospital said that she often camped out on the reservoir during the summer months on her days off from work. She told me that she went fishing on a boat and caught lots of fish. She was very enthusiastic about how big the lake was—it is one of the biggest lakes in the southwest region of New Mexico.

As I became more used to all the situations at the hospital, I started to tease the nurses, doctors and custodians around me. They asked what made me decide to cooperate with them and change myself and start living. I said, "I do not know, did I really change?" I never noticed that I had changed. It was mostly the nurses aides and custodians that I joked with.

One late afternoon, two nurses aides helped me to go to bed to relieve pressure from my sitter. I asked them, "How does my butt look?" They looked at one another and started laughing hysterically with their faces blushing as red as a strawberry. One them said, "It looks like a regular butt, just a little lighter than ours." And with laughter, I asked them if there were red pressure marks where I had been sitting. After asking them this question, they just started joking about my butt and saying that being nurses they'd seen too many bare butts, and that they all look the same. They told me, "There is no pressure area and no red marks. But in the meantime we will just put some lotion on there like baby magic." I told them, "I don't need baby magic." And they said, "You're our baby here." After that I asked for the name of the lotion that she was going to use. She showed me a pink bottle and it really did say "Baby Magic," and that my butt would be as smooth as a baby's bottom.

It was a big transition for me, to depend on somebody to do things, especially rubbing your butt and private area. If I was able to move I wouldn't have let anybody put lotion on me in that part of my body. We joked around for a while after they finished with their task. They both told me that I had changed a lot in my attitude. They were more comfortable and happier working with me and they told me to keep this attitude and not to go back to old habits. They said, "You should've seen yourself and heard yourself when you first came into this hospital. Your attitude was so bad that nobody wanted to work with you. We tried to ask you questions and you wouldn't answer. Or you would never agree with anything. You didn't want to be bothered or you wouldn't let anybody ask you any kind of questions. You were like a wolverine or a stubborn donkey, and to tell you the truth, even a rattlesnake would be better. We saw one yesterday in the parking lot and we ran away from the snake as fast as we could run. Some people saw us and started to laugh at us. And they told us that all we had to do was tell the snake to go away and not bother us."

One day the head nurse of the whole hospital came in. She told me that I should take a lesson in being a comedian, an actor, singer or a songwriter. After that she told me that there is a school for all these things and I could go to school and take classes. The questions she asked me just puzzled me and rumbled around in my head. It made me wonder how I could go to school and attend a day of classes in my condition. She came back another day and asked me if I had thought about the questions she'd asked. I told her I hadn't and asked for the questions again. She told me the question was simple. She asked me if I wanted to go back to school and finish up with the remainder of my high school years in the hospital. I guess she was trying to cheer me up with this idea of going back to school. But I told her, "I used to love going to school back on the reservation, when I was able to walk and able to ride the school bus, but I don't think I can go to school now, because who has all the time in the world to transport me from home to school?" I also told her I thought it would be a lot of work for me and my family.

She explained that she was telling me to go to school because there was a school in back of the rehabilitation hospital. This was to be a great transition for me. I'd stay in the hospital and go to school during the day so I wouldn't get bored. It was very simple for me to be transported to school. She said that the teacher would contact my counselor at the local high school on the reservation and they would talk with one another to see what courses I needed to finish up the remaining years of high school. I asked her if it was really that simple, that what she told me sounded like a miracle or magic. What would somebody like me do who couldn't move nothing, not even to pick up a pencil?

Early one morning, I was surprised by a couple of student therapists when they rolled in a gurney and said to me, "It's time for you to go into the stainless steel Hubbard tank. You will like this therapy because it is warm mineral water. It will make you feel like you're swimming. The whirlpool will also stimulate your muscles to relieve all the aching areas."

I was glad when one of the hospital therapist's staff who had a good disposition came to observe them transferring me to the gurney. She was always joking with all her patients during her routine rounds. She encouraged me by telling me, "You will enjoy your short time in the whirlpool once you get accustomed to the warm water. It will make you feel good and you will be relieved of your stress. I bet that you will not want to get out. But you don't want to stay in there too long or you will look like a prune."

I questioned one of the student therapists, "What is stress?" She told me she would get back with me sometime in the evening.

In my adolescent years in the hospital with no family close by, I had no knowledge of what "whirlpool" meant or what it looked like until I experienced it on this particular morning. Two qualified staff members were able to operate the electric hoist that elevated me first in the air, with a chain attached to the four corners of the stretcher. Like removing an engine out of a vehicle, they slowly swung me across the room and gently lowered me into the Hubbard tank filled with warm mineral water.

After completion of the first stages in lowering me into the tank, the motor was turned on to start the water pressure. Thereafter, the water started bubbling against my body, I could feel the gush of warm water as it put pressure against my body where I had some limited feeling; this procedure was for therapeutic purposes.

Later, the student therapist I had asked about stress came back and tried to explain it to me. She told me about herself first and how stress affects her with school, especially at the end of semester when preparing for the final exam. How she cannot think straight or sleep worrying about the final test. She asked, "How about you, how does stress affect you?" I told her, "I don't know what stress is, we don't use that word on the reservation." She looked at me with a puzzled face, and went outside to get some fresh air.

Three days each week shortly after I had my breakfast the physical therapist would come to my room to assist me in doing range-of-motion exercises on all my limbs. Also, she exercised my fingers, helping to prevent them from getting stiff. Pam, the physical therapy director, was an older lady. She was serious about her work and she didn't joke around. Lisa, who was younger, would always joke around and tease me. Lisa would say, "It is time for you to get out of this room and get out of your shell. All you look at is the four walls and the ceiling. What else do you want to see?"

I would respond, "I'm listening to you. What are you going to do with me today?" while I was lying on the long black gurney with a white sheet covering me. It seemed to me that the white sheet covering me represented a trip to the morgue. But, in reality, it was for a lengthy ride to the physical therapy department where I would get a warm mineral bath. I got used to this daily routine and I always looked forward to going to the whirlpool.

Ruben and Bobby were the two employees who operated the recreation department. The two men rotated their duties. At times, one worked in the office and the other entertained the patients in their rooms. Their primary purpose was to provide activities to meet their patients' interests with what little available resources the recreational department had on hand. No matter how severe your disability appeared or the adversity you were confronted with, the two men were always there to lift up your spirits. They had the gift to make people smile and laugh by telling jokes about what they had experienced in life. They would banter with patients while we were in the recreation room. The two men never failed to make an effort to bring some happiness to the patients throughout any day when they were on duty. During the daytime, they were schoolteachers at a nearby school called Hot Springs High School; later on in the evening, they would wear a different hat as recreation therapists at Carrie Tingley Rehabilitation Hospital.

Their profession in working with different types of disabilities was tough and required a lot of patience. Their knowledge as well as compassion to care for all disabled patients was extraordinary. They also volunteered their time, especially on Sunday afternoons after church mass, to work with their patients on unfinished projects. Neither man showed disrespect to anyone with a disability. They were always looking forward to working with us in the evenings. The patients with extensive disabilities, with developmental disabilities, the physically challenged, people with braces or missing limbs or severe recent injuries were always given extra attention by these two hard-working men.

The recreational therapists made their rounds in the ward during the week, and they would ask patients for suggestions of movies they would like to see on Monday of the following week. Bobby or Ruben would then operate the equipment to show movies in the dining area on Monday nights. On movie nights, student volunteers from Hot Springs High School came to help with the entertainment for the patients. While one of the therapists operated the movie from a little booth overlooking the dining room, the other therapist managed the serving of the refreshments that were provided by the hospital cafeteria. The canvas screen was big. It required two maintenance men to pull the screen down. This was usually done right after supper to get the room prepared for the big event. Next, an overhead film projector was loaded with a specially selected movie for us to see. Everybody was welcome to the free showing of the movie. The nurses and doctors who stayed upstairs at the hospital would come down and join the patients to watch the free movie of the week. Some patients were in bed, some were walking, and a few patients came in their wheelchairs. On other nights, volunteer students also helped entertain the patients so that we wouldn't get bored or homesick.

Every day, for the duration of my stay at the rehabilitation hospital, I saw the occupational therapists communicating diligently with some patients in order to find out how they were adjusting and coping with their hospital stay. They would ask: "Do you like it here? Is there anything you need to make your stay more comfortable?" The medical staff never inquired about the patients' ethnic backgrounds. The therapists' main focus was on evaluating their patients' progress at the hospital. The therapists reported back to the doctors on their findings.

The old jukebox in the recreation area at Carrie Tingley always played Spanish music. The patients who were paraplegic were able to play pool in the recreation room with one another or sometimes with the hospital staff. Some patients who were paraplegic would go to a room, a very small room about twelve feet by twelve feet, where they would work on models such as aircraft, ships or cars. After completion, they would paint the models themselves. A patient named Freddie, who worked on the models constantly, loved to sniff the glue and took the open tubes with him when his class had ended. He was finally caught by one of the nurses.

For other recreational activities, which usually happened on weekends, the therapists would invite some of the patients to go on a field trip for a few hours to Elephant Butte reservoir or cruise in their wheelchairs outside the hospital area or walk around the hospital to learn about the adobe structures and observe different landmarks in the area. I really liked the scenery outside. The landscape was different, with no mountains. It was isolated, and had a hot desert climate. Overall, it was very different from what I was used to—hills, mountains with trees and plants, and different types of domestic animals running in groups throughout the reservation.

The smell in the summer evenings outside the hospital was vivid in my mind and senses. A fresh cool breeze erupted from the water sprinklers on the lawn surrounding the hospital. The aroma took me back in time; it reminded me of my home on the reservation, the northwestern desert climate of New Mexico, where I was accustomed to the effects of the rain showers. The sprinklers brought out the fresh smell of the wet lawn, and the beautiful display of a colorful arched rainbow. Back home on the reservation at Twin Lakes, New Mexico, this fresh scent was the way it used to smell right after a thunderstorm. The Twin Lakes region had lots of rain showers during the hot summer months in 1975, and after the rain shower, the aroma from the lawn evaporated in the hot desert air with the force of the heat.

In addition to the recreational therapists, some of the hospital staff who worked with patients were empathetic and really friendly. They knew the patients well and treated them as if they were their own kids. Sometimes, they would take the patients to their homes for a home-cooked meal. I was invited to go home with staff several times and I enjoyed those chances to get away from the hospital and meet other people. However, the majority of the patients who lived nearby yearned to go home. In my case, Carrie Tingley became a second home where I finished out my adolescent years. I had a good relationship with the staff members at Carrie Tingley. Everybody knew me because I was a long-term patient. The staff was always willing to help me in all aspects of the treatment. I became content in the environment with the staff as my custodians.

17

HIGH SCHOOL GRADUATION

I missed my Indian classmates and friends at Tohatchi High School back on the reservation. I wanted so much to graduate with the class that I had started with as a freshman, but at that point, I had no choice but to get on with my life and complete my schooling at Carrie Tingley. I encountered many obstacles in the pathway to achieving my vision goals. Every day, I felt the need to overcome my horrible recollection of my painful accident. I turned to the professional medical staff and dedicated social workers to guide me and encourage me to have more faith in myself. It was lonely and hard for me to make decisions about the rest of my life without talking to other people.

To make my life easier and to give me some mobility, it was determined by the medical staff that a motorized wheelchair was essential for me to get around independently. Thereafter, a unique wheelchair was designed for me; I went everywhere I needed to go, and even some places where I had not gone before in my able life.

While it may seem that I was fully accommodated through technology and devices, it did not make my body whole. I needed others to assist me in my daily routines: in preparing to start my day, and other minute tasks such as wiping my tears or blowing my nose. I was unable to do the simplest small things for myself.

Alone in my room, I questioned myself out of frustration. How could I do my daily schoolwork when I could not do the simplest task for myself? Why did I take on such a huge challenge? The walls would not answer me. Most of the time I felt school was time wasted and it was too much effort to get a diploma. Why would I need a diploma since I was a quadriplegic? After I got acquainted with my teachers, I often argued with my favorite teachers about why I was expected to do all the assignments on time, when I didn't have the right technology to help me. Eventually the frustration grew within me. It was the loneliest situation on earth. When I think back on how difficult it must have been for them to teach a student in my condition, facing all the overwhelming challenges that I faced, I appreciate all their efforts to educate me by overcoming my resistance and refusing to let me give up.

At first I felt worthless and thought there was nothing for me to accomplish in my situation. Then I began to notice that in all of the books and movies they showed us, there were no Native Americans who could be role models for me. I asked several times if there were any Native Americans who had the same condition that I had, and I was told that the staff there could not find even one Native American author with quadriplegia or paraplegia. I realized that there was no Native American mentor for me, and it was then that I decided that I could be a mentor to other Native Americans with disabilities by sharing what I had gone through and encouraging them to do what they wanted to do. Once I had this idea, I was determined to complete high school.

There were two young ladies, my speech therapist Julie, and Kate, an occupational therapist, who always had bright smiles on their faces in the morning. They would say, "Hello, how are you? How do you feel? How was your night? Did you have a good night's sleep? Would you like to do something else other than going to school every day? Are you bored with going to school?"

At first I didn't reply, I just looked at them and went to class. Then one day I said that my main goal was to finish the remainder of my high school years there at Carrie Tingley.

I worked with Kate for half of the day, and she encouraged me to do other things. She said, "This is what rehabilitation is all about, doing different things and not only going to school."

Kate introduced me to drawing with my mouth. She showed me books with pictures of some other people with quadriplegia doing their drawings at other rehabilitation centers across the country. After observing all the drawings in the books, I became interested in drawing with my mouth. I did some drawings with her by placing a mouth stick between my teeth. After that, I got accustomed to drawing different things such as animals, landscapes, and different objects she placed on top of the table for me to sketch. My first drawing was of a purple moose that I drew with a marker. I kept drawing until the marker was dry. When I was able to do drawings for an extended period of time at Carrie Tingley Hospital, I finished two drawings that she kept for herself.

Kate always worked with my hands and arms, trying to exercise them to strengthen and stretch them so they wouldn't get stiff. She would attach two metal rods behind my wheelchair that reached over my head and hung in front of me. She then attached two long springs with a cuff to my wrists that helped me to try to move my arms. My left arm started moving first, but then later my right arm took over. It made me feel and look like a puppet sitting in a wheelchair. After working with her for a number of weeks she ordered a metal ratchet brace for me, which enabled me to pick up small objects like forks, spoons, and blocks, and it also allowed me to control the electric wheelchair that she ordered for me. I never used a blow-tube to navigate and command my electric motorized wheelchair like my friend Kevin. I use the little movement I have in my right biceps and gravity to control my chair.

When I got used to driving this wheelchair I went all over the hospital, even going to areas that were restricted to all patients. It became almost impossible for the nurses to keep up with me and to keep a close eye on me. The only way was to put me back in bed and park the chair away from me.

I argued with the nurses in frustration and said, "Now you want me to stay in bed, and not be up in the wheelchair? You nurses always wanted me to get in my wheelchair and get out of my room. What is the idea of taking my wheelchair away from me?"

They responded, "Don't worry, we'll get you back in your wheelchair after supper. You need to rest or take a nap so you can relieve the pressure areas on your sitter so you won't accumulate pressure sores."

Julie, the speech therapist, was the most inspirational and motivational individual I had ever encountered in my life. She took extra time talking with me even when I was in a bad mood. She would ask various questions relating to my current situation and about what I used to do at home when I was able.

She asked me, "Do you like school?"

I responded with no second thoughts: "I like school sometimes because it keeps me occupied and out of trouble, but not all the time. This is what I chose to do for myself while I am recovering from my severe injuries."

Then she asked me, "Do you want to pay a visit to Kevin? He's doing some drawing in my office almost every day."

I then asked, "Why isn't he attending school?"

"Because Kevin is so far behind in his school years that it is hard for him to keep up with other students his age. But you are so near to graduating from high school and this is your final year."

Another time, she said to me, "I would like to provide both you and Kevin with a pencil and a piece of paper so you can try to determine your future goals and put them in order."

Kevin and I parked our wheelchairs beside one another outside in the shade. It was a very pleasant day, a hot mid-afternoon toward the middle of April in the year 1977. I was nearing my graduation from high school. The coming events relating to my graduation were the only thing I had on my mind. At that point in time, I didn't know what college was all about, because no one in my family had ever experienced college life.

I wrote just a few sentences that read: "Julie, I want to continue on with my schooling. I want to go to college. But I do not have the slightest idea about how to enroll." I had gotten the idea to continue on with my education from advertisements on TV. They often spoke of students earning their degrees, and made it sound so inviting, easy and interesting.

A couple days later, Julie and some of her co-workers came to my room and asked me, "Where do you want to attend college?"

I replied, "Where do people with disabilities go to college?" Then she brought in a lady named Betty who had muscular dystrophy and was also confined in a wheelchair.

Betty told me, "I went to New Mexico State University, in Las Cruces. However, this corning year I am going to the University of New Mexico in Albuquerque to work on my master's in business administration."

I had no idea what she was talking about. I asked Betty to come back in a little while so I could visit and talk with her by myself.

When Betty came back, I asked her, "How do you get into a college or university? How are they different from one another?"

She said, "The colleges are just branches of the whole university, and the university is just one whole school. I will call down to New Mexico State University and ask for a registration packet for you if you are interested."

She told me New Mexico State had a good program for people with disabilities and special needs. At NMSU there was a group called The Barrier Breakers, a small community looking and lobbying for help and resources for the people with disabilities who attended the school. Such help and resources included wider sidewalks for wheelchairs, door openers, dining and cafeteria accommodations, campus enforcement and other changes to make the school more accessible for students with disabilities.

A few weeks later, she received a batch of forms relating to school registration and brought them directly to my room. I completed a number of forms with assistance from her, and Julie mailed the forms back to the college.

I was not informed of any new developments concerning my applications for a long time, and I thought Julie had abandoned my plans and me. I was anxious during my wait for a response from the university's admissions office. I waited for two weeks before Julie came to visit and wickedly startled me awake from my nap. She had come to congratulate me in person about my acceptance to the university. Apparently, she had requested that New Mexico State inform her of any essential information regarding my application. She told me that my acceptance letter was in the mail and that I should be receiving it within the week.

Suddenly, everyone at the hospital knew about my acceptance to the university. I was pleased, and inquisitive as to what college would be like. I asked my nurses and doctors what I should expect and how to manage my college life. Many of them did not want to talk about my acceptance to NMSU, so I kept a lot of my thoughts to myself. But I was made to understand that avoiding the many distractions at university, keeping up with homework, and attending classes were very, very, very important.

Before I graduated from high school I was given a psychiatric evaluation at the rehabilitation center. A short bald-headed Anglo man who was all dressed up in formal wear came in with a briefcase with all kinds of pictures. He displayed white cardboard cards smeared with black ink, asking me what images they reminded me of. He performed this evaluation in a small enclosed room with no windows.

"What does this remind you of?"

I just looked directly at him and said, "Did you just smear some ink on that paper and fold it in half to get that image like a butterfly?"

Then he inquired of me again what the ink smear looked like on paper. He knew instinctively what I was thinking, so he didn't come all the time to see me. I only saw him twice: when I first got injured, and in my final year of high school.

My mom had been trained to provide care for me at home on the reservation, and she then trained other members of my family. They started us off with a week-long visit, then two weeks, which was the most I could be away from the hospital. My dad and other siblings caught on quickly with tasks like transferring me from the truck to the chair, then chair to the bed, and changing my position side to side.

Meanwhile, the staff from Tohatchi corresponded with Carrie Tingley by way of fax or mail to send and receive homework and assignments. The curriculum I was taught at Carrie Tingley was designed to parallel Tohatchi's, but the education I received at Carrie Tingley was actually better, because the teacher-student ratio was basically one-to-one. Also, Tohatchi concentrated not only on academic curriculum, but electives such as physical education, wood workshop, band and sports, whereas at Carrie Tingley Hospital School, concentration was centered solely on our studies of academics such as English, math, reading, and history. The staff there provided rehabilitation for my injuries, but they also helped me to continue with my education. Carrie Tingley, being a state hospital, was allowed to collaborate with Tohatchi High School in my home district to insure that I met their requirements for graduation.

In May of 1977, I was finally released from Carrie Tingly Hospital where I had been confined and watched like a hawk. I returned to the reservation. The driving time between Tohatchi and Carrie Tingley took about a whole day. My teacher at Carrie Tingley had already made contact with my counselor at Tohatchi High

School, informing him that I would be returning home to Twin Lakes. My counselor had made all the arrangements so that I could get Tohatchi High School credit hours while I attended Carrie Tingley Hospital School.

The feeling of being back in high school was a bit nerve-wracking, and I wondered if I could compete with the normal students. I did not participate in any of the school events such as spring formals or prom, pep rallies, sport events and student gatherings. The only high school event I attended was the finale of high school life, the graduation ceremony.

I had been home for a week when my counselor, whose name was John, and a couple of high school students came by to visit me. I used to go to school with these two students before my accident. They both told me that this was their first time seeing me in a long time, and they thought that I had died! While we were all in my room together, my counselor then said to them, "Don't bring out the bad memories. Let's just look forward to the graduation ceremony."

He informed me that I was going to be graduating with seventy-seven students in the class of 1977, and that I would be graduating in the top ten. When I asked him how that could be, he replied, "You went to school in a different district. You were in the district for Hot Springs High School, and at Carrie Tingley Hospital school you were taught one-on-one, so I think you have gained a lot more knowledge. Your teachers there said you are a very intelligent student."

Despite an unwanted new challenge in my life situation, I had been determined to continue with my schooling. From my rehabilitation stay at Carrie Tingley Hospital I had made it back to Tohatchi High School at the end of my senior year to graduate with the class that I started with as a freshman. I wasn't any different inside when I was a freshman than on my graduation day. I just wanted to get my diploma from high school and move forward with my life as a disabled individual. This had been my ultimate goal ever since I had regained my consciousness from my severe accident. I didn't want to be at home wondering what life had to offer or assuming life was just going to pass me by. Paralysis is not a choice that I made for myself. It was the result of a sudden, unexpected accident. I had worked with many individuals to get where I wanted to go. I mentally picked up my journey walking stick and was ready to graduate in an electric motorized wheelchair at the age of nineteen.

The day finally came and I was excited beyond comprehension. When I arrived at the high school, I noticed that I was out of sync as far as high school fashion was concerned. Many of the students were well dressed in dresses and skirts and suits. Some of the guys that I knew from high school looked like penguins in their black tuxedos. I had picked up my cap and gown at the school and begun our long wait. We waited for two hours, and I remember feeling that time was barely inching its way forward. I could feel the cold air from the nearby mountains blowing on my face. I became extremely cold before I got inside the gym where it was warm.

The principal and counselors were arranging the student body based on honors and grade point average. I was anxious to complete my high school years, and grateful when the wait ended and the line began moving. As the ceremony progressed through the national anthem, the honorary mention of graduating students, scholarships and grants, and keynote and other guest speakers, I took mental notes of the school, the faces, and the size of the audience.

I caught the term the faculty and student body used for disabled students, "special student." When I heard the term, I was offended at the use of the word "special." I remember thinking that I was not special in any way. I was just a normal student who was graduating that day like everyone else. I did not want any kind of special recognition that was spawned by sympathy toward my condition. But my anger subsided when the graduation theme began and we moved toward the podium to receive our diplomas. Then a shock of self-consciousness took hold of me when I realized that the focus of the audience's attention was on the center of the auditorium and the podium I was approaching, and this realization made my heart pump faster. My counselor, John, presented my diploma. I forgot that I was disabled and confined to a wheelchair during that moment. I felt that I had accomplished a normal goal like any able-bodied student. This was the pivotal moment I had waited for, and the hours of waiting seemed to fade to seconds in no time.

One week after my graduation I started coughing constantly. Over the course of the next few days, I noticed symptoms of what I thought was just a regular cold: congested nasal and chest cavity, coughing up yellow phlegm, headaches and chills. As the days slowly went by, I noticed that I was feeling worse. At nightfall, my symptoms seemed to magnify in intensity. Eventually, I had fever, started coughing blood, and my breathing became labored.

My dad was worried and couldn't do anything to help me so he quickly transported me to the emergency room at the Gallup Indian Medical Center before my condition got any worse. I was immediately admitted to the hospital for observation and treatment. It took the doctors a long time to figure out what was wrong with me. They did a lot of examinations on me, including x-raying my chest, and later diagnosed a severe case of pneumonia. A doctor then informed me that I was going to be hospitalized until my lungs were clear of inflammation and infection. He stated, "We're going to put a tube down your nose so the machine can siphon and clear out all the phlegm down in your lungs caused by the infection." I had this tube going through my nose into my lungs for a few days, and afterwards I began to feel a lot better.

When I was about to be released from Gallup Indian Medical Center, the doctor there informed me that he was considering transferring me to a nursing home called Mckinley Manor in Gallup.

I informed my parents that I wanted to go back to Carrie Tingley Hospital, because my immune system was no longer used to the high elevation or the cold climate back on the reservation. I asked my social worker at Gallup Indian Medical Center to try to contact my primary doctor at Carrie Tingley to see if they could allow me to return there for the remainder of my recovery. I was in the Gallup hospital for another three long days before finally I received word that Dr. Lehman at Carrie Tingley Hospital wanted me to return there instead of going to the nursing home. My dad had volunteered to accompany me on a small charter airplane back to Truth or Consequences.

A month after I graduated from Tohatchi High School I returned to Carrie Tingley Hospital.

I had been advised by various doctors and nurses at Carrie Tingley to postpone my quest for higher education for another year due to the time required for recovery from my severe injury and recent pneumonia. However, Julie wanted me to continue my post-secondary education while I was still fresh out of high school. She said that a gap of a year or two between high school and college was undesirable and would lessen my opportunity to receive a full Navajo Tribal Scholarship.

Julie was knowledgeable about how the gears worked within tribal governments concerning scholarships. She was in close contact with the scholarship office at the Navajo Nation headquarters and had filled out a number of applications for me to obtain assistance with tuition, books, and room and board. Julie informed me that I would have to go to Las Cruces and take a placement test known as the SAT. Another month passed before I received word on my test date.

In the middle of June, my mom received a phone call from the Navajo Tribal Scholarship office in Window Rock, Arizona. She was informed that I had been awarded a full scholarship to New Mexico State University! My mom notified me right away and I asked her to send me the whole packet of information about the scholarship.

I came back to Twin Lakes for what would be my last visit for a while. I wanted to stay home and visit with my family for about two weeks before I moved on to begin higher education at New Mexico State University at Las Cruces. I informed my parents that it would be better for me to go to the college from Carrie Tingley, and not go straight from the reservation.

I had made the choice to experience something beyond high school, home life on the reservation, and confinement at Carrie Tingley Hospital. I can honestly say that my time at Carrie Tingley provided an excellent experience as I learned to interact with the nurses, doctors, cooks and maintenance staff. Now I really wanted to understand and experience college life to the fullest: the loud early buzz of the alarm clock indicating it was time to get up and start preparing for my first class with the aid of my caregiver, the new and interesting diversity of students, the mass stampedes between classes, the trips to the cafeteria or campus bookstore, the campus buildings, and the many languages spoken that sounded like birds chirping in the trees. No one else in my family had the opportunity to go to college. I was the first one to do so, and I was looking forward to my new destination.

While at home, I lounged about and did little things to occupy my mind. I mostly listened to music on the radio because I did not have a computer like I have today. I enjoyed the atmosphere and environment on the reservation, and the simplicity of life. I was also still waiting for the green light that marked completion of arrangements for me to begin college and confirmation that the funds were available to pay for tuition, books, room and board, and other expenses.

My parents and family wanted to have a traditional ceremony performed for me in accordance with Navajo customs. The purpose of this ceremony was to build a sacred path for health in body, mind, and spirit. Any time a member of Diné leaves the protection of the four sacred mountains, a ceremony for spiritual protection, good health and a good journey is called for. This was my last duty before I began my educational journey, physically and mentally, to New Mexico State University.

18

NEW MEXICO STATE UNIVERSITY

Before starting classes at NMSU, I visited the school. I made my first journey into what would be my exciting new world in late June to visit the university grounds and to observe the accessibility and accommodations for an individual with a disability such as mine. My intention for this trip was to take my SAT and ACT examinations so they could determine what classes I had to take or could skip. My advisor at the college had scheduled these two tests for the same day, a situation which was uncommon and detrimental, they are usually scheduled at least one month apart. Incoming freshmen usually begin a slow process of studying for these tests prior to taking the exams, but on the day of the tests, I hastily browsed through the test pamphlets and used the first answer that came to my mind for each question. My resulting test scores were not satisfactory for several reasons: the strain caused by completing both tests on the same day; my impatience to find out what classes I would be enrolled in; and the physical and mental stress caused by my recent injuries. The last reason was that I had such great confidence in myself and my ability to handle the two tests without preparation. I was fresh out of high school and felt that I had all the knowledge that I needed.

My second trip to New Mexico State in late July was to register for my classes and tour the campus. I had a registered nurse, Joe, who was employed by Carrie Tingley, who assisted me and drove us to the early registration events. As was ordinary for every college and university, the early registration opportunity attracted a stampede of students. Long lines of aggravated, impatient students crowded the registration office.

Julie provided some shortcuts to make my day of registering more convenient. To aid me through the chaos, she made a list of all my anticipated expenses, to be submitted for payment prior to registering. These included tuition, books, and room and board. She called in advance to speed up the registration process for me. Some of the classes that I was able to snag were prerequisite classes that I wanted to deal with first. Those classes were English, mathematics, and history.

Next it was time to tour the campus to become familiar with the surroundings and to memorize where my classroom buildings and dormitories were located. After I'd enrolled for classes, I was assigned a dormitory room in Regents Row at University Park and given a key to my room. My tour began with an exploration of the dormitory. Regents Row was three stories high and was located on the opposite side of the health center from the registration building. My room, which was located on the first floor, was of a decent size. I had my own bathroom and shower. My window looked out onto green tennis courts and the track field, where I saw a few runners and a few other athletes on the field practicing track events. There was also a large tree that grew in the yard in front of my window.

As I viewed my room, I realized I was hungry and decided to continue my expedition to the snack bar, which was located below the bookstore, to feed my growling stomach. The main student cafeteria was located north of the snack bar across the large parking lot. I noticed that the Garcia Annex Building was next door on the south side, which was my next area to visit. The Garcia Annex was a two-story building that housed the headquarters of Services for Students with Disabilities (SSD). This building was located on a steep hill that I would not attempt to climb by myself even though I had a motorized electric wheelchair. Joe was considerate enough to guide me up the steep hill.

All the while between my adventurous trips and during the long hot summer days, I was anxiously waiting at Carrie Tingley Hospital in anticipation of the start of the fall semester. I was at the hospital for a majority of the summer. Aside from my trips to NMSU, I spent a lot of the days watching films produced by different universities. These films were usually about their institutions' programs to assist and accommodate individuals with disabilities. They documented everyday college life, including the normal daily routines of waking up, preparing for meals, commuting to classrooms, and one-on-one assistance. The universities' films competed with one another for prospective students based on the level of quality services provided to the disabled individual.

I was still lacking a consistent caregiver to assist me with my daily needs and morning preparations for class. Julie had written an advertisement for a qualified individual to monitor and care for a physically challenged student. She placed these ads in several places across the campus hoping to hire a qualified student with a considerable amount of experience. There were a few nursing students who responded to the advertisement. About two weeks before I left for New Mexico State, a student nurse from the university came to visit me at Carrie Tingley Hospital. He was a Mexican-American guy from Tyler, Texas. He said it was his third year as a nursing student, and that he was competent enough to take on the responsibility of caring for me and assisting me with my daily needs in the dormitory for the upcoming academic school year, and he needed a job since he required some extra income for his nursing supplies, and other things.

He brought a friend and a pizza to share with me in hopes of getting the job. I gave him and his friend a tour around the hospital while he expressed his interest in the job. He seemed highly motivated and friendly. He talked constantly about his experiences and skills as a third-year nursing student. I made sure I revealed all the hot spots at the hospital for a disabled individual who was confined to a wheelchair. He gave me the impression that he was qualified enough, meeting all the criteria and questions that I had. He said that he would take excellent care of me. I selected him from a batch of twenty prospective caregivers because he demonstrated at the hospital in front of a registered nurse that he was able to lift someone like me. While he talked endlessly, his attitude and knowledge about nursing seemed overwhelming.

It was around the middle of August when Julie told me to start getting myself prepared for school within the next few days. It was time for me to go on my educational journey. Julie arranged for my transportation, a State of New Mexico station wagon, to take me on my road trip to the university. Julie and Joe were to be my friendly escorts to the land of college. They packed all my belongings: clothing, medical supplies, my schoolbooks and other small items.

I gave my farewell to the staff members of Carrie Tingley and they wished me luck. I was very important that day because I was the first patient in Carrie Tingley history who was able to finish high school and continue on to higher education. The staff members were there to wave their farewells, as if they were seeing off a white-sailed ship leaving dock and harbor for the wide open sea. Joe lifted me into the car, and Julie steadied my wheelchair at the same time. After that they took my chair apart, folded it, and put it in the back of the car.

As the three musketeers were leaving the front yard of Carrie Tingley, I glanced back at the hospital and began leaving memory crumbs behind, hoping that I would not need to find my way back to this place in the future. We departed and drove off for a long, hot and highly anticipated journey to Las Cruces, the home of the Aggies at New Mexico State University.

We stopped at a local restaurant on the way into Las Cruces to get some Mexican food because Joe had a dangerous craving for hot green chili grown in Hatch, which was located nearby. The restaurant offered a buffet special and Julie and I decided to have buffet Mexican dishes as Joe ordered Mexican food with extra green chili from the menu. With our stomachs full after our delicious and satisfying lunch, we continued the drive to the NMSU campus.

Throughout the trip, I listened to endless lectures about college life and its responsibilities, and warnings about its pitfalls, from both Julie and Joe. "Now, Gilbert, you are on your own. I don't want you cutting corners. Be serious about your schooling and be responsible for your actions because actions have consequences. When it's time for you to go to class, go to class. Show those other people that you can do as well or even better. Study one or two hours at a time."

Julie and Joe warned me about slacking and cutting corners in my schoolwork, but their lectures went in one ear and out the other. Once I got to the university, my mind and my inhibitions just slipped out the door. I came to find out that Julie was keeping tabs on me, and she contacted me when I had a little trouble during my first month. Apparently, she was speaking with my counselor from time to time, and I also got concerned questions from my professors.

It was the most negative thing I had ever done. I went to class, but studying—I hardly ever studied! There was always someone coming to visit me, and they would say, "Let's go over there; we will walk around the campus, let's go check out my pad and listen to some tunes, or do something else. Let's go watch a basketball game or to a concert in the park." Students who lived off campus would say, "Let's go to my apartment." So I did that and joined them most of the time instead of studying. When I got the wake-up call from my professors after my little run-in with peer pressure, I began hitting the books.

I found some good friends at New Mexico State. I became close friends with the Hispanic professor who taught my art class, which I loved. This professor took extra time and effort with me and looked at the abstract drawings that I did with my mouth.

Another friend who I met there was Toby, who also had a disability. He suffered from multiple sclerosis. Toby is from Santa Fe, and he roomed next door to me on campus. His mother was part Native American from the Pueblo tribe near Santo Domingo and his father was Hispanic. He was the second oldest of the children in his family and had three sisters and a younger brother. His brother was the youngest and also had multiple sclerosis. It seemed that the disease was carried in the male genes in his family. Like me, Toby had a caregiver who aided him in his everyday routine and activities.

Toby invited me to visit with him and his family more than once during the holidays and school breaks. I remember that my first visit was very pleasant. Toby introduced me to his whole family, including his grandparents, aunts, uncles, and cousins. I met them all. At times there was a language barrier because there were three languages spoken among them: Spanish, English, and some Pueblo. They spoke in Spanish most of the time, but no matter which language they used, there was always someone to translate. Toby had a very nice family, always welcoming, and they always offered me a place in their home for a week or so during holidays and breaks. When I got to know his family well and had made several visits there, it was hard to leave them when it was time to go back to the university, having become accustomed to their hospitality.

Toby introduced me to a lot of his buddies, who soon became my buddies also. From the time I met Toby, I began to notice that a majority of my friends were Hispanic and from Santa Fe. When they referred to the city of Santa Fe, they would call it "Santa" and then they would burst into loud laughter in appreciation of their heritage. Toby is a good and close friend of mine to this day.

I came across few Native Americans on the NMSU campus and in the surrounding area. I became aware of the fact that there were not very many Native Americans attending school there. I wondered why Natives were not seeking college education. With no more than a high school education, they would find it hard to get gainful employment anywhere. High school seemed to be the ultimate goal of education for most of them. I supposed that they were held back by their beliefs in their ineptitude, their perceived lack of intelligence and skills.

Most of the Natives I did come across did not seem to be as open to friendship or conversation with the other students. They were quiet and self-contained, as if blind to the presence of others. Some were fairly nice and somewhat talkative, but they confined their conversations to their academic studies. Some of them turned out to be a bit on the stuck-up side and appeared to have a selfish attitude. Even though I was acquainted with some individual students from the same high school where I had graduated, I never attempted to make a Native American a friend at New Mexico State.

All of my personal needs were assessed and administered to me by my caregiver. Initially, he was doing an adequate job, performing the necessary routines. At times, he would inquire as to how to do a certain job, and I would walk him through the duty. I was constantly reminding him to do routine inspection and duties. He was lacking in organization, attention to detail, skill and experience. I should have known that he had exaggerated about his skills, especially for a third-year nursing student. I think that he had gained his knowledge about nursing from reading literature, classroom textbooks and lectures only, without actual one-on-one experience in caring for someone in my condition. His emphasis on his education rather than skills when we first met should have put up a red flag. As months passed, it seemed like the work required to provide care for someone in my condition was just too much for him, and he decided that he couldn't handle it. It seemed that the only thing he had been looking at was the amount of money the job paid.

Despite his incompetence, we were becoming acquainted with

each other, and I was letting him slide on certain issues. This opened a pathway for a personal relationship rather than a professional one. He took advantage of this leniency, and our roles seemed to flip—he became the master. Once that happened, aggravation and impatience followed. Our schedules soon came into conflict, and he began to put himself first before me, breaking the understood client and patient contract. One of the main reasons that I was late for my classes many times was that I had to wait for him to arrive and get me prepared for class or scheduled events.

From time to time, I consulted with Julie and my advisor about his behavior. They advised me to speak up for myself and see if I could remedy the situation. But the problems continued and the situation escalated. His attitude deteriorated, and his rude behavior was getting more intense. I had to terminate his services as a caregiver at the end of the fall semester.

In the beginning of the spring of 1978, I acquired a new caregiver who was introduced to me by a friend who was also confined to a wheelchair. The new caregiver was already awaiting my arrival at school. After we introduced ourselves I instructed him on my daily routines and care, including the importance of getting me prepared for my early classes so I wouldn't be late. His only problem was that he loved to sleep in, and it was hard getting him motivated early in the morning.

I was having a grand old time studying into the wee hours of the night at NMSU when disaster struck. After the consequences of last semester's slacking off in class and short study periods, I had become diligent in my schoolwork and studies. I spent a lot of my time in the library and long hours in the study room. Due to the long hours of sitting, I accumulated a huge pressure sore which I came to find out later was about the size of a baseball but wasn't too deep. I did not think it required medical attention. I just thought it was something that would heal itself after it ran its cycle.

Despite the pain and the odor of the sore, I continued to go to classes. I began having symptoms from the pressure sore, such as headaches, intense sweating, and chills. Near the end of the spring semester the days and nights became longer because I had to endure every second with pain. At night, I had difficulty falling asleep, wondering what the pressure sore looked like.

Throughout the semester, I fought against the urge to go to the emergency room. I did not want to be admitted into any hospital. I just was not ready for confinement again. I had spent more time in the hospital than out since my accident and I did not want to go back. Finally, the semester came to an end. I had no choice but to go to the emergency room with the help of one of my caregivers. By that time the pressure sore was severe enough to require medical attention and confinement in the hospital for a number of months.

19

TIME OUT

Once again, against my will, I was hospitalized at Carrie Tingley Hospital for a few months. I had been diagnosed with a severe infection stemming from the pressure sore. It is common sense and common practice to annihilate infection prior to any kind of surgery. My body was already fighting this infection, and to have surgery would overload my immune system. I had an IV line running continually into my vein, containing antibiotics to destroy and inhibit the growth of the infection.

The doctors waited for the infection to subside and then disappear before performing surgery to remove the sore. I began to lose my appetite before my surgery, and I lost it completely after the surgery. Feelings of letting nature take its course no matter the outcome began to kindle in my heart. I did not care at all. My condition deteriorated severely. The medical staff had no choice but to run an IV line to provide nutrients and fluids to sustain me. This incident was my first encounter with a huge pressure sore, and I was confined to the Intensive Care Unit for a couple of weeks after the major surgical procedure was completed.

I was in the hospital for six months after I had major surgery done on my sitter. It kept me from sitting up while I recovered. Six months was a long time to be confined in a hospital. The days and nights became too long, almost driving me to the point of insanity.

The only places I could see were the four walls and ceiling in my isolated room while I restlessly and impatiently lay in bed, feeling more and more claustrophobic. My doctors had ordered no visitors at all for my room.

I was upset and angry with myself. If only I had gotten up a few times, and if I had a more experienced and consistent caregiver during that first semester, I would not have gotten myself into this predicament, requiring extreme surgical procedures, recovery, and my current deplorable state. To make matters worse, the medical staff was always at hand to make disapproving remarks. This had been the major reason I did not want to return to Carrie Tingley, knowing that there was going to be a landslide of never-ending negative comments about my condition. I felt a bit ashamed and embarrassed. I did not want to share with anyone the extent of my suffering from such an infection caused by the huge pressure sore that accumulated by sitting for long hours at a time.

I was glad when a few of the nursing students from college came to visit with me while they were learning medical practices under their director and the supervision of the medical staff at Carrie Tingley Hospital.

These nurses had been undergraduates the previous year. We had endless conversations about college life in general, duties they performed at the hospital, and other classes they attended at university. I was usually entertained and distracted from the boredom of my room when they came by to visit with me. Many curious questions came up concerning my experiences of life on the reservation, the transportation, food, the water system, the government, and family life. One student nurse even asked me if a passport was a requirement to travel on the largest Indian reservation, which was a hilarious question. When all these questions were asked, I told these students that it was not another country and that the reservation was part of the United States.

When the student nurses were not there, I thought about all the events from the beginning of my first semester to that very moment. I wondered about the reasons for the things that had happened and how my decisions had affected my life thus far. I was sure everything started with my prior stubborn caregiver's neglect. The spring semester's caregiver had been fairly responsible and made sure that I got up out of bed more often and into my chair so I could enjoy my surroundings. However, my condition had already started to deteriorate by then.

I did like New Mexico State and I liked the college life I had experienced there, but the weather in Las Cruces was just too hot for me. My body couldn't take it. Every time I went out in the sun, I got sunburned, and I was also warned about getting dehydrated. For this reason I carried a bottle of water with me at all times. Most of the time I stayed indoors where it was cool, but if I went outside I would stay under the shade of a tree or building. I also needed an escort at all times because of the hilly terrain on the campus. There were steep hills as far as my eyes could see, and traffic was terrible on campus. There was one time when I was crossing a street with some other students who were my classmates coming back from class, heading to my dorm room, when a vehicle almost hit me. The vehicle was traveling above the speed limit as it approached the student-crossing zone where we were already on our way across the street.

I began asking the summer interns lots of questions about the University of New Mexico. My questions and concerns centered on the location, accessibility, and accommodations for disabled students. In talking about aspects of college life at that university, some of the nursing students said that it was a fascinating school with many benefits and accommodations for disabled individuals. First off, the university is situated on a level portion of land so I would not have the difficulty of steep hills and numerous steps. This would mean that I would not have to have an escort at all times while I was out and about.

The weather in Albuquerque was usually warm or cool and did not have as many hot days as Las Cruces, which was a plus. Dormitory rooms on campus had air conditioning that ran all day, which was not common at New Mexico State. However, during winter, I was told that it would become cold enough to wear a jacket or sweater. I already expected that as I came from an area of seasonal weather changes. I was used to cold weather when I was growing up, but had not been exposed to it much since my accident.

The upside of attending the University of New Mexico was that there were hospitals and rehabilitation centers all around the periphery of the campus, all situated within a five-block radius. The university had its own hospital, which was fully equipped and was adjacent to the Albuquerque Indian Health Center. There was UNM Hospital on the north side, Saint Joseph's Hospital on the west side, a Presbyterian hospital on the south side, and Lovelace Hospital on the east side. I wondered why I had decided to attend a school that was located in the middle of the southwest desert where there was not a hospital nearby that could provide adequate care to anyone in my condition. I must have shown keen interest in the University of New Mexico because one of the nursing students was generous enough to volunteer to compile all the forms for transfer, admission, and registration documents and have them sent to me at my home.

At NMSU I had made a lot of loyal friends who were very hospitable and considerate of my condition. They found ways to improve my living and helped to provide daily necessities. When a friend goes beyond the boundaries of courtesy in voluntary and selfless acts, this friendship is true and worth keeping. When I was thinking about transferring to UNM, I was torn because I did not want to leave my friends behind. Needing to recover from the trauma of surgery and the long hospital stay, I finally made a reluctant decision to journey back to Twin Lakes and stay around the reservation at my parents' home to get my bearings. I found it essential to return to a place where I found peace, comfort and silence.

At home I pretty much lounged around every day, and had long conversations with my grandmother. She shared many of her old stories with me; some of these stories would go on through a whole day. During this time I had the chance to ask my grandma, "What is this about not talking about your disability, being a Navajo?" She got upset with me and told me, "You can't talk about anybody's disability of any kind, as you know in the future it might affect you." She said that by talking about it you might bring some bad luck to yourself. It was the same with planning for your death. She said, "That is for the white man. Navajos do not talk about our disabilities or anything to do with future death planning. Anything we say about those things might affect us sooner or later." She kind of put me down.

My neighbors on the reservation had never seen anybody confined to an electric motorized wheelchair. This is one of the reasons why it is very challenging living on the reservation. Every time I wanted to go somewhere or just to get some fresh air outside, my neighbors in the community would be standing outside or looking out their windows. They reminded me of the times when I was able, and I would get up very early in the morning and take a jog across the fields to keep myself physically fit. I would see prairie dogs standing in the fields, staring at me. I didn't have the slightest idea what was going through my neighbors' minds, but it didn't matter as long as I hibernated in the house, only looking out through the window. I isolated myself from the whole community, since this was the only way to avoid all the attention and the stares that I attract. I still have the same uncomfortable feeling about going outside, because people will stare as though they have nothing better to do.

My mother was constantly working and my dad and brother were the ones who looked after me at home. From time to time, I would take short trips to my family's ranch where there were sheep, horses and other livestock. There was always something to do there. I enjoyed being there. However, during this period of self-reflection I made a decision to go back to school. I came to the conclusion that I would transfer to the University of New Mexico in Albuquerque, and I began my application process with the help of my mom and brothers.

As promised, the student nurse at Carrie Tingley had sent me the application for admission and other related documents. I visited the campus twice prior to making my final decision. UNM was a very big university, much larger than New Mexico State. New Mexico State had a population of around fifteen thousand at that time, and UNM had a population of thirty-five thousand or more.

I began researching by telephone and seeking resources that could aid me financially in attending UNM. I had gained knowledge from the process Julie and I experienced in applying for NMSU. I knew how to enroll, how to apply, how to fill out applications, how to get a Pell grant, and how to apply for assistance to help pay for my schooling. My mother and I sorted out all the applications by priority and we got everything finished before the deadline.

20
THE UNIVERSITY OF NEW MEXICO

I was accepted to the University of New Mexico in Albuquerque at the end of July 1979, and I started that fall. When I first arrived at the university, I went to the dormitory to find the room that I was assigned. As it turned out, my name did not appear on the dormitory list. Baffled, I went to registration to find out what the problem was. At the registration office I waited for a while and then was informed that I was not registered or even enrolled. I was not sure how that came to be. A lady there informed me that I could still register, as the deadline for registration was not until the following week. I felt a little hopeless and lost, like a baby lamb in the meadow. I didn't know what to do next.

That day, I stayed around the campus until nighttime. I had arranged transportation from my home to Albuquerque through services provided by Navajo Vocational Rehabilitation. Now I had to wait for my long sad journey back to my hometown on the reservation, again with the services of NVR.

Back during the middle of the summer, someone from NVR had informed me that he could help in obtaining some necessary assistance for my educational needs. At the time he said he was working on my applications and that I would be assisted before my admission to UNM. Now the fall semester was starting and I had not received any aid, as he'd decided to wait a year to make sure I got all the proper documents and paperwork done well ahead of time. I did not want to wait for NVR to go through all of their red tape to get assistance when registration was just around the corner. So while I was waiting for transportation, I managed to apply for a loan through the university's financial aid office. The lender was the Federal Direct Loan Program, to whom I signed my life away, and am still paying back to this day. I did not want to wait to continue my education, so I applied for the loan, which was the last thing that I wanted to do. Also, to my dismay, I lost a lot of credits when I transferred from NMSU, even though I was transferring to another state university.

With the day's mess of matters behind me, I went home, and the next day a lady called me at my parents' residence. She was a counselor from the New Mexico Division of Vocational Rehabilitation (NMDVR) in the Albuquerque office. I took the phone call and she introduced herself and asked me to come back to Albuquerque and meet with her. She also said the man from Navajo Vocational Rehab was going to be there, too. Apparently, she demanded that he come to Albuquerque and make sure all paperwork and assistance was worked out and provided. He was going to fix all the paperwork to get me enrolled and get my dormitory room as he had promised before, though I had already paid for my room and board through the National Student Loan. I was assigned a room in Hokono Hall, Room 172. I still remember that.

The counselor also inquired of me, "Who is going to help you through the semester? Is there a caregiver who can assist you?" I thought about the possible individuals who might be able to set aside time to assist me while I attended the university. I thought my cousin Truman might be able to help. When I brought this idea to his attention, he was interested, as it would enable him to get off the reservation and have a chance to live in a big city. I had thought of him because he lived alone near his mother, and he did not have a wife or children to support. State DVR was willing to provide compensation for his assistance, and Truman readily agreed.

Truman, my brothers and I had grown up together on the reservation. When we were little kids, we did all kinds of things together, like traveling on horseback all over the back country. We also herded sheep for my grandma and helped my grandpa with his cattle. His mom and my mom are sisters, which is why I called him my older brother. Truman and I got along together very well, and he was an excellent and consistent caregiver.

However, you can't control your immune system against the cold wintry weather. I completed my fall semester at UNM, but in the middle of the next semester I got sick with a cold. The beginning of the spring semester was very nice and warm, but later the cold weather snuck up on everyone, and I had no choice but to endure it. What made matters worse was that there was air conditioning in the classrooms where I had afternoon classes, and I noticed that several students already had colds. As a result of the cold weather and the germs that were airborne from the sick students coughing in class, I contracted a virus.

Again, I thought that I was going to get over this common cold fairly quickly, but as a couple weeks passed, my cold got worse. I went to the Albuquerque Indian Health Center because I had developed a fever. A doctor there informed me that I had pneumonia, so to my dismay I was admitted to the hospital. They transferred me to St. Joseph's Hospital, where I stayed for at least a month. They cleared my lungs by suctioning out the phlegm, and I underwent physical rehabilitation as I had lost a lot of my strength and weight. I was not able to continue with my schooling until the following fall semester in 1980.

Although this was a big setback, I made friends at St. Joseph's Medical Center who would remain an important part of my life ever after. First there was Doyle, who shared a room with me.

When I was moved into this room, I demanded of the hospital

staff that I occupy the bed nearest the window so I could view the city. I saw that there was another vacant bed near the entrance as I came into the room. I woke up a few mornings after my transfer and noticed that I had a roommate. He seemed to be very much in pain and glistening with sweat, yet he still had enough cheerfulness to start an ongoing conversation with me.

We exchanged introductions and I knew him as Doyle. He was a realtor with a real estate business and home in Albuquerque, but was originally from Colorado. I remember telling him where I had lived, and he asked if I had seen one of his real estate signs depicting a black key with the name in white: "Pargin Realty, Inc."

I noticed that Doyle was a television channel surfer, a true tube fanatic. I wasn't too much interested in watching the tube while I was recuperating from pneumonia. Doyle spent most of his time in recovery watching the television while I slept and gave the nurses a difficult time.

Around lunchtime on the day he was admitted, Doyle's family came to visit bearing get-well flowers and cards. Doyle introduced me to his wife, Margaret, his daughter, Lynn, and one of Lynn's friends who came with them. They greeted me with generous handshakes and general questions as to why I was admitted into the hospital. They inquired about how long I had been there and how long I was going to be staying in the hospital. I remember Margaret was the interviewer. She asked where I had lived, and she knew that I was Native American. She wanted to know what tribe I was from. Apparently she had seen my electric wheelchair, and her innocent inquisitiveness took hold of her. She questioned if I was able to walk or if I was confined to a wheelchair.

I decided to tell her my tale so that I might avoid the flood of questions flowing from her curiosity. I informed her that I was quadriplegic, meaning that I was paralyzed from the neck down with only a little movement in my upper right arm, and had been so since my accident at the age of seventeen. Her initial questioning and curiosity concerning my life was new to me. I had never come across anyone who had wanted to know so much about my condition and me.

Lynn was the next person to speak up. She kept looking over at me with curiosity, as if she was trying to recall something. She walked to the middle of the room, pretending interest in a television program. I noticed from the corner of my eye that she tried to get a better view of my features.

She became breathless and excited when she finally realized that she had seen me somewhere and said, "I know you from somewhere. I have seen you at the university. That is where I have seen you, cruising in your wheelchair from class to class on campus!"

I didn't want to open a conversation with her right away because I was uncomfortable with her parents there. Margaret's attention was mostly on her husband, chit-chatting and asking a new line of questions directed to her husband's condition. Lynn became comfortable after recognizing me and stepped over to the window to look outside from the ninth floor. From the window, the view overlooked downtown Albuquerque around Central Avenue. She was pointing out to her friend various locations where she had been.

After a whole day of visiting, the Pargin family left for the outside world, leaving Doyle and me imprisoned with some veteran older nurses of Saint Joseph's medical staff. Doyle spent two additional days keeping me company and updated with all the local news from the tube before he was discharged. On the day of his departure I felt miserable because I had gotten used to his companionship.

Margaret offered to be of assistance, as they had accepted me as a family member. She said, "If there is anything you require or that you need help with, here is our phone number and address. You are welcome to our home any time; call us ahead of time to see if we are home so that we may prepare for your visit. Do not hesitate to call or come by for a short visit to at least say Hi."

Thanks to her authentic offer, I became a bit more open to outside help from others. There was a certain sense of kinship that radiated from their pleasant personalities. Even some of my roommates that I lived with for a number of months still felt a bit like strangers. But there are certain individuals who can became friends over a few days.

Truman had gone back to his home on the reservation while I was in the hospital and rehab, and I got a new caregiver once I was released. He was not able to assist me on a regular basis because he had classes to attend and our schedules were not compatible. I found myself helpless at times, trying to get prepared for class, so I would ask someone who was passing by my room in the dormitory to put my books in my backpack, and then I headed to class. In my classes, I knew I could not pick up a book or a pencil even though I wished to, but there was always someone who offered a helping hand to me. Usually, I carried a big tape recorder in my backpack to all of my classes so that I could record the professor's lecture—with the professor's permission, of course. When it came to my overwhelming homework assignments, I usually had a student note-taker who would assist me in typing my papers. If no one was around to assist me, especially when I needed to write an essay, I would spend the whole day typing it, letter by letter, using two chopsticks taped together and held between my teeth. It was very frustrating, and completing my assignments required diligence and patience.

While I was living in the dorm, I worked out a way to do art. I was capable of doing oil painting on canvas by holding the paintbrushes with my teeth, with the assistance of some friends who were also attending the university. My caregiver would set up my canvas and my makeshift easel formed from a music stand that I got from the university art building. After I was tired and done for the day, I made sure my caregiver or someone who was helping me cleaned the paintbrushes with turpentine while the paint was still wet. I would complete a 2'x3' painting within one week when I had the right idea and would sell it to someone who was in the market for a particular painting. The finished paintings were placed in an area high and free from traffic to dry for several days. I sold them at an average price of two to five hundred dollars for an individual painting. This generated some extra spending money while I was going to school and living in Albuquerque. I painted landscapes and old famous Indian chief warriors like Sitting Bull. I discovered that the most sought-after paintings were of famous Indian warriors and chiefs, the Virgin Mary, and Southwest landscapes. I never drew the Virgin Mary until an individual approached me to draw one for her so she could hang it on her living room wall.

When I was in my room, there were times that I wanted to leave the dormitory all by myself. However, because I could not open the door from the inside or outside it was impossible for me to leave. During that period of time, the university hadn't installed electronic door openers on many entrances and exits. I found that from the inside, it was not a problem because there was always someone around to open the door. If I were outside, I would sit in my chair for at least a few minutes, waiting for someone to pass by, and then I would ask the first passerby, "Excuse me, would you please open the door?" That was the only way I could enter any building. They would reply gently, "Yes, sure I'll open the door for you." But when it came to the Native Americans, they just stared at me and walked away in a different direction. I don't know why it was like that. It may have been because of the superstitions and taboos in the Navajo traditional stories, but my disdain for other Native Americans on campus increased.

I made and kept a lot of friends at the University of New Mexico. At UNM there were people from all over the world. I knew so many students that I could not make an estimate of the number or try to name them all. I made friends with them, and I still remember a lot of those faithful friends and wonder at times where they are now. They helped me a lot with all kinds of things. I took classes with some of them and they would help me with note taking. We would go to class together, me in my wheelchair and they walking beside me. Some would say, "I will walk with you to school and then go on ahead to my own class." They were very faithful about that, but I still had to struggle with a lot of things in my disabled life trying to educate myself and keep my mind occupied.

Not everyone was nice. There were so many times that I would drive over a thumbtack on the floor and get a flat tire, I think some students threw them there on purpose. I had to go into my classroom with a flat tire going "flop flop." It got me mad but I could not do anything about it, and I did not know who was to blame; there were a lot of students, like a stampede of cattle. The instructor asked me why I was late and I tried to tell him that I had a flat tire. A few professors would accept an excuse but most wouldn't. The ones that didn't take excuses said the students were all treated equally. I guess the professors believed in equal opportunities, although the disabled didn't have any at all from my point of view. Today all or most of the wheelchairs have air-free tires, but that makes the wheelchair heavy. You can get a big nail and hammer it into your wheelchair tire and it will not go flat and still keep rolling.

Of all my experiences going to the university, I had the hardest time doing my homework, like doing an essay, when I cannot write. I used a typewriter using a long mouth stick and tapping on one key at a time like a chicken picking worms. An essay would take me two nights because I had to backspace and use a correction tape to make my paper perfect so the professor could give me a good grade and some kind of acknowledgment. Reading my books was another barrier. Most of my desks were not high enough for my wheelchair to go under. The only thing that helped was a drafting table that I purchased from a nearby yard sale. Going to the dining room was complicated too. The girls that worked there already knew me from class and helped me out with my tray. They made it a lot easier for me when I went there by myself straight from class because I was hungry.

When I first moved into the dormitory at UNM, I met another disabled student there named Paco Flores. He became a good friend, one whom I know and maintain contact with still. Paco was from Mexico and he roomed two doors down from me. We began talking and visiting with one another on a daily basis. We decided that we wanted to rent a house together because we shared common interests and we had both acquired so much junk that we didn't have space to store it all in the dorm. We were determined, and we discussed ways to save enough money to rent a house.

We found a four-bedroom house near the university campus that we were able to afford by dividing the expenses in two. The reason we rented such a sizeable house was that we wanted to hire caregivers who would be able to room with us and provide assistance to us on an almost twenty-four hour basis. We were both confined to electric motorized wheelchairs, but Paco was able to do a lot of things on his own, such as moving to and from his chair, driving a vehicle and opening and locking doors.

I met a lot of friends through Paco. Some were able bodied and a few of them were disabled. A lot of foreign students came by and asked permission to stay in our house while they looked for their own apartments. We allowed them to stay on condition that they helped us, such as by transferring us from our beds to our wheelchairs. They would also go grocery shopping and run errands for us. Some of the foreign students would come and hang around and spend time at our house because their apartments were too far to get to within the hour or two break between each class period. They would just stay around and study or spend some time with us doing chores, anything to keep themselves occupied. Sometimes on the weekends they would organize a big party where they would cook their own traditional foods and have a good time. They brought their languages, customs, and music into the household.

When that house was full, I could hear all kinds of different languages being spoken. They always asked me to say a word or phrase in my own language. Some of the students never knew that I was an Indian from the United States—they thought I was an Indian from India, as Paco told them I was an Indian but he never specified that I was an American Indian from the Navajo Reservation. I learned some words in the different languages that were spoken in our home—just enough to carry on a little conversation. We later named that house the International House.

I even had a girlfriend from Spain; the Spanish they speak in Spain is different from here, it has a very strong accent. She taught me a lot of Spanish, and so did her sisters and brothers. They became some of my best friends, and the relatives were close; I got along with them very well. My girlfriend wanted to take me back to Spain but I did not say anything when she asked. I told her, "I'll think about it." Today when I think about it, I think twice about my decision. I could have visited Spain or even resided there. I lost one good opportunity for living in a different country in Europe.

I was the only Native American Indian among the house full of foreigners, but this did not bother me in the least. They kept me occupied and entertained so I would not have feelings of home-sickness and boredom, and through our common interests and genuine need for companionship we became friends. Paco and I stayed at this residence for eight entertaining years, until our landlord, without informing us, sold our International House to another real estate agency. Today, I remember our crowd as good friends who were reliable and dependable caregivers.

I was happy living in Albuquerque. Although family is important, I was content being away, and my schooling occupied most of my attention. When the summer break arrived, my trips to visit my family became less frequent because of the difficulty in finding transportation going back and forth. I did not keep in close touch as I intended at first, because I didn't have access to a phone at that time.

I struggled a lot during my time at UNM, and I went through a lot of transitions. My memories of my schooling at UNM are of hard work and a lot of studying that had to be accomplished to achieve a decent grade. Studying hard meant a lot of time sitting in my chair, sometimes throughout the night. I knew without a doubt that sitting for long periods of time would be a health risk. I knew my health should come first, but sometimes I neglected it because I was expected to get my assignments completed on time just like other students who were able-bodied. The professors never cut corners for me because of my physical disability.

Sometime in the middle of the semester, I began to feel under the weather and I could sense that some kind of sickness was taking over my immune system. I had firsthand knowledge of what was happening to me because I had experienced all these symptoms in the past. Even though I knew what was wrong with me, I never expressed my concern about my condition to anyone because I did not want them to know that I was sick. I usually started sweating and had headaches off and on and also muscle spasms. My headaches and spasms got worse week by week. I tried to treat these symptoms by taking extra medication that I purchased over the counter from a local pharmacy. I wanted to finish a full semester of school, so I went beyond the boundaries of obsession and neglected my health. A few times my friends at school had to call an ambulance and I had to go to the emergency room for a diagnosis.

The reason they called the ambulance, some of my friends told me on one of these occasions, was that I smelled like raw meat that was spoiled. They knew that something was awry and that this was a serious condition that could not be ignored. I never smelled it myself. Pressure sores are common among quadriplegics because they cannot move to relieve pressure areas on their own bodies. I knew from experience that having a pressure sore could mean hospitalization for several months if not treated right away. This time, the doctors at St. Joseph's performed multiple operations to close up my wound. Before I underwent surgery, I was given a large quantity of antibiotics to clear up most of the infection. I spent six months in St. Joseph's hospital. This was my longest confinement in a hospital since starting college, and it was my second experience involving a pressure sore on my sitter.

Some doctors would get after me and ask me, "Why do you spend so much time in your chair?"

I would tell them, "I'm attending school at a university and cannot afford to withdraw from my classes in the middle of the semester." I was determined to finish a full semester of classes!

After my operations, one of my chief surgeons informed me that he was going to order a wheelchair for me that reclined like a bed, and that would alleviate the pressure of sitting for so long. The doctor moved away and his order was never fulfilled. I was never able to get in touch with him, even though I left many messages for him to return my call. So I had to use an electric motorized wheelchair with a standard back for the duration of my classes at the university.

There were numerous times I became ill in the middle of the school semester and I needed to withdraw from classes. Most of the time I was unable to do so because I would be admitted to the hospital with such urgency that there was no time to inform my instructors. As a result of a late withdrawal, my professors would select a "withdrawn/fail" mark on my record or a "fail" for the class. A few of my professors were lenient and understanding enough to assign a "withdrawn" mark as long as I took the course again. But when I received a "fail" mark, I would become depressed and delve into my emotions, searching for a sign of comfort and relief. I did not want to give up and succumb to the negative feelings.

Every time I got better from my illness I continued with my studies. Even though I got sick and went to the hospital many times, I would go back to school, re-enroll for classes and never give up, because I knew without a doubt there was always another chance. I did not allow other people's pessimistic attitudes or any negative feeling of being unable to succeed to change my mind about returning to school.

Sometimes I would finish a full semester without getting sick. That sense of accomplishment was uplifting, and nobody could take that away from me. One of my ultimate goals was to finish my higher education and receive my Bachelor of Arts degree, even if I had to go half of a semester at a time. I kept telling myself that one day soon this goal will be accomplished with God's willingness and my effort to do so. The thought of giving up never appeared in my mind.

21

A REAL VACATION

It was like a dream come true, turning another chapter in life, going to a country where I didn't even speak the language. But I would be going with my friends from Spain and Mexico, who were fluent in Spanish. I would be the only Native American going along.

I had been invited to take a trip to Mexico with Paco and a few other friends during our Christmas break in 1984. The only thing I lacked was a caregiver. Paco told me not to worry, Mexico was far different than the United States, and people there were always friendly and helped one another. He also assured me that he would find me a caregiver once we got situated, on one condition: that I learn how to speak Spanish. I had already heard Spanish spoken a lot in the dorm and at our International House, and though I had not planned to learn the language, I was picking it up quicker than I thought I would.

Now Paco, myself, our buddy Mike, and four other students, were setting out on a long journey for a vacation to Guadalajara, Mexico. I was very eager and excited to go, even though I knew very little Spanish. This was going to be my first long vacation outside the United States. Paco and I had been planning this trip for two months, but still we didn't have the slightest idea when we were going to return. I also had no passport or personal ID except my university ID. The students who made the trip with us were very helpful in assisting me with eating and drinking and sometimes transferring me around.

Paco could drive his own van that was equipped with a hand control device and an electric wheelchair lift. He had invited a friend of ours who was a mechanic to go with us, but he said he couldn't leave his family behind. We asked him to assist us in preparing for the trip, so he filled up both gas tanks for us, helped pack our clothes, and put water and snacks in the van to accommodate us during this long trip. Once everything was organized, we packed ourselves into the van like a can of sardines.

We drove nonstop down to Las Cruces for five hours, which was extremely exhausting for me. Sitting in an upright position in my wheelchair, it seemed as if the highway stretched even further. When we got to Las Cruces I felt like a statue. We stopped for a breath of fresh air and then continued across the dry desert to Deming, NM. The other students started to get tired, too. They wanted to stretch and go to sleep, but there was not enough room to lay down, with two wheelchairs in the van plus seven people.

From Deming we set out for Palomas, Mexico. It wasn't hard for us to cross into Mexico because Paco had friends working at the border checkpoint. Paco and I and two of the students went into Mexico first. Mike dragged behind with two other students. We informed him that we would meet them in Chihuahua, Mexico.

From Palomas, Paco phoned his uncle, who lived in Ascension, in the state of Chihuahua, which was close to the border of Palomas. His uncle and a couple of his friends came to guide us the rest of the way. "Oh what a relief!" I thought to myself, as I was tired and exhausted from the seven-hour drive.

We finally arrived at Ascension, where Paco's uncle invited our group into his house. In addition to being very tired, I had a headache. I went to sleep right away and slept for at least five hours before I was awakened by one of the students checking to see if I was hungry or thirsty.

Paco's uncle informed him in Spanish that he had a guest house available, which was located about a block away. "You can all stay as many days as you need. Get some rest before you continue on your journey to Guadalajara. My workers will assist you with whatever you need for the remainder of your stay."

This extra house that we stayed in was utilized by people who worked for Paco's uncle on his ranch and in the oil field. We had first priority to choose what rooms we wanted and which beds we wanted to sleep on. I was able to get plenty of rest and enough to eat before our long journey down to Guadalajara, in the State of Jalisco. When Michael and his gang hadn't shown up after a couple of days, we decided to continue on our way, since the students we were with only had a couple more weeks for this vacation. We left late in the evening because it was a lot cooler, and were joined by Paco's cousin Santiago, who helped us on the long ride.

During our journey, we were entertained by the two women students who sang Spanish music, they told me that they had been singing since they were little kids, and they knew their songs by heart. It reminded me of a Spanish choir. By nightfall we were on the freeway driving into Chihuahua. When we arrived in the city, the ladies wanted to make a stop here and there. It was late before we knew it, so we had dinner and rented rooms there in the city of Chihuahua. The ladies enjoyed a night on the town. They had invited me to go, but I was exhausted and wanted to rest. The next day we left for Guadalajara around noon. We were about halfway to our destination and still had a quite a ways to go. During our drive, the ladies shared their stories with me about their night out. We laughed and talked most of the way while I was laying down in the back seat of the van.

We made a stop in Durango to grab a bite to eat, we were all very hungry. We stopped at a roadside stand, where we watched the people prepare our meals. It was very interesting to see how they prepared our food. I noticed a man behind the tent who was peeling the skin off a snake. I instantly turned my back, as I had been told by my grandmother that it was our Navajo tradition not to watch or participate in such events. After this, I completely lost my appetite. All I wanted was something to drink, so I bought a soda and a beer. It grossed me out even more as I watched my friends eat their orders without knowing that they could've been eating snake meat. Paco told us to eat all we could, because our next stop wasn't till Zacatecas. However, I knew he had to stop for fuel somewhere along the way, because that was another eight-hour drive, so I wasn't worried about not eating much. The ladies were tired from their night out; they were out like logs after they ate, laying down on the floor beside me and using me as their pillow. I just wondered if they had eaten a snake taco or burrito.

We arrived in Zacatecas late in the evening. It was a small town, however there was a lot of traffic. I asked Paco how much longer before we got to Guadalajara. He looked at me and said, "Early' tomorrow morning." He advised me to lie down and take a nap, because we still had a long drive up the mountain. I took Paco's advice and took a nap in the back of the van. I woke up around three clock in the morning and glanced around the van and noticed we were still driving. I looked around and Paco and one of the students were still up talking. Santiago was tired so he lay down on the floor with a blanket and made his sleeping bag his pillow. With five of us in the van, we still managed to get comfortable and get some rest for the next day.

On the outskirts of Guadalajara we stopped at a gas station for fuel. I awoke when I heard Paco talking to the attendant. Paco asked him how much further it was to Guadalajara. The attendant told him it was about eighty to ninety kilometers further up the road. The ladies finally woke up, and began combing their hair and washing their faces with wipes. I yelled out to Paco from the back of the van, "Paco, we need some coffee!" Everyone agreed, one of the girls mentioned pastries, coffee, and milk! So we stopped along the way to grab some coffee and pastries. About thirty minutes later, Paco yelled out, "We're in Guadalajara everyone, it's now eight o'clock in the morning! We have about fifteen more minutes before we get to my family's house, where we all can relax and get some fresh air!"

When we arrived at Paco's family's house, Santiago and the girls opened the gate as we drove into their family's yard. They had a big field that looked somewhat similar to a soccer field. Later, I found out that this really was where his family played soccer. Paco's mom and Paco's sister Jackie greeted us. They were very happy to see me because they had met me in Albuquerque before I finally came to visit them in Mexico. They continuously hugged me and made me and the other people feel very welcome. They quickly prepared breakfast for us while we unpacked.

Paco's family was pretty wealthy because they owed oil fields and a large number of cattle. The maids helped prepare the table where we ate. This was the best meal I had eaten in a long time, especially after experiencing the situation with the snake burrito or taco. They had prepared quite a large meal for us all. I never ate so much food in my life. Then Paco's sister gave us a couple of roll-aways that we placed outside in the field while they prepared our rooms. For the remainder of the day, we all lounged around. No one felt like going anywhere. It was a day to rest. Paco's mom told us that if we needed anything there was a store located about a block down the road. Even though I was exhausted, I went along to the store to grab some Mexican beer. The beer was very bitter but refreshing. It was nice to have a beer with the ladies after such a long trip.

Towards evening, near dinner it started to rain. The phone rang and Paco's sister answered. She asked Paco, "Who's Mike?"

Apparently, that was Mike himself on the phone. He got lost and forgot what street we were on. Right away, Paco's sister Jackie offered to direct him back while we ate dinner. She and Santiago left to assist Mike. After about twenty minutes they returned. From the window I saw Mike walking back in with Jackie. Mike had a big grin on his face. I could tell he was a bit embarrassed but he greeted everyone in the front room. I heard him ask for me, and the group told him I was in the living room watching TV. He came into the living room with a big mischievous smile that I knew well, and gave me a hug. He had told me back in Albuquerque that he wanted to have a grand time in Guadalajara, and I knew he was ready to party. We headed out to a disco joint, where we got separated from one another. I was looking for him and he was looking for me too. We met all kinds of people at this disco place. We had a blast! We returned to Paco's around two-thirty in the morning and quietly went to bed.

The next day we made plans to see the places that we wanted to visit while staying in Guadalajara. Mike and I went to a local corner convenience store and purchased a bottle of genuine tequila. The label on the bottle read Jalisco, and we asked Jackie how far the distillery plant was. She pointed southwest and said it was sixty kilometers. After Mike asked her various questions about how to get to Jalisco's distillery plant we decided to plan one of our sightseeing trips there.

We had a fantastic time going to the tequila distilleries where we were given some samples to taste. They showed us how the tequila is processed from the Agave tequilana plant, which only grows in the southern part of Mexico in the State of Jalisco. We also visited some other little pueblo towns located near the distillery plants.

We slept in the next morning and didn't wake up till after ten. Mike and I went out to grab a bite to eat. I had a sandwich that had beef, chili and Mexican white cheese. It was delicious. We went back to the house and everyone had left. I heard Paco's sister yelling my name. I asked Mike to see what she wanted. Mike interpreted what Jackie said: She had good news for everyone, we were going to Colima beach tomorrow morning! Paco's dad had offered to show us the area around Colima and get us a room there.

Mike was excited to go. He was jumping up and down like a monkey, and he couldn't wait to spread the news to the rest of the group. I asked Jackie where we could wash our clothes, and she said, "You can wash your laundry here. The washer is up in the attic." Then she directed Mike where to go. She asked me where everyone else was, I replied in English, "Somewhere cruising around!" She understood very little English, but she understood what I was trying to say. She replied, "Driving?"

"Yes, but I don't know where," I said.

Mike came down from the attic, and Jackie asked where we had gone the night before. Mike had a big smirk on his face as he responded, "To a disco." She said she knew of a better place we might enjoy, a bigger disco joint. She told Mike she would show us the place when we returned from Colima.

We left for Colima beach around mid-morning the next day. Everyone was excited to see the beach. Colima beach is south of Guadalajara on the west coast of the state of Jalisco, about a seven-hour drive because of the rough terrain through an area like a rain forest. Once we arrived on the beach, Paco's dad accompanied us to our rooms. These hotel rooms were nothing like what I was used to in the States. They were made out of straw so that the cool breeze could enter the rooms. They were similar to beach houses with two beds in each room; Mike, Jackie and I shared a room. After settling in, we walked the beach of Colima. Mike and I found a local tavern where we grabbed us a bottle of tequila. We sat away from the group and enjoyed the nice cool breeze. After taking a few swigs of tequila, I asked Mike to put a blanket down by the beach and lay me down so I could relax. I looked up at the bright stars in the sky while listening to the sound of the ocean waves. I wondered if I'd ever come back to this unique place. Mike and I tried to identify different astronomical formations in the sky.

I remember saying to Mike, "I bet in ten years, a motel will be built right where we're laying, or this place will be a dock for ships. So enjoy it while it lasts and since we are both here. I will never forget this place. Let's get the best of it now, Mike!"

During the day it was too hot to stay on the beach, and the only way we could cool off was by taking a dip in the ocean. I asked one of the lifeguards on duty who understood English for a life jacket, and asked if it was okay for a person in my condition to get into the ocean. He told me, "I don't see why not." So two of my Mexican friends got me out of my wheelchair, put me into my shower chair and rolled me out onto the shore and into the water. They kept a good close eye on me, so I didn't hesitate. This was the first time in my life that I had ever been into the ocean or a large body of water; this was paradise for me!

As soon as they put me into the water, the undercurrent got hold of me and pulled me under the water for less than minute. When I finally came back up, I was about ten yards away from where they first put me in and all I could taste was the saltwater in my mouth. I was amazed at how powerful the force of the undercurrent was. I wondered how I could swim back to the shore when I couldn't move my arms or legs, even though my friends were swimming around me and keeping a close eye on me. I floated in the sea with the support of the life jacket around me for about thirty minutes.

My friends dragged me out of the sea and onto the beach to rest from the constant rolling of waves. I lay on the beach for another half hour trying to calm down my adrenaline from experiencing the rush of being in the ocean. After I had finally calmed down, my friends buried me in the sand on the beach to protect me from the scorching sun. My head was the only thing that was left exposed above the ground like a turtle so I could breathe and look around. The sand on the beach felt very cool and comforting. After I had taken a nap in the sand for about an hour, they pulled me out of the sand and put some dry clothes on me. We were all pretty hungry by then, so we went to a nearby tavern.

After finishing our dinner, Mike, Jackie and I decided to go for a walk in the plaza and look around, not for anything particular but to just sightsee. Mike got tired after a while, and wanted to sit down somewhere. He pointed in the direction of a cantina, where we all sat down to have a couple of beers. We socialized with some local people and shared our trip experiences with them. Mike and Jackie talked with them more because they knew more Spanish; the only time I spoke was when I was asked a question. After a few hours we left and started walking back. We looked for the other group members, not knowing that they had left with Paco's dad for a drive up the mountains to see active volcanoes that were spewing ashes. While waiting for them to show up, we grabbed ourselves some more beers and walked back to the beach. We built a fire and sat around and wondered what we would do next.

A day after my wonderful swim in the ocean, Paco's dad came by and informed us that he was going to take us to Acapulco to sightsee. This was the most exciting invitation that I'd ever had to see such an exotic place. Paco's father had taken a week off from his work to spend some time with his son.

I truly had an amazing time during my vacation on those beautiful sandy beaches. I was even able to see one of my favorite rock and roll bands, Journey. That was a wonderful experience, especially since they were singing in English!

It was a short couple of days at Colima beach, and already it was time for some of the group members to return back to Albuquerque to continue school. They needed time to pack their belongings and make their long journey back home to the States. I was relieved that we were headed back to the city, because I grew tired of the continuous drinking. The smell of sea water was beginning to make me sick to my stomach, and my hangover wasn't helping. On top of everything else, I began to feel the pain of being burnt from the scorching sun, and this headache was killing me! From that time up to the present, I never again drank so much tequila!

I stayed around Guadalajara with Paco and his family while Mike and the other students returned to Albuquerque. I became bored and got lonely because I missed my buddy Mike. We had been down there for the whole month before I asked Paco, "When are we going back?" for the first time.

Each time I asked he would reply, "Next month."

I was already growing used to Guadalajara, and I was speaking more Spanish because that was the only language that was spoken around me, and it was essential for me to learn. After asking Paco over and over about when we would return to Albuquerque, I finally gave up and didn't want to ask him anymore. Time went by so quickly. Before I knew it four months had passed, and it was my turn to head back to Albuquerque.

22

LIFE IN MEXICO

I had enjoyed my vacation in Mexico very much, but I was relieved to return to Albuquerque. Paco and I hung around visiting some of our friends we had left behind. We renewed our lease for the house we lived in before we left on our journey, the white, four-bedroom house with a large back yard close to the university, our International House.

Residing in the city has perks that are not available on the reservation. There were not many opportunities to occupy myself on the reservation in my physical condition. If I were able to walk, I could be outside doing yardwork, helping my brothers or just being out and about. In the city there were many accessible options such as seeing a movie at the theater, going to a library and reading a book or doing research, window-shopping at the mall, or just going for a simple cruise in the park.

The house that Paco and I were renting was only about two blocks away from the university. But there were many times in the city of Albuquerque when I had no personal caregiver, even though it was a bigger city and people said it was easier to obtain any kind of services for individuals with disabilities. Paco and I forgot to think about our physical needs for help with the daily tasks that should be provided by professional caregivers, who were a rare breed at that time. There were times when I would stay in bed for a whole week with a little help from Paco bringing me water and emptying my bedside urine bag.

Paco owned a number of used Volkswagens, and he and his friends worked on them, getting them back in running condition. At one time, he had more than ten Volkswagens parked outside and along the street. Because of city ordinances that allowed only running vehicles to be parked at a home, he had to get rid of most of them or take them somewhere else for storage. The city threatened to tow them away, so he had to rent a place to store them. Paco found it difficult to find space for all his engine parts. To my dismay, he began to put them on kitchen surfaces, tables, counters, and chairs. Eventually, he used the laundry room as his alternate storage room and garage. Trying to follow the placement of engine parts and bolts kept me busy and out of trouble during my school breaks.

Paco was getting very annoyed and bored staying in Albuquerque, doing nothing and having only a little help off and on every other day or so, trying to do his mechanic work. Paco expressed his feelings to me about the situation that we were in and said that in Mexico we wouldn't be having such a hard time, as he had a lot of cousins and friends who would be willing to help us. One of the main reasons that we decided to go on an extended journey down into Mexico was to search for a better living situation. In Albuquerque we could hardly get anyone to help us on a daily basis or to give Paco an extra hand to rebuild his old Volkswagen engines. I didn't have any interest in working on the Volkswagens because I had my own agenda.

When Paco and I had saved up enough money, we made a second trip to Mexico in the summer of 1986. We talked about this trip with our friends over and over again. Some of our friends would not consider going, because to them Mexico seemed to be a ghetto place, and they didn't care for the sanitary conditions they would be faced with. However Paco's cousin Juan and another friend named

Jesus agreed to go, and we were well prepared to take this trip once again! I was very excited the day we left. I thought about all the places I would visit, all of my friends I had left behind and would be with once again. Once again we did not know how long this trip would last.

The journey down was similar to our first trip, long and tiring. We only stopped for gas and small snacks along the way. I didn't worry too much about the drive; I slept most of the way in the back of the van. Our companions alternated with assisting me and Paco during our journey. They helped reposition me and helped me sit up when I needed to. I liked the fact that we cruised down during the evening when it was cool.

It rained a lot, especially through Zacatecas to Guadalajara, but there was very little traffic. Paco drove all night into the early morning hours nonstop, but his passengers kept him awake. I remember him stopping for coffee a few times, but he drove all the way down himself. I woke every now and then when we hit rough roads, and would bug him, "Paco, where we at, we close to Guadalajara?" He would snap back and make smart remarks, but I knew I was keeping him alert.

I conversed with Juan when I was awake. He wasn't very fluent in English, and he asked me why I liked Mexico. I told him I liked the country because it didn't seem like an expensive place to come for a vacation, and you can do whatever you want to do, and there were plenty of beautiful places to visit and see. I emphasized how beautiful Guadalajara was and some of the things I experienced there from my last trip. I also stressed how friendly the people there were to one another. I explained that Mexico was a far different environment than what we were used to experiencing in the States.

Juan invited me to his home in Chihuahua, but we never made it to his house. He and I quickly became close friends, and he told me he would take care of me during this trip. I told him I'd like that very much, and I'd appreciate any of the help he could offer me and others during this trip. We talked about all kinds of things during the trip down; our conversation was long and interesting. He asked if I was a smoker. What tribe of the Indian nation I belong to. He told me that there were Indian tribes that lived in the mountains of Chihuahua. He also spoke of the Aztec Indian tribe that lived near Mexico City. He asked me again what my plans were when we got to Guadalajara. I told him I had various friends I wanted to meet up with again. Lastly he asked if I had met Paco's family. I told him I had, twice, once in Albuquerque and again during our last trip.

Paco interrupted our conversation because he needed Juan's assistance with stretching. He pulled over at a gas station where Jesus and Juan helped him get out of the van while he stretched his legs and stood tall for a few minutes. He seemed to be having spasms and cramps from the long drive with no rest. While Paco was stretching, we munched on some snacks from the cooler. We had lunch meat sandwiches, soda, juice and water. Once we were back on the road to Guadalajara, it seemed like the road had gotten even longer. We weren't too far from Guadalajara, but were driving up the mountain now. Paco told me to go back to sleep and I gladly took his advice. I was sleeping like a baby, when I heard him yell, "Indian, get up, we're in Guadalajara!"

I called back, "You woke me up from my beauty sleep, I was dreaming I was back in the States."

We stopped at a gas station to fill up and get some coffee and sweet rolls. Paco asked Jesus to call his mom and tell her we were coming, and that we weren't too far from where she lived. When we finally arrived at Paco's family's house, he honked his horn, and they opened the automatic metal gates for us with the press of a button from inside. I was curious to know why they had such tall gates and guard dogs that were on top of their roof. I asked Paco why they had to keep things so secure here. He said there were many drug cartels in his neighborhood.

Paco's nephews introduced their dogs to me while they fed

them, two huge male Rottweilers. These guard dogs seemed to be very vicious, and I did not like them looking at me at all. They watched me as if I was their breakfast that morning. The dogs were very mean to all visitors and strangers, however, it seemed to me that they obeyed their owners very well and were well disciplined. Their barking was very annoying, but I tried my best to ignore them during the time we spent there.

Paco's family were very welcoming and pleased to see us all again. They asked if I could move down there and live with them. I told them, "I'll think about it!" After meeting everyone again, we had breakfast with them and talked about our long trip. Paco's mom asked him how long we planned to stay this time. He told her we were going to be down there for another six months, or maybe more.

I gave Paco a suspicious look. The number six was Paco's favorite number, I guess. She mentioned she owned an apartment complex that was a block away that we could possibly stay at for the duration of our time down here. She told us, "Don't hesitate to come over and spend time with us." And she generously let us stay at her apartment rent free.

We accepted her offer and moved into a three-bedroom apartment that was located on the ground floor. It had a small kitchen and two bathrooms. We hardly ever used the kitchen, most of the time we ate out with friends. We had plenty of privacy here; we came and left at any hour of the day or night. We didn't hesitate to invite our friends and visitors. It was a nice quiet apartment complex. I felt comfortable at Paco's family's place, and we were able to rest up there for a few days before we moved into our apartment. For three days all we did was eat and sleep. One thing I appreciated during these three days was that Paco's parents' house had hot running water and I was able to take hot showers in the morning. In Mexico most people didn't have hot running water due to the climate. Most people took cold showers and they were used to this condition. Our apartment didn't have hot water either.

On the third day after our arrival we moved into our apartment. Paco's mom gave us both a set of keys and directed us where to go. The apartment complex was white with metal security doors and gates that surrounded the complex. The gates had locks on both ends, which allowed us to enter and leave only with our keys. This made it difficult for me when I was home alone. I always needed someone by my side to aid me with the key. I couldn't rely on just anyone. A lot of people were strangers to me, as I was there in a third world country vacationing, and I didn't trust just anyone with my keys. My friends were a lot slower than my electric wheelchair; They would arrive shortly after I did, and I had to wait for them to assist me.

Having to rely on someone else all the time seemed almost impossible for me. The friends that I made down here didn't mind assisting me at all, but I had to pay them for their assistance through meals or by other means. I didn't mind buying lunch for them; it was a lot cheaper than what I would pay for a meal back in the States. Amazingly, almost everything was less expensive here. However, I still had to budget my money properly. The expense of our trip home was constantly on my mind. I knew I had to save enough money to get back to the States. Whenever I thought about budgeting for our trip home, I was also concerned about my house that I was renting with Paco back in Albuquerque. I often wondered if I still had a place to live, and how our friend was maintaining our house. I reminded Paco occasionally to call back to Albuquerque to inquire how our friend was caring for our house, and to ask if our utilities continued to be paid. I didn't want to lose that house! I had lived in there for quite some time and it had become a place I could call home. A lot of times Paco wasn't concerned with these subjects, he seemed to be in his own little world here in Mexico. However, I was still very apprehensive.

It seemed like every day Paco wanted to go to his friend's garage in Guadalajara to hang out or work on his van. Paco had grown up with this friend since childhood. Sometimes I enjoyed going along just to get a glimpse of what they were doing, but mainly I enjoyed conversing with the guys at the garage because I wanted to increase my Spanish vocabulary and get acquainted with other mechanics who worked there. I estimate that about one time out of the month Paco's friend raced his stock car. To get ready for one particular event, he would get prepared by doing tune-ups and test runs. This was a special event that occurs only once a year. Stock car drivers from surrounding areas showed up with their cars. Admission was free to us because Paco would be towing the car. We were eager and honored to be part of Paco's friend's racing team.

The big racing events were west of Guadalajara in the rural area about forty miles from the city. Paco and his sister would gather munchies together for our day-long trip. Jackie made sure there were plenty of snacks and soft drinks. We wouldn't come back home until late night, usually weather-beaten and exhausted due to heat, the high altitude and thin air. It was amazing how many people I saw from the United States taking part in the races. Before they raced a lady sang the Mexican national anthem. It was alright with me, it did not bother me at all.

The day after the big race, Juan got a call from his family telling him that they wanted him back home in Chihuahua. After the phone call he immediately came to my room where he was assisting me with my daily needs. I could see the gloomy look on his face while he quietly continued where he left off getting me ready for the day. After he got me up on the side of the bed, he transferred me into my chair. He said, "Let's go to the store and get something to drink."

I said, "So early?"

So we walked to the park and sat down for an hour or two just chit-chatting and eating our lunch. I could tell that he was sad and that he had something to tell me by myself. He hesitated for a while. After I asked him what was wrong, he took a deep breath and told me, "My family needs me back home right away!"

I told him, "Don't feel bad, things like this happen all the time." I told him that his family was more important than anything else in the world. He agreed with me.

While we were walking back, he asked if there was anybody around that was going to be helping me with my daily needs and activities. I told him nicely not to worry about it. I said, "I will manage to find somebody, but in the meantime let's go back to Paco and Jesus and let them know about this concern." Before we got back into the apartment he quietly mentioned to me he was low on cash. I said to him, "Don't get too stressed about it, we'll figure something out when we sit down with Paco."

After analyzing the situation, we figured out how to get him home. We all pitched in money to help purchase his bus ticket to Chihuahua. Juan had been very thankful, helpful, and friendly during our trip. I didn't mind at all having to pay for his bus ticket home. To show him we appreciated his friendship and help, Paco and I gave had him some extra cash to spend on himself. He was very happy to be heading home but at the same time he didn't want to leave us all by ourselves. He had become attached to us in that short period of time. During this time I wasn't worried about finding help. I knew from past experience that people were most willing to help with anything. Paco told me his cousin and his family would assist me with anything I needed. Jackie told me that if I was alone at the apartment I should come to their family house and watch TV.

The night before Juan was leaving, I went with him to a local laundry to wash our clothes. He was pretty thrilled for his trip back home the next day, almost like a little kid on Christmas Eve. When we were done with our laundry we went to a restaurant and had a very delicious dinner. The food was so delicious that before you arrived, you could smell the aroma a block away. After eating we cruised around the streets and did some exploring while he said his goodbyes to some friends he had made there. On our way home we stopped by a local tavern and grabbed a twelve-pack of Mexican beer he wanted me to try. It was one of his favorite beers. When the liquor kicked in, I got tired and told him I was ready for bed. He helped me and said, "I just realized this is going to be the last time I'm helping you into bed."

I laughed and told him, "Well, tomorrow you still have to wake up early and get me prepared to get you down to the bus depot." Paco and Jesus were already fast asleep when I told Juan good night.

I had a wonderful time in Mexico. It was full of joyful adventure and memorable experiences. Strange people from a different country became my new best friends. I had a feeling this would be my last trip there, so I made the best of what I could during this trip.

There was a little pueblo just outside Guadalajara that was one of my favorite places to go, because in it there was a natural fountain on top of the mountain that came from a natural spring. It seemed like the mountain was touching the sky there, with the clouds covering the tip of the mountain, and it was foggy most of the morning. This little town was way out east of Guadalajara. In our spare time when Paco was not working on engines with his friends, we liked to go up there.

Sometimes I rode around with one of Paco's friends and we would check out the movie theaters and cruise all over the city. Sometimes during the nighttime Paco would invite me to go with him into pueblos on top of the mountain where you could see the volcanoes that were active in the distance. We would go up there and watch a volcano spew ash into the air. It seemed like some of the ash was going to blow towards us, but the active volcano was far in the distance. Never in my life did I dream that I would experience anything like this. Some of the Mexicans I got to know there informed me that the volcanoes were only active during the summer months.

I was able to view a lot of natural exotic places in this country. There was a large body of water in the valley. We went there to visit

Paco's friends who had invited us to a fish dinner with their family. They always spoke to me in Spanish. I just looked at them with big questioning eyes, wondering what they were trying to relay to me. There were times I tried to respond to their remarks, but my vocabulary was very limited. I had no alternative but to keep trying to learn their language. I told myself that when I got back to the United States I would take a course in Spanish, which I did, even passing with a decent grade.

Paco introduced me to one of his buddies named Luis who was also confined to a wheelchair. In Mexico, Luis had earned his master's degree in business administration. Once we got acquainted, Luis and I became true close friends and spent a lot of time together. He worked part of the day, and when nighttime came he would always come around and see if I wanted to cruise around in the city with him and his helper. He also had his own family, a grown-up son and a young daughter. His wife was always very polite. She would always call Paco's sister's place to invite me to come over and have dinner with them.

One night when I was eating dinner at his residence, Luis's older brother had come also. He was a teacher at a local school. While Paco spoke with him, Luis asked me in Spanish, "Do you know how to play chess?"

I looked at his son, because his son knew how to speak English. His son said, "Do you know how to play chess? Do you want to play a game of chess with my uncle?"

I said to him, while looking at his uncle, "I don't actually know how to play, but I have played a few times."

We started to play, and the game went on for a couple of hours. I don't know what kind of approach I utilized, but I beat a part-time chess teacher in Mexico. He invited me to his school to demonstrate to the students how to play chess. I told him that I was not comfortable speaking in front of others and didn't have the patience to demonstrate the skills necessary to play chess to someone else, especially in Spanish.

On the final day of our vacation in Mexico, my friend Luis declared to me that I was welcome at his residence any time that I returned to Guadalajara. I got the impression that he wanted me to stay a little longer. He also offered to buy my wheelchair from me, and said that maybe the next time I returned to Guadalajara, I could bring him a wheelchair like mine. I told him that my wheelchair was my only means of getting around. He said that it was very difficult to get additional parts for wheelchairs in Mexico. In the United States, individuals who are physically challenged are fortunate enough to be able to get the equipment they need to make their lives easier. In Mexico, individuals must purchase their own medical equipment and necessary medical supplies to be able to live a decent life. Many times these essentials are hard to obtain.

When we were preparing to leave to come back to the United States, the friends we'd made and had spent some wonderful times with were sad for us to depart. My old friends wanted me to stay longer. As before, I always felt welcomed into their homes, no matter what the circumstances might have been. They offered me food, shelter, and assistance with my daily needs. These friends of mine never seemed to let me be alone. I was always out doing something entertaining with them. That kept my mind occupied and not worried about my own family in the States. We went to movies, enjoyed bar-hopping and discos, soccer games, and took small trips out of town. Paco's whole family had gotten used to me being around the house, and I also got used to them, like my own family back on the reservation. They would ask me to come by the house so we could have dinner or go to out together. I can say that this was the best time that I have ever had in my physically-challenged life.

We finally left with some friends who assisted us on the way back to the border. When we reached the border we paid for their bus fares back to Guadalajara. I was lying in the back of the van because I was tired from the long and exhausting trip.

We had an easy time crossing the border back into the United States from Mexico. Upon our arrival back in Albuquerque a lot of things seemed different, and we learned that many changes had taken place. We had reserved a place to stay in Albuquerque before we departed for Mexico so that we would have no problem upon our return. It was December. We had been gone a year and a half.

23

LIFE IN ALBUQUERQUE

My time in Mexico was one of the happiest and greatest times in my life. Despite living with paralysis and being a quadriplegic, I did almost everything that an able-bodied person could do. I had lived in a country that I really didn't know about. Despite not knowing the language at first, I had forced myself to learn and understand in order to communicate with my friends. I ended up learning more Spanish when I came back to Albuquerque, because I lived with mostly Latinos and Mexican people who spoke Spanish frequently. When I took a couple of courses in Spanish, a semester apart, I aced both of them.

After taking Spanish classes I mostly spoke English and Spanish while living in Albuquerque. I felt my Native American people were just ignoring me, but that was really of no concern to me. Whether they were going to ignore me or acknowledge me, I wasn't going to lose sleep over it. Later on I found out that most of the Native American students thought that I was Spanish because I only hung around with Spanish-speaking people, and by that time I spoke the language fluently, too.

Six months after my return from my long stay down in Mexico, there was a great downfall for me that overshadowed a big achievement which came at the same time. I had finally earned my bachelor's degree, but when I left the university neighborhood my troubles started.

First I moved to the North Valley area of Albuquerque, where I again lived with Paco. I didn't like living in that part of the city, as it was too noisy there. There were train tracks located about a hundred yards away from the house that we were renting. At four o'clock in the morning, when the train rolled by, it would rattle the house. Because of my dismay at the constant noise, I moved to a different location in the same vicinity.

I had become acquainted with a guy named Jesse, who was a paraplegic and could still use both of his arms. He was also in a wheelchair. He lived in the North Valley with his wife and two young kids. I asked him if he and his wife could be of assistance to me. He said he would have a discussion with his wife about my condition and need for attendants. A couple of days later they came over to notify me that they had both agreed that I could move in with them. This took place in 1988.

I wasn't aware of what he was doing at that time to keep himself occupied. All I knew was that he was a longtime friend to Paco from when they were in rehabilitation together in Roswell. Jesse was Hispanic and was married to a woman from Santa Ana Pueblo. I found out that there was a lot of drug trafficking in that area. There were people constantly coming by every day, even at nighttime and through the wee hours of the morning.

Well, against my better judgment, I experienced what Jesse was involved in and addicted to. I tried most of the drugs that Jesse was dealing with and I started abusing alcohol. I felt dismayed about this, but at the same time wanted to be accepted as one of the crowd. I just let myself go for a few months into the pit.

I had lived with Jesse for about a year when I got tired of the traffic and realized that I was going too far into substance abuse. A friend of mine who went to school with me at one time, and who then worked with the Bernalillo County Housing Department, told me about housing for people with disabilities in Albuquerque. I had kept in contact with her, so one day she called me and asked me to come to her office in the South Valley and apply for an apartment. After I submitted my application with her assistance, I was able to get a two-bedroom apartment in the South Valley of Albuquerque. After a long wait for the paperwork to be completed, I was able to move into my new apartment in July 1989. A lot of people I knew helped me move.

I advertised for a caregiver in a local newspaper. An African American guy responded to my ad and agreed to be my caregiver. His name was Derrick. He was a good caregiver in the beginning but he never stayed around at night. In the daytime I would talk with him and go around visiting different places with him. But during the nighttime as soon as I would go to sleep, he would sneak out and do the same thing that Jesse was doing. He wouldn't return until early the next morning. He told me that he was at work across the city at a nursing home. I later found out through an acquaintance of his that he didn't have a job, and that Derrick owed money to the individual with whom he visited all the time during his absences at night.

I would hear the door slam very early in the morning upon his return, and he would holler, "Are you alright? Do you want anything to drink right away before I fix you some breakfast? Before I go to sleep I will fix you something to eat and get you ready for the day."

I would ask him "Where have you been?"

He would simply reply, "I was at work, and on the way back I visited with my girlfriend."

Well, that was none of my business. There were times I would give him money and ask him to pay the bills, like the gas, lights, and rent. He did it responsibly a few times. Then a disaster occurred. I found out that he spent all the money on himself or his debts. The landlord from the housing office called and informed me that my rent had not been paid. The electric company sent me a notice informing me that they were going to cut off my utilities since they also had not received any payments. I found out later that Derrick was using my money to buy crack cocaine.

It was a big setback for me. I called the Albuquerque Independent Living Resource Center to inquire about assistance and they helped me out with the rent money, the lights and the gas. As a result of my misfortune I ended up in a nursing home for two weeks after I dismissed Derrick as my caregiver. It was like a nightmare living there, listening to all kinds of moaning and yelling all hours of the day and night. These sounds reminded me of horror movies that I watched when I was a teenager. I could only rest during part of the day, as these noises kept me awake at night.

I wanted to get out of there so terribly because of my sleepless nights that I asked my social worker to advertise for me to get a new caregiver, and also to try to contact an individual I knew previously to see if he was available and willing to take the job. This friend of mine agreed to take care of me.

I only spent two weeks at this particular restless nursing home. After my release, I didn't look back, and I was very happy to return to my apartment where I could rest quietly and comfortably with no disturbance. Bernalillo County Housing had held the apartment for me. This time the housing authority ran criminal background checks on all applicants who wished to be residents at that housing complex. Around that time, my old friend Paco moved into the same residential complex, right across the street from where I lived.

Rod was my longtime friend from UNM. He was still taking a few courses there. He helped me out a lot by being a good caregiver. The only problem he had was alcohol addiction, a problem that was aggravated by his friends who came by with a ready supply of a variety of drinks. As long as his close friends did not come by or visit, he was alright. Some of his friends who lived in the North Valley would come by and they would offer him all kinds of drugs. By that time I knew about these drugs because of my past experiences.

One night there was a tragic incident at my apartment. On that night we were at another residence up the street, having a grand old time. Rod heard that someone had broken into our apartment and he borrowed a gun from someone at the party. He ran back to the apartment; I followed him, trying to keep up with him. They had broken the window by the front door and taken off with my stereo and my art supplies. I was disappointed, and instructed him to put me to bed so I could go to sleep.

When I woke up early the next morning, I noticed something different and strange about Rod because he usually never woke up early. He looked scared and sort of paranoid and said that he was going back to his mother's house because he feared the police were looking for him. He knew that they were going to arrest him when they located him. He had gotten himself into a lot of trouble with that gun, because he had shot another guy in the arm. The cops did arrest him at his mother's house.

Arturo was another Mexican whom I met through Paco. He was from Chihuahua. When Rod deserted his position as my caregiver, Arturo volunteered to take over the job before I was taken into a nursing home, since that was the only alternative at my disposal. After Arturo became my caregiver I had to give him precise instructions on how to care for my personal hygiene and daily needs. Even though the only language that he spoke was Spanish, he caught on quickly in comprehending my instructions, and we were still able to communicate. I learned more Spanish from him than when I was vacationing and lived in Mexico. Arturo became one of the finest, most consistent caregivers I ever had while living in Albuquerque, with the exception of my brothers.

Arturo was an illegal immigrant living in Albuquerque in quest of a better existence for himself. He had no green card, so he could not legally find work here in the States. All he had was maybe a phony social security and identification card, which we never discussed. He moved into my apartment as a live-in caregiver. The only thing that used to really concern me was that he smoked a lot of cigarettes. I did not like the smell or smoke of cigarettes. I warned him to smoke outside the apartment, but he didn't pay attention. I told him to at least smoke in his own room with his window open.

He would have his friends over for a visit and they would try to communicate in Spanish with me. I would pick on his friends and they would pick on me, and it made it easier to get along with them. His friends would tell me stories about Mexico, and how wonderful it was to be down there. I already knew about the conditions in Mexico, having resided down there for about two years.

Because of all the trouble I had gotten myself into, I was given eviction notices by my apartment manager a couple of times. I was three months behind on the rent. My electricity was turned off that same summer. My friend Paco was living across the street not too far from me and I asked him if I could use an extension cord to use his electricity, and that's what I did.

I kept holding off on rent, until the supervisor came to my apartment and told me himself that I had to move out. I didn't know what to do or say when he showed up, but I wanted to get out of there.

I called my younger brother at his work site. He worked as a part-time silversmith in Gallup during his vacations from his job as a welder in a shipyard in Louisiana. I discussed my circumstances with him over the phone, and he asked me what I wanted to do. I asked him to come over to Albuquerque and pack my belongings and take me back home to Twin Lakes on the reservation where our mother lived. At that point I didn't know what to do or where to go. My caregiver was planning on returning to Mexico the same evening that I contacted my brother. Arturo didn't like living in the United States. He wanted to get away from abusing alcohol, illegal activities and conflicts in Albuquerque.

My brother and his brother-in-law came over that same night, but it was really late so they had to spend the night with me at my apartment. Since everyone was so tired from packing, we all slept in until noon the next morning. After making sure that we had packed everything I had, we departed from Albuquerque. We arrived back at my mom's that day.

I felt uncomfortable being back at home after being away for so long. Everything looked strange to me. Even hearing my native language being spoken around me sounded strange and foreign. The only thing I could see was the desert and the clear blue sky above. My mom had been expecting us and had prepared a room for me. This was in the middle of the summer of 1990 when I came back to the reservation in Twin Lakes.

My brother was a great inspiration to me despite the fact that he is younger then I am. He would pay attention to me when I told him about my problems and the situations that I was going through. He was one of the only brothers who would never argue with me or give me a talking-to, even when I was in the wrong. He would take some of my suggestions—not all, but some.

As the summer wore on, I was just at home sleeping most of the day; and in the evening when it cooled off, I would go outside to get some fresh air. I was getting bored at home with nothing to keep myself occupied. One day in August a thought clicked in my mind and I decided to take a chance and re-enroll at UNM. I called that day and requested all the necessary enrollment documents and class schedules so I would be able to look through them and pick the classes that were required for my master's degree. I enrolled in a few classes to keep myself occupied so I wouldn't think about what I had done to myself when I was living in the South Valley. Living in the South Valley was a negative experience for me.

I needed and was searching for a dependable, consistent caregiver in order for me to continue with my education. I had no one else in mind but one of my brothers who had been working only a few days out of the week. One evening while he was visiting at my mom's residence I approached him with the idea of his becoming my personal caregiver. I informed him that I had re-enrolled at UNM and asked if he would like to go back with me to Albuquerque to help me out as my caregiver.

He responded to me quickly by saying, "Yes, I want to try living in Albuquerque and searching for a side job there just to get off the reservation. I could try it for a couple of months or maybe a year. Perhaps I'll like it there a lot more." At that point in time he was having family difficulties that he was trying to resolve.

Prior to moving back to Albuquerque, my brother and I went to search for an apartment a couple of times on weekends. The second time we went into town we located an apartment which was near the university and convenient and accessible for a wheelchair. My brother took on the duties of being my caregiver for one school semester at UNM; he also found a side job as a silversmith.

We both discussed what I had done wrong before I got back into school at UNM. He told me that I should have gone back to school before I made my move down to the South Valley area. He told me that I could probably have already started classes towards my master's degree.

I went back to the University of New Mexico with eagerness, like a little kid starting preschool. I was so anxious to start graduate school that I visited all the buildings where my classes were to be located. I lived in a small two-bedroom apartment located on the ground level so that I would have access in my wheelchair. Every day I drove my electric motorized wheelchair to and from school. I had enrolled in some courses that were required for my master's degree. I finished one full semester in the fall and returned home off and on, because my brother wanted to see his family almost every two weeks.

I attended the next semester of summer school, but I got so tired after the semester that I got sick and was admitted to the hospital. I tried to con my way out of the hospital, but I was too tired and stressed out. The doctor told me he was admitting me because I was losing weight and very fatigued from busting my tail and neglecting my body by not eating routinely the way I'm supposed to. I was fed intravenously on the doctor's orders, without my consent. I spent six weeks in the hospital.

My future goal at the time was still to obtain my graduate degree from the University of New Mexico. Once I completed my studies at the university I planned to attend law school to benefit and assist individuals with disabilities who are deprived of the essential resources that are available and allocated for them. I wanted to attend law school because I noticed that many issues that need to be addressed related to services for people with disabilities on the reservation require some legal background and knowledge. There are a large number of physically challenged people living in remote rural areas who are overlooked by the tribal government.

After I was released from the hospital I got another apartment and moved in with a new caretaker. All I did was lounge around. Most of all, I just wanted to come back to the reservation. My rent was going up, and I could not pay for rent and my caretaker at the same time. The only reason I lived in Albuquerque was because of school, but I was not well enough to continue.

24

LIFE IN THE NAVAJO NATION

I kept thinking about going back and living on the Navajo reservation. I thought about this for a long time, and it was a tough decision to make. I had grown accustomed to living in the city where everything was easily accessible and accommodations for individuals with disabilities were available. I knew the reservation was not wheelchair friendly and the house that my family lives in was not accessible. I couldn't cruise around freely in the house because of the narrow halls and doorways. I would always need someone to keep an eye on me. I remembered trying to avoid the soft dirt but always getting stuck in the sand dunes behind the house where I liked to kick back under the two big cottonwood trees. I never complained, sometimes I just reclined in my chair to take a nap for a while, but I'd wake up sunburned and looking like a lobster, with dust all over me. That would keep me in the house for a few days from the pain until my skin healed. At least it was a relief from the neighbors, who will not keep away from their windows when I go outside. They just have to see who's out there in the wheelchair that goes around by itself. Going back home meant I would once again be the entertainment of the day for them. Some things never change.

I finally made a decision to return to the Navajo Indian Reservation to the place where I grew up as a young child. My caretaker in Albuquerque had helped me out a lot while I lived there. Now he helped me pack up my belongings and move back to the reservation. I talked with the landlord and we put the apartment in my caretaker's name. After that a friend moved in with him and helped with the rent.

In June of 1994, I returned home to Twin Lakes, New Mexico, to my mother's residence. I remember it was a scorching hot summer, with no fan or air conditioning circulating the air in my room. In my room at that time, things were not situated for my disabled needs. For example there was no TV to keep me occupied, just a small transistor radio for my entertainment. No one came by to visit me because at first no one knew I had returned from Albuquerque except for my immediate family. I didn't have a phone or a computer in my room. I had never wanted to get either one of them.

One afternoon in late July an elderly missionary came by after talking to my mom where they attended church. I guess my mom was tired of me laying in my room with no one coming to visit me. I did not have a consistent helper at the time. That missionary came and talked with my mom. I heard her ask for me and my mom said, "I'll introduce you to him." My mom introduced Sue to me. She asked me some questions and I told her I was blessed by a missionary at my maternal grandparents' house, I was baptized in a Mormon church. "Do you still go to church?" she asked." "Yes I used to go to several different churches that talk about the same things in the bible when I was living in Albuquerque. I went to several churches that were not Jesus Christ of Latter Day Saints." She said, "Now you need to find your real church and start reading the book of Mormon." I told her I could not hold a book.

She asked if I would like for her and her husband to give me lessons. I said yes. Most of the day I was bored and I was not doing anything. So they gave me a big box of cassette tapes so I could listen to the Book of Mormon when I was not doing anything, which was almost every day. I listened to some of the tapes but sometimes caught myself falling asleep.

The following week in the afternoon, both elderly missionaries came by. Sue introduced her husband Arlo to me. He was a quiet and humble guy. He was nice and shook my hand and they both gave me lessons on the book of Mormon.

I stayed in my room all the time, where I hibernated and became claustrophobic trying not to be noticed by any visitors that came to call on my family. I got tremendously discouraged with my living conditions and wondered why I had come back to the reservation. The only thing that kept me here was the desire to re-learn the Navajo language. I was kind of losing it when I was living in Albuquerque speaking English and Spanish with my friends and not being able to exercise my native language.

Now my mind was only set on going back to Albuquerque, that's one of the reasons I was mostly bedridden; my thoughts were stuck on that idea, and I didn't tell anybody my situation. It was during this time when I was keeping to myself in my small, dry and boiling hot room at my mom's place, that I experienced my first bone break since my accident. In these long sizzling summer months, water was a necessity for me to cool and hydrate my body, but water in this terrible incident became the villain. My bed was an electric hospital bed with controls right by my side. There was a glass of water for me to drink to prevent dehydration. When this glass tipped over, the water spilled inside the control unit. My bed came alive and went haywire like an electric bucking barrel that's used for practice at rodeo training school. I couldn't control it, so I had to yell out to one of my brothers to come unplug the electric cord. When my bed bucked, I heard a loud crack as if one of the trees outside my window had broken a limb. At that time, I was going through constant back pain. When I heard that crack, the pain in my back diminished, and I believed at that moment that my vertebrae had realigned. The sound actually came from the femur in my left leg that had fractured, as I was informed later.

After all the crazy commotion, my brother asked me if I was okay, and I asked him to pick up the glass. He told me my bed was wet all the way to my shoulder. He wanted to change the sheets but I told him to put a dry towel under my shoulder so it could soak up all the wet area. With the back pain disappearing I was feeling reasonably comfortable and sleepy.

After it got dark and was cooling down from a long day of summer heat, I decided to turn in, maybe have a good dream or sleep quietly. My brother came in to turn me over to my left side—that's the common side for me to sleep on, as it gives me the freedom to move my right arm with the little movement that I still have since my injury. My brother was the main one who put me to bed and did all the transfers after I came back home from Albuquerque. He moved me gently to turn me, and he heard a weird noise like two stones rubbing together. He quickly stopped moving me and called my mother to my room. She came in slowly, half asleep. My brother asked her, "What is wrong here? It looks like his leg bone is broken." Now my mother was fully alert and terrified.

It was eleven o'clock. My brother said, "What are we going to do? We can't just stand here and look at him. We have to take him to the hospital emergency room right away to see what's wrong. He's sweating and has a headache." Then he hurriedly dressed me in my warm-up and a regular tee-shirt and went out to park the truck in the driveway. He asked my mom to open the door to the truck and quickly carried me out. He told my mom, "Let's go, we can't wait too long." And then off we went.

I never thought I'd be in the Gallup Indian Medical Center ever again in my whole disabled life. I never thought I would be alive this long.

After a long examination, the diagnosis was made, and later that night I was admitted for a stay of six long weeks. As you may have guessed, I was not pleased about the bitter air, the white walls, and the cafeteria food that never became an acquired taste to me. My femoral fracture was pressure-wrapped with cotton wraps and ace bandages that held it together.

With my disappointing admission to the hospital, there came the doctor's complete regimen of rehabilitation procedures, including medications and nutrition. I had no alternative but to follow the strict orders of the doctor, because I had a whole staff of mean nurses assigned to me for my care. After careful consideration and discussion with my doctor and others, my doctor decided against the surgical procedure of placing a metal rod in my leg. There was a possibility that infection might occur that could lead to amputation.

During the last week of my hospital stay the orderlies started getting me up into a standard wheelchair and wheeling me outside the hospital so I could get some fresh air. I could look over the horizon and see the skyline of Gallup. As always, the ride was short and I wanted extra time to be outdoors. The small excursions I had were still appreciated because I needed to get away from the hospital environment. The nursing staff knew I was quite bored and claustrophobic, because all I did was sleep and eat small portions of my food.

Most of the time I was irritable staying in such an environment, which I feared was to become my second home. Some nights I was rudely awakened from my beauty sleep by loud laughter and bright lights coming from the nurses station that was located right across from my room. I really sincerely wanted to get out of there as soon as possible. I wanted to go back home to be in my own little white room where I felt comfortable and secure. At home I could do pretty much anything I wanted. I could eat whenever and whatever I wanted. It makes me pleased to have my own choices of what I want to eat, and how much I am able to eat, without nurses dictating over and over, "Gilbert, eat all your food now." That's not my idea of living comfortably. I detested having someone trying to force-feed me and intimidating me with threats to feed me intravenously.

The weeks passed by slowly and I was still confined in the hospital. I was awfully anxious to hightail it out of there. My doctor finally reached a decision to release me to my home. My doctor was especially friendly, and he always listened to my individual concerns.

He inquired, "Are you prepared to go back home where you can be comfortable and not bored?"

I replied spontaneously with no second thoughts, "Yes, of course, I want to depart this prison ward."

My doctor made an appointment with nurses from Rehoboth Mckinley Home Care Services to come over for a demonstration of how to wrap my leg. I did not have a hard cast because I could not feel my legs. He explained that he could not put a cast on my leg in case it might swell up and I wouldn't feel a thing. That could jeopardize the healing process and the blood circulation.

A nurse and an aide came by that same afternoon to see the demonstration of the wrapping on my leg. My doctor was nowhere to be found, so they called him on the intercom. As soon as he came in, he greeted the nurses and told the nurse to help him hold my leg in place while he demonstrated the wrapping. He told them not to wrap it too tight, just to make sure my femur bone lined up so my leg bone would grow back; it might not be as straight as it was, but it would be straight enough. He showed them a couple of times with the same wrappings. After that he told the nurses to come to my house twice a week.

On the day of my release, I woke up very early, eager to leave. I refused to eat the large amount of breakfast that was prepared for me. I waited impatiently like a caged wolf, frequently looking out the window for a family member to come pick me up. At long last, shortly before noon, my youngest brother came to my rescue to steal me away from my confinement. Rolling down the hallway of the hospital ward in my wheelchair, I saw the familiar faces I had gotten to know. I said a quick goodbye while my eyes focused only on the hospital exit. As I reached the exit in my wheelchair, I felt like an animal being re-released into the wild after capture.

The evening before I left, my doctor notified my family over the phone that I needed to be on a good diet and drink a lot of liquids in order for my bone to heal properly. I had been willing to do what the doctor told me to do while I was confined in the hospital, but when I got home all the words went out the window and I was back to my normal routine. I absolutely ignored my doctor's orders. I ate only one large meal a day, which was my normal everyday appetite, but for sure I drank plenty of water to prevent dehydration and any additional type of infection. In my condition being a quadriplegic, the most frequent infection is a urinary tract infection.

I kept going back to see my doctor for scheduled appointments for x-rays to determine when I could get back into the wheelchair again and go wherever I desired to go. But it was already winter and too cold for me to be out and about. My body cannot tolerate an excessive amount of cold weather.

I did not like being on the home healthcare nurses' schedule. Most of the time I was sleeping from the pain pills. I did not like to be interrupted when I slept, or to have anyone messing with me. The nurses told me, "This is the only time we have to come in this direction, we have a couple of other patients down the road too." I told them that twice a week was too much to be bothered with, why not make it once a week? The head nurse looked at me and said, "Doctor's orders. When you go see your doctor for your next appointment, ask him if he can make it once a week. I'm sure they will make an x-ray first before he will decide. He can tell us what to do after that."

This nurse was right. When I went for my next appointment my doctor told me that my femur bone was healing well, he even showed me the x-ray. I told him that I was getting frustrated getting visited by two bothersome nurses who woke me up twice a week, and he said he would limit the visits to once a week. I was happy after my exam with the doctor, knowing my bone was healing right and soon I would not need the wrappings.

I liked teasing the nurses when they were wrapping my leg. One would be pulling my leg gently to keep the bone aligned, and the other one would be wrapping it quickly. I would joke and toy around with them in reference to a Thanksgiving turkey dinner, "Make your wish," or, "If you take my leg out, you had better make a good wish," which made them both laugh hysterically.

I'm glad to say that some of these nurses and aides are still part of my life. They have transformed from "health care professionals" to extended family. The new nurses were initially intimidated by me, so I tried to use humor to make them more comfortable. Most of my efforts were rather pathetic, but they still helped to ease frustration and manage anger. Sometimes I would pretend that I was sleeping, trying to escape from their visits. But, no, they would always wake me up, and I didn't have any choice but to cooperate. I don't know why I had to give all these dedicated nurses a hard time. These were gifted health professionals who visited patients from home to home, covering about 150 miles per day. Some used their own vehicles and others used company vehicles. They traveled throughout rural areas of the Navajo Nation. I would say these are angels brought down from heaven to work with some severely disabled patients like me, despite brutal dangerous weather and road conditions. I guess it was just my nature to be trying my best to be a tough character, but that didn't always work. If the nurses didn't come when they were scheduled, I missed them.

There was one nurse who got along with me very well. She was very nice and kind; she looked for every possible way to take care of my needs. She understood patients in my condition. When I was in a bad mood, she just did her job and asked me one question at a time. Sometimes she would get me out of my day's dark mood. I guess that's what every individual with a spinal cord injury goes through, from stubborn silence to barking at the nurse. I was trying my best not to get too close to the nurses. All I wanted was for them to do their job and be on their way to the next one, because I knew they had many more patients to see even through the nights and weekends. Someone would always be on call. And still, they would sometimes put their own good times aside to check on patients on the reservation.

Nurses are often scorned for things like being late with medicine or not coming the instant they're called. Yet they might be holding their bladders because they don't have time to use the restroom, or starving because they missed lunch. They're being peed on, puked on, pooped on, bled on, bit, hit and yelled at, and are missing their family while taking care of yours. They may even be crying for you. The minute you read this, nurses all over the world are saving lives, sacrificing the little family time they have to care for anybody that comes their way.

25

ONE STEP BACK, TWO STEPS FORWARD

Despite the care of the home health nurses while I was living at home, in 1998 I developed a pressure sore that worried me, as it did not heal. This pressure sore began during the wintertime when I was transferring into a car. One leg had dropped down and hit the bottom of the door panel. After being transferred into the car, I asked one of my brothers to see if I had any raw areas on my shin. After his examination, he informed me that there was nothing wrong and for me not to worry about it, so we left that morning for a drive to Farmington.

A few months later, I noticed that there was a dark area on my shin with a bad sore, and I knew that it warranted medical attention. I went to my doctor who, after he examined me, sent me to the hospital in Albuquerque. I was worried that if I did not receive immediate attention and care to heal the sore on my shin, my leg might be amputated.

One afternoon after I was admitted to the hospital, I placed a call to the Pargin family to notify them that I had been admitted to the hospital again. Margaret and Doyle began visiting me. They greeted me with get-well cards and cheerful smiles. During every visit, they asked me if I had any requests such as books and magazines or food. Since Doyle and I had met while sharing a hospital room, they knew that hospital food was not that great.

One Sunday after church mass, Mr. and Mrs. Pargin came to visit me and said that they had a suggestion. That suggestion was that I should gather all information about my adventurous story, from childhood through my two worlds of being able-bodied and disabled, and have it transcribed. My story would then be formed into a book.

Margaret insisted that I start working on putting together all the information that would be put into an autobiography, because I had an amazing survival story that demonstrated persistence, patience, and goodwill balanced by pain, frustration, and stress. She reasoned that my life story and survival could be meaningful to many Native Americans living with disabilities and could give them insight and resources for dealing with such a condition. It could give them motivation and hope to live a life without the stigma associated with disabilities. She got me started on my book by providing tools that would assist me in my venture, a voice-activated tape recorder, and some bundles of cassette tapes.

Somehow my adopted mother already knew that I wanted to write a book about myself. She gave me the green light of encouragement. "After all," she told me, "you went to UNM, so I'm sure you took English."

The Pargin family, Doyle and Margaret and their daughter Lynn, have been a true spiritual inspiration for me and kept me motivated to reject fleeting thoughts of giving up on my disabled life. They definitely contributed an abundance of understanding and comfort as I coped with my disability. Margaret would call me every so often to check on my progress and to see if I had begun my recordings, but it was not until two years after her initial suggestion that I felt motivated to initiate telling my life story to the tape recorder.

Around the year 2000, the millennium year, I was lying, stress-free, looking at the four blank white walls of my modest room. I was determined to jumpstart my rusty mind on a time-consuming, challenging journey, an ultimate mission where nothing is impossible. I started dictating my whole life story on a small black VOX voice-activated tape recorder. It was not easy for me to press the on and off buttons to start and stop recording. I could forecast that this incredible task would hold many obstacles, from frustration with the process to the depression of recalling memories from my past.

I had thought about this for a while, where and how to start, how I would write or record my own voice, how it would come out and sound. It was quite a challenge to remember everything that I did in my past when I was a young teenager, back when I didn't know what to expect next or what harm would come to me. I was just living life at ease on the reservation, my home.

I attempted in a short period of time to remember all the pleasant memories of a time when I was still able to walk. As much as I would have liked to record, there were just too many memories to dictate all at once in a hard day's work. I was trapped by the desire to return to the time of my memories of when I was able to walk, and to avoid thoughts of my quadriplegic state. I would become so discouraged recalling my past memories that I would just fall asleep while the tape recorder was still on, so that all it recorded was my snoring.

This task of extended recordings took me a long, tough eighteen months that produced only four ninety-minute tapes of my life. It seemed like these early memories were all that I had left in my life that I wanted to reveal and share with other individuals in my condition. I sensed that these tapes did not do justice to the details and experiences I had in living my two lives. I had to take steps to fully elaborate on the experiences of my whole life so that people would have a better understanding and feel for the adversity of learning to live with a major disability.

Thinking long and hard, recalling almost every tiny detail in my whole life was exhausting and brought me to long hours of restlessness and recurring hurtful memories. Wondering how to lead a productive life while living with a disability, and dealing with the ignorance and closed-mindedness that people have towards me can lead me to anxiety. I had to look at every possible angle of my life and where I stood at each particular crossroads.

When I finally finished the recordings, I asked a sibling to send them off to Margaret Pargin, who had offered to be my transcriber. I didn't have much confidence in my potential to produce good recordings. It was hard to talk into a tape recorder with hard-to-push action keys. My voice sounds robotic and dull and void of human expression because of the pointer device in my mouth at all times, which I need to operate the remote control for my television and to answer and dial the telephone. I also needed access to some resources for editing my work, which could not be found in a tape recorder.

I remember the day I asked my niece to turn on the tape recorder for the first time so I could hear my own voice. When I listened to it, it scared me and I laughed so hard and wondered, "Is this really me talking or is it somebody else?" After that I never played back my recordings that I did on the tapes, I just sent them to my adopted mom and she transcribed them. I still have those old tapes and the transcriptions in my drawers somewhere in my room, treasured up with mouse droppings.

While I was waiting to hear from Mrs. Pargin, doing absolutely nothing but looking at the four walls and soap opera episodes on TV, a fresh idea popped into my mind. I decided to inquire about what new technology was available at that time to support people with disabilities like mine. With new enthusiasm I began my research by making inquiries to different agencies that provided services to individuals with disabilities. This process lasted almost a year.

My Uncle Toney, my mom's youngest brother, is an attorney who was working with me on some legal issues at that time, and he told me that voice-activated computers had been produced for physically challenged individuals in Europe, and he suggested that I research this. I thought this was a major step up from using a voice-activated tape recorder. If someone could create a piece of machinery to could go into space, visit the moon and bring back rock samples, I reasoned that a piece of machinery that operates on human voice commands and handles secretarial duties could be invented. This would be another avenue of independent living for me to share with other people living with disabilities.

During late September of 2002, I embarked on my mission of seeking the necessary technological equipment to assist me in my endeavors. I contacted numerous entities, agencies and organizations, including universities and rehabilitation centers, asking for any information, collaborative services and suggestions. I received a couple of positive responses regarding the possibility of such assistance for the disabled, but most were doubtful. Everywhere I had called there were no concrete responses indicating that voice-activated computers were available to individuals or accessible to the public. It seemed like my efforts were futile.

Finally, I came across an opportunity while talking with a local social worker from the Rehoboth Mckinley Home Care office. She advised me to make contact with a gentleman named Virgil at the Mckinley Independent Living Center. I hesitated to call him for a couple of months because I was feeling a little under the weather and I wanted to build up my strength before I continued with my effort.

One morning I woke up in good spirits, ready to pursue my mission. I placed a phone call to the Rehoboth Mckinley center, and a young lady answered the phone. At first, I was hesitant and toyed with the idea to end the phone call, but I believed in myself and reasoned, "What harm can it do?"

At the woman's greeting, I inquired, "Do you know anything

about a voice-activated computer?" She didn't have any knowledge about such a computer, but referred me to the same individual whom the social worker had referred me to, a man named Virgil.

Little did I know at the time that this gentleman would become a prominent figure and mentor in my life, providing solutions to various problems that I would come across. Virgil was the director of the Independent Living Center at that time. I spoke with him over the phone for the next few days. He had a positive attitude and a genuine willingness to help me. He stated, "We can assist with your needs for independent living. But I know of a resource in Albuquerque called Career Services, Inc. that is funded under the New Mexico Division of Vocational Rehabilitation. Career Services provides assistance to Native Americans with all kinds of disabilities to help them achieve self-employment and to become successfully independent. You can discuss logistics with the director there. Her name is Denise. You need to contact her and explain what you desire to do for self-employment. Then respond back to me."

A few days later, I followed his advice and began long conversations with Denise over the phone, which continued for the next few months. We discussed my strategy of incorporating the use of a computer to jumpstart putting my life story on disk and having visual access to the document. After our in-depth conversations, she told me, "I will send an assistive technology specialist out there to your home so she can observe and make an assessment."

Denise also suggested that I should apply for services directly with the national DVR, which is focused on aiding those with disabilities in searching for employment or furthering their education to become self-sufficient. Programs under this federal entity are able to provide technical assistance, training for employment or the uses of necessary equipment and tools, guidance and counseling.

I was hesitant to apply because the Navajo Nation VR had already closed my application for technology assistance because I was not able to perform the skills needed to operate a computer. When a counselor from NMDVR reviewed my case and came to visit me at my home a couple of times, he too denied my application because I was so severely disabled. I had been denied by both the Navajo Nation and the state of New Mexico without accurate assessment or a physical evaluation, and my next course was to appeal my case to the state and to the Native American Protection and Advocacy Project.

About two weeks later, I received a letter making an appointment for the supervisor for the counselors for Area Eight of the NMDVR to visit me at home along with my current counselor, Bob, out of the Gallup office. She wanted to make a full assessment and evaluation before re-opening my case. She wondered why I had been denied before and why my case had been closed. Her understanding was that my cognitive skills were still intact despite my physical disabilities. She wanted a sample of my work to include in a review alongside my appeal. A week later, I received a letter from her stating that my case had been reopened and that I had now qualified for assistance through the New Mexico Division of Vocational Rehabilitation.

Applying for assistance with vocational rehabilitation from the Navajo Nation Office of Special Education and Rehabilitation Services (OSERS) proved to be a harder egg to crack. I had already waited patiently for two years. I was attempting to appeal the closure of my case that year. The attorney from the Native American Protection and Advocacy Project who was assigned to help me in the appeal requested a lot of paperwork, including notarized documents and signatures, which all seemed too difficult. Taking into consideration the time it would take to assemble all requested items, it would take two more years to finally have approval for Navajo Vocational Rehabilitation to provide me services. I had my attorney deliver documents to the executive director, and finally my paperwork began its circulation through the processes of approval to receive assistance for the necessary technological tools and equipment. My adamant demands for appeal and approval got the ball rolling.

With my constant hounding, I was able to get any dragging feet to shuffle to a sprint. It also shed light on the internal processing and mentality of the agency employees. It seemed that most of the approvals were based on favors directed toward their consumers who happened to be relatives or acquaintances. After I had demonstrated such determination to overcome the obstacles and trials I faced, the VR of the Navajo Nation paid closer attention in making detailed assessments and evaluations, and advocated a higher quality in written works and work ethics.

Denise had told me that she would be sending over an assistive technology specialist. So I waited patiently and alertly for a few weeks or a month for a visitor or a phone call to schedule an appointment. One late afternoon, a lady by the name of Kathy called to schedule an appointment for an assessment of my skills and abilities, my environment and daily routine. About two weeks later she came over to visit me at home, in my little congested white room.

This was a turning point for me because it was my first actual one-on-one meeting with an outside authority. When she arrived, she asked my mom for directions to my room. My mom told her where I was, and she walked in with no hesitation.

She asked me numerous questions and then said, "I heard you want to write a book about the story of your divided life."

I replied, "Yes, I do."

Her initial reaction seemed to be doubtful of my capabilities to achieve my intended goal.

I answered all questions to the best of my knowledge. Most of them were questions that had been asked multiple times before by other interviewers. I decided that I would show her the first layout of my transcribed dictation on paper.

Immediately, she said, "You are already doing the work. That shows that you have motivation and are determined to see your work through to the finished product. Let me see how I can assist you. I will sit down and have a discussion with Denise and get back with you as soon as possible. I hope we will be able to provide what you anticipate for your assistance."

After Kathy's first visit to my home, she and Denise both visited with me for an evaluation just a few weeks later. These two ladies seemed to have an endless line of questions for me about my preferences and what necessary tools I would need for a successful result in creating my autobiography. Kathy also later brought another technologist to aid her in assessment. Connie had worked with Kathy in Florida. I named her the Spring Chicken because her favorite food was southern fried chicken.

One Sunday afternoon in the middle of May 2003, Kathy and Connie came bearing big, unexpected eye-opening gifts provided by NMDVR through the Career Services program. These boxes of gifts were a brand-spanking-new IBM computer with up-to-date software, along with a printer. Kathy informed me, "You can start training this software on the computer with your voice with some help from me and Connie."

They finished assembling the computer, but to our dismay, the CPU was malfunctioning. They disconnected the processor to take it back in for repairs to Albuquerque. I didn't see another CPU for a month until Kathy and Connie visited me once more with a functioning unit. I realized that these two women were genuinely dedicated and determined to help individuals with disabilities to meet their goals; they traveled countless miles to volunteer their time to be of assistance to me. They set aside their own time and funds for gas to visit me, even on the weekends, rain or shine. Never did I hear any kind of complaint or disagreement, only plenty of fruitful advice and encouragement voiced by their cheery personalities.

I started my episodes of voice training with my new computer. I was being educated to make use of the computer in conjunction with a microphone that is voice activated through software called Dragon NaturallySpeaking. The software allowed me to use the computer with different voice commands, and I could dictate into a microphone on my headset and the computer would transcribe every word that I spoke. I exercised with the software so it might come to recognize my voice. I read numerous sample tutorials so that it would recognize my speech patterns and pronunciation. The more one reads, the better the chance the software will recognize your voice. This was a surprising and exhilarating experience, being able to dictate into a computer and produce a document. Based on my knowledge and experience, I could honestly say that this was the greatest thing that has happened for independent living.

Connie routinely started driving over to Twin Lakes to train me on the software from late morning to the middle of the afternoon. She would have me read numerous tutorials throughout the day with a break every couple of hours. She taught me the procedures for using the all-in-one printer that was capable of printing, copying, scanning and faxing. I was competent enough to operate the computer on my own with no assistance. It seemed that the possibilities were endless, and I could touch base with practically everything, utilizing only my mind and voice.

Those hours of learning were long, tiring, and stressful because we ended in the afternoon, a time when the sun inflicted its worst heat waves, but the end result was beyond priceless. Before I had fully finished my training of version five of Dragon NaturallySpeaking, Kathy brought to my attention that Career Services had purchased the seventh version of the program. This version was basically the same but with faster response in transcribing, grammar suggestions, and spell check. So I had to deal with intense instruction in learning new software, as is the price of sophisticated technology. I like the experience of learning and the entertainment of new gadgets, so this was another welcome, motivating challenge.

While training on my new computer equipment with voice-activated software, I was like a kid waiting for Christmas morning to open his presents. Every day, I looked forward to learning something new and incorporating that new skill or concept into my writing and implementing it in my daily living. Learning information from the Internet became almost an obsession. If my daytime hours were not fruitful in productivity, I would be up in the middle of the night surfing the web, researching and gaining new knowledge. It was mind-boggling to know that there is never-ending information that is readily available on the Internet.

Cyber-surfing for knowledge is an endless journey of learning, just as you would imagine that the universe is a continuous expansion without end. When I think about the possibilities, I recall a feeling from childhood, when I was attending boarding school and had seen and held a globe for the first time, knowing the world I lived in was an almost unthinkable enormity.

Of course, there are pros and cons to the Internet and its access to numerous sites with a wide variety of information and entertainment available. While happily working with my new computer, I experienced a double disaster. Apparently, my computer had contracted a virus through the Internet and email. As it was going through the motions of crashing, lightning happened to strike nearby. An electrical surge went through my computer and burned out my modem from my dial-up server. I was devastated because I was unable to continue with my work on my own.

I contacted Kathy right away at her office. Once again she came to my aid regarding my failed device. Kathy called IBM to arrange to have it repaired in a few days. The repair technician put the project off for two months until Kathy became adamant about having better service. Finally, after waiting impatiently with nothing to do, my CPU was returned and I had my life support back, as if this piece of hardware was a ventilator keeping me inches away from death. I remember I had nightmares of never being able to use a computer again. It goes to show how much dependency I had developed on the use of a computer and its software.

26
ADVOCACY AND ACTIVISM

Back in 1998, my home health nurses introduced me to a graduate student from the University of Arizona who was doing her practicum and internship studies at Gallup Indian Medical Center. She was the coordinator of a spinal cord injury support group focusing mainly on Navajo people with spinal cord injuries who lived in and around the Gallup area. She invited me to attend her meetings at the hospital to get acquainted with other people in my condition. As I was already involved in a peer support group in which I talked with other spinal cord injured individuals, I did not want to attend a lot of the meetings I was invited to.

The first two or three meetings were worthwhile as I was able to talk with some of my peers concerning their specific problems relating to disability. Other times I didn't care for the meeting because it was always on the same issues that had been covered previously. We never seemed to go forward, we were always stuck on the same matter when we discussed topics relating to spinal cord injuries. There was always some individual there who felt sorry for himself or herself.

I felt that a lot of Native Americans gave up hope for themselves because there were not enough groups advocating for them across the reservation, especially in rural and remote areas. They needed more exposure to innovative concepts so that their minds could

275

explore and open themselves to the challenging world out there and ways to improve their lives. Disabilities affect all ages from young to old. You have to struggle a lot when you are challenged with any manner of disability. There are many aggravations in life that you face when you are trying to get in contact with some of the resources that are supposedly available and allocated. You try to get in touch with the people who advertise that they provide services for all disabilities. They ask you to keep in contact at all times, but most of the time when you call they are not in the office or they just ignore you and say they are too busy with other consumers. Some people have to travel long distances just to make a phone call.

This was often on my mind, that the Navajo Nation needed to wake up and support the people who are challenged with disabilities. It was past time to start providing adequate services and doing what is right for the physically challenged people of the Navajo Indian Reservation. I'd had the same ideas about the needs of physically challenged students when I was bumping over all those curbs in Albuquerque, back before the Americans with Disabilities Act, but it was still easier to live and be accepted in the city.

Whether in the city or on the reservation, I continued to live my disabled life one day at a time, never giving up. Why give up when there is hope and there are future goals still to be accomplished?

Now it was 2003, and I started shining on the Navajo reservation like the morning star. People were calling me on my home phone. My phone wouldn't stop ringing day after day and I couldn't ignore it. My mom was getting annoyed about the calls because they were always for me. Many people called asking if I would do a presentation, keynote and master of ceremony or become a board member. There were also letters in the mail asking me to be affiliated with their organizations, and invitations to disability conferences. The interest started from the roots of the reservation and went to the state levels.

It all started when I wrote a poem that I presented to one of the attorneys who worked on a closure case on my behalf against Independent Living Services, part of the Navajo Nation Office of Special Education and Rehabilitation Services (OSERS). A domino effect began when this lady sent my poem all over the Navajo Nation.

In July I received an unusual phone call from someone who introduced herself as Madeline. She said that she was a paralegal employed under the Native American Protection and Advocacy Project. She worked at the Hopi Legal Office of NAPAP in Keams Canyon, Arizona. She asked me if I would be able to do the keynote speech at a conference for the Office of Special Needs Hopi Early Intervention Program.

I said, "What's a keynote speech?" She told me it's like a presentation. I asked if it was like the presentations I had done in school at the University of New Mexico in a classroom. She told me that this one was not going to be in a classroom, it would be in an auditorium in front of a large crowd of people. I asked what I would be talking about. She told me she had heard about my experience living with severe disability on the reservation, and a poem I had written the year before. When I asked her how she got hold of my mom's phone number, she said, "Through one of the attorneys that you were working with." Then she told me that my poem had circulated throughout all the OSERS agency offices on the Navajo and Hopi reservations. After that I had nothing to say except, "Okay. I will do the keynote about my life experience and read my poem to the audience, even though this poem still needs work."

This was my first experience in public speaking on the reservation. I did not prepare a formal speech for this conference because I wanted it to be genuine, words that had meaning that came straight from my heart. The ride into Hopi country was hot, long and backbreaking, but I enjoyed the scenery of the countryside.

I saw the evidence of floods in the formation of the top layer of sand. Along the way, there were road construction delays for repairs of the highway. When I arrived at the site of the conference all I could see was sand devils blowing dirt all over.

At the conference I was treated with respect, and I was honored and felt fortunate to do my very first presentation in front of the Hopi people. Before my introduction, I was anxiously battling my nerves and gathering my wits. I had not a clue as to how to begin my speech. I had no plan, strategy or outline to go by. But when I saw the microphone and I was before it, my only thought was of the encouragement that the people in this conference expressed for me. When I realized that there were some who had confidence in my presentation, I began my speech without hesitation. Besides, I was already up at the podium and I couldn't hide or back out! So, as the saying goes, I had to do what a man's got to do.

As soon as I began, the words began spilling out of my mouth like a raging river, and before I knew it, my time was up. I was bombarded with a flood of questions from the audience after my presentation, and I was delighted to answer them to the best of my ability. At the end of the conference, many people approached me with questions about how I got started or even thought about writing in my disabled state. I was asked questions about when and where my next presentation was going to take place.

I enjoyed meeting people from various cultures, mostly the Hopi, who were very friendly and enthused to meet with me. It was like living in Albuquerque with my many friends and roommates from other countries. These were just human beings with feelings and inspiration just like myself, looking for another avenue to succeed in life. I met other people in wheelchairs, but none as severely disabled as me, a quadriplegic. I went home feeling pleased about the experience I had just gone through and a bit exhausted. This was just a taste of what my future held in public speaking in front of large audiences at conferences.

Within this same year Kathy, Assistive Technology Specialist at the Career Services office in Albuquerque, wanted me to write a short summary of my background and my major life experiences living with a severe disability. With the help of my eleven-year-old niece, Moe, I composed a short letter describing my history including my background and the experiences of transitioning into life with a disability. After long hours of brainstorming, we produced a finished, informative letter, and Moe and I emailed it back to Kathy. She carefully reviewed it and then forwarded it by email to a lady named Maria who worked for the Navajo-Able Consortium at the OSERS office in Window Rock, Arizona. This letter was to provide information to support my participation in the Rez-Tech Conference in Kayenta, Arizona, to increase the awareness among individuals with disabilities that all things are still possible, no matter how difficult the obstacles might be. Inspired motivation and hope for achieving something better in life was my message—that we shouldn't settle for something less than what we are satisfied in having, but rather strive for something better and journey over the horizon into hope, and away from giving up our own dreams.

I soon received a formal letter asking me to speak at the 2nd Annual Rez-Tech Conference that was to be held on Saturday, October 4, 2003, on the Navajo reservation. Marie organized the conference to bring to light the availability of many tools to make life easier for the disabled. My presentation, titled "The Power of Family, Friends, Agencies, and Assistive Technology: With Technology Nothing Is Impossible," followed Kathy's presentation, which addressed the technology assistance provided by the Career Services office to aid Native Americans with disabilities and give them the opportunities to work and enjoy leisure activities. And so I began my new role as an advocate for awareness and education in independent living at various conferences throughout the reservation.

Without preparation except for arrangements for transportation and assistance, I left my home at Twin Lakes on October 3rd, 2003, with one of my cousins. Again, I did not carry out any preparation for my speech because I only try to speak the truth about my experiences from the heart and what is in my mind. On that day, it was rainy and windy, and I didn't want to go because I was ailing from aching bones and my sinuses were acting up. Also, I had another excuse for not going. I did not possess the information of where the conference was to be held. But Kathy had encouraged me to attend and give my presentation alongside her, and I could not let Kathy down because there had been so many things that she had done for me. I felt I had to go, and my cousin encouraged me to go no matter what, rain or shine. I had to call the OSERS office that morning for directions.

My cousin and I left in the early afternoon for a destination that was quite a long way away, and it was still drizzling all the while, even when we passed through Chinle, Arizona. As I looked about on the way to Monument Valley, I saw both extremes of life's existence. Going through the Saint Michaels area, I saw many forms of life, plant growth, trees, animals, and humans. Driving through this country, a person could feel the interest for life beating within the bark of tall pine trees, within the hides of squirrels, horse, cattle, and sheep. Life seemed to exist in almost everything within sight.

On the other hand, later down the road as we traveled north through Chinle, it seemed like nothing grew around that area. It was devoid of any life. Water, life's sustenance, was flowing all about the red desert sand, free flowing with no boundaries, no dams or levees. But it seemed that there was no life to feed. It resembled the photos of landscapes on the red planet Mars. There was one place where we had to wait alongside the highway for the water level to go down so we could drive through the paved road. Still, nothing seemed to stir except the flowing and constant downpour of rainwater.

When we arrived in Kayenta it was already dark and still drizzling. It looked like we had missed the major downpour there because there were huge puddles and muddy dirt roads. We looked around and tried to locate the people we were supposed to meet for the conference. We didn't catch sight of anyone, and we only noticed tribal vehicles in hotel parking lots. To be honest, I didn't know that region of the reservation. All we could do was find the cheapest and the nearest hotel that we passed by. The last available hotel was Holiday Inn. We decided to turn in there for the night because my cousin and I were tired and my sinuses were getting the best of me. We booked a room and also left a message for Kathy at the Quality Inn where she said she was going to spend the night.

I asked my cousin to call to the front desk and ask if room service was available at our hotel, as I was feeling under the weather and didn't want to venture out into the crowd. It turned out that I would love the room service at that hotel. I ordered a rack of baby back ribs, which were very delicious. My cousin wasn't so lucky with his order of pork chops. He began looking at my dinner like a stray dog waiting for something to drop from the table. I could not finish my meal as I was ailing, so I only ate half of it and I offered the remaining portion to him. He soon had a big smile across his face while rubbing his tummy.

Later that same evening, after our bellies were satisfied and I was dozing off into dreamland, my cousin was kicking back with his eyes glued to the television, when he heard a knock at the door and woke me up. Kathy and Connie had arrived. My cousin invited them in, and they introduced themselves to him while they made themselves comfortable and conversed with us about the next day's conference. They told us that they had been on the lookout for us the whole day.

Our minds moved to the big event. I wondered who would attend and whom I would meet. Kathy and Connie gave us directions for the location of the school where the conference was going to take place.

The next morning my cousin and I woke up and got prepared for the big event. I was still feeling under the weather. I didn't eat too much from the breakfast buffet because I didn't have much of an appetite. After breakfast we headed on over to the conference site, which was at Monument Valley High School located a little bit north of Kayenta.

We inquired with various passersby and local townspeople as we charted our way to Monument Valley High to discover its precise location. Kathy and Connie had only given us the name of the place and not very much information or specific directions. We looked for multiple white vehicles with the Great Seal of the Navajo Nation on the center of their doors. If we caught a glimpse of one, it would make it easier to locate the high school, because there were a large number of Navajo Nation employees who were also going to attend the conference. We saw a parking lot with a few vehicles with the logo and we assumed this was the location of the conference. The parking lot was full, and I noticed a few school buses toward the end of the lot. Apparently, a volleyball tournament was taking place simultaneously with the conference.

There were a few stragglers outside the parking lot who were making their way inside to the conference. A couple of these folks came over to us with interest in meeting me and asked several questions about who I was. I hesitated to answer them right away, because I was too busy preparing myself to be lifted onto my wheelchair, and my cousin was also too occupied unloading my wheelchair.

When we got into the school, some of the people who were attending the conference started coming over to greet us, saying, "The main person is finally here." I told them we had a hard time finding the conference site and that I had been about ready to turn around and go back home. Then Kathy said it was time for us to do our presentation in a few minutes.

We did our presentation in a classroom full of people from many agencies throughout all parts of the reservation. Teachers, social workers, parents, and counselors were some of the guests in the audience. Our presentation was long, but apparently interesting, and we were applauded and honored at the end.

This was the first time I was a bit nervous speaking in front of a large audience with so many faces and eyes focused directly on me. It was unnerving, especially when the audience was quiet and so intent on listening to every word that came out of my mouth. After my presentation I was flooded with a tremendous number of questions. It wasn't difficult for me to answer any of the questions that were thrown at me.

One day as I was browsing around the Internet, I spotted a website that caught my interest, it was for a national conference called Consortia of Administrators for Native American Rehabilitation (CANAR). This organization was created exclusively for vocational rehabilitation services providers serving Native Americans. I asked my niece, Moe, to copy the phone number down for me. A week later I finally decided to call. The contact person named Phyllis was located at Northern Arizona University in Flagstaff. I inquired of her about the dates for the next CANAR conference and how to make reservations to attend. I told her that I was fortunate enough to have come across their organization on the Internet and that I was interested in learning more about these service providers. After my long conversation with her, she said she would call me back the following week with more detailed information.

A week later she returned my call and informed me that she had contacted the Navajo Nation OSERS and conversed with the executive director in Window Rock. She said they talked about the various locations where CANAR held conferences, from Boston on the east coast to New Orleans on the south coast and Seattle on the west coast. The convention on the west coast was the last conference of the fiscal year and coming up soon. However, after Phyllis reported her long conversation with me, the executive director of the Navajo Nation OSERS said that it was feasible for me to attend the conference.

My attendance was approved only for the reason that I had become one of the members of the Navajo Nation Advisory Council on Handicap-able. This was the first time that CANAR invited anyone not in the employment of the federal government or a tribal entity to participate in their conference. The executive director of Navajo Nation OSERS had advised the coordinator of the Advisory Council on Handicap-able Trust Fund to check on the budget and make sure that all my travel expenses for attending CANAR were going to be paid in full and taken care of without delay. It wasn't quite that simple, but the expenses were covered—after all the arrangements were already made.

One afternoon I decided to call Kathy at the Career Services office in Albuquerque because she was still working with me when issues came up about my computer and other things. I told her, "Do you know what, Kathy? I'm going to go to CANAR, which is one of the largest Indian conferences on vocational rehabilitation, in Seattle, Washington."

She replied that she and Denise were making arrangements to attend the conference too. I could sense her excitement through the phone that day. She informed me that she'd get back to me soon with more details on the conference. For about a week or two after that, we informed one another about the upcoming event by phone and email. One afternoon, Kathy called me and said that the only way she and Denise were going to be able to go to Seattle was to give a presentation, because Denise's supervisor would not provide for any financial arrangements for them just to attend. Kathy asked me if she and Denise could do a presentation along with me.

Denise, Kathy and I had to decide quickly on the content of our presentation, who was going to do what part of the speaking, and who would be sending the proposal to CANAR in Seattle for approval. Kathy submitted the proposal. Denise's part of the presentation was going to be focused on New Mexico's statewide career services for Native Americans with Disabilities to become self-employed; Kathy's presentation was targeted on assistive technology; and my presentation was on how assistive technology was helping me to reach my goal of writing an autobiography and advocating for people with disabilities on the Navajo Reservation, including how I work with my computer and Dragon Naturally-Speaking, use a mouth stick to navigate the telephone keys to make phone calls, and my TV remote to watch any channel I wish. One afternoon, Kathy called to tell me that our proposal had been accepted.

Kathy arranged all my travel plans including hotel reservations for me to attend CANAR. My expenses were covered by Navajo Nation OSERS. Now all I had to do was get prepared to do a presentation at one of the biggest conferences on Native American vocational rehabilitation.

When Kathy asked me who was going to be my caregiver at the conference, I told her, "I think my brother-in-law is going up there with me." However, when I asked my brother-in-law to be my assistant, he said he was terrified of planes because of the events of 9/11.

Just at the right moment, my cousin moved back home from Santa Fe to his parents' residence on the reservation near me. I told him that I was going to Seattle for a whole week for a conference. I asked him if he could be my assistant. He responded right away with eagerness that he wanted to go, as he hadn't visited that part of the country yet.

After a long discussion with my cousin I called Kathy back to let her know that he was going to be my caregiver at the conference. The NMDVR was going to pick up my cousin's expenses for his plane ticket to travel to the conference. Kathy was on the ball and confirmed everything for my cousin as well as for me without any hesitation. After confirming all the arrangements, Kathy also picked up the two plane tickets at the Albuquerque airport and brought them to my place while she was en route to Window Rock to attend a meeting. Without Kathy organizing all of these arrangements, I would not have been able to travel to the conference.

This was one of the few times that I had flown on an airplane during my disabled life. I was not too worried about leaving home at the time, but I was struggling with sinus ailments. I had some thoughts of canceling the trip.

My cousin asked, "Why cancel when all the expenses are fully taken care of?" So I had to drag myself through preparing for the adventure.

My cousin packed my belongings that I was going to take along with me on the journey. We both stayed at the Garden Express Hotel in Albuquerque the night before we departed for Seattle. The next morning we went to the airport early to make sure everything was in order. I noticed that the security protocols had intensified since the 9/11 terrorist attacks. There were intense security checkpoints involving luggage search, x-rays, and handheld metal detectors. The Southwest Airlines employees were fairly hospitable and helpful. The last time I had taken a flight was more than a decade ago when I had flown back from Mexico on an international airline. Now we got on a direct flight to Seattle, Washington in the late morning; our flight was to take three hours.

When we arrived in Seattle, the weather was a combination of stormy rain, sleet, snow, wind, and bitter frigid air. The moment my senses picked up on the climate, I didn't like it. I just wanted to turn around in the terminal and get back on the plane and come straight home. I already knew that the cold weather had the best of me because of it tightening up my muscles and making my bones ache, and I was already sick from having the flu, which started two days before I left New Mexico. To make things worse, my body was sore and restless from the long flight. All I wanted to do was forget about the whole conference and lie down, rest, and fall into a deep sleep.

My cousin encouraged me to go on through the three long agonizing days of the conference. My presentation was scheduled on the last day of the conference in the late afternoon. The conclusion of my presentation was about living on both sides of the fence, meaning living with ability and disability. To this day, I look back and wonder how I ever got through my presentation when my nerves almost got the best of me. I was relieved when I was finished and I finally got to relax from my stress-filled day and enjoy the remainder of the evening. That night, we prepared for our journey back home to a warmer and nicer environment. The CANAR conference was another mark on my walking stick in meeting my vocational rehabilitation goals, but I remember this as one of the most horrible trips that I have ever experienced in all my disabled life, because I was ill throughout the conference and had no interest in going sightseeing with my cousin.

The next morning we all packed up our luggage and took the late-morning ride to the airport. Our flight was scheduled to depart from Seattle-Tacoma International Airport early that afternoon. As soon as we boarded the plane I was happy and content that we were finally en route to New Mexico. The flight back to Albuquerque was a lot smoother and seemed quicker than coming up to Seattle.

27

LEADERSHIP

I had received a letter in July of 2003 from President of the Navajo Nation, Dr. Joe Shirley Jr., saying I had been selected to serve on the Navajo Nation Advisory Council on Handicap-able. I was astonished by this letter and couldn't wait to go to my first meeting to see who else was on the board. Our first meeting was to be in late July. I didn't know the policies, procedures and bylaws of the Navajo Nation. I said to myself, "It's about time I get my feet wet with my own tribe." I started to read and study the bylaws over and over, day and night. I wouldn't stop reading it until I understood every word written on that paper.

When I started my term there were only three members and a coordinator. It seemed like we didn't do much at all except go through some paperwork called an affirmative action plan, trying to reword, implement and revise this plan. When I went to some of these board meetings I would memorize a lot of what they were talking about, so I was one of the outspoken ones at any meetings that I attended. One of my significant responsibilities was to advocate on behalf of Navajos with disabilities, and I wasn't interested in this affirmative action plan. To me it didn't have any teeth at all. How much could it do for all the individuals that lived on the reservation when it wasn't an act or a bill? All it seemed to be was a way to put in a complaint about how an entity or individual is treating anyone with a disability. However, we finished revising this plan and sent it to President Shirley to sign. Our coordinator also sent a copy to the Department of Justice, but we never heard back.

Later on down the road, the coordinator quit her job and we were left with no leader, so everyone looked to me. I was chosen by the majority of the board members to be president, maybe because I was the only one with a higher education background. This was a three-year term, and whether I liked it or not I had to put on my thinking cap and dig in. This was my first time being a president of any committee or board and my first shot at being a leader. I had to write my own agendas as well as work at getting more members involved from different agencies. I was relatively new to tribal policy and procedures, but by then I was also on the board of the Statewide Independent Living Council, so I compared the two policies, studying them closely to try to bridge them together.

I had asked the director of OSERS in Window Rock to see about getting some other members involved to be a vice president and secretary. I went to a lot of conferences on the reservation and met many others who were disabled. In my first year as president in 2004, I chose a vice president and a new secretary, people I had met during a conference in Window Rock.

In February 2005 we had our first meeting with some new members in Farmington, New Mexico. It was snowing from where I lived all the way to Farmington, but I made it to the meeting that day. Most of the members were there so we started the meeting, and the first thing I wanted to do was change the name from Handicap-able. It was the first item on the agenda and the two choices for the new name were Disability and Accessibility. I knew that Accessibility would not work, but I wanted to test the board members. All the members agreed on the word Disability, and the Executive Director also agreed to changing the name. The change was implemented throughout the bylaws documents. Now the name became Navajo Nation Advisory Council on Disability.

My council members and I traveled throughout the Navajo reservation holding meetings in all five agencies on the reservation at different Chapter houses. At a few locations the Chapter houses were old, with no electricity or running water. At some places that I visited, a wheelchair could not get through, and we'd need help to get into the local Chapter house. There would be rocks, dirt and weeds growing at the entrance; it looked like there was no one to maintain the Chapter house, and some had broken windows and broken doors. I made my way in even though they weren't wheelchair friendly. At one Chapter house I asked the custodian and secretary there, "What is the reason that you don't have a sidewalk? Don't you have any disabled people around here?" They just looked at me curiously, like, "What?" I knew the first thing they would say is that they did not have enough funding and the tribe in Window Rock does not give them enough revenue to fix the Chapter house or fix the sidewalks. One of them suggested that maybe our Chapter officials were better than theirs. This just made me laugh, and I told them I was from Twin Lakes, New Mexico, where there is no sidewalk leading into the front entrance either. I didn't even know who the Twin Lakes Chapter officials were, maybe because I didn't go to meetings at the Chapter house with no sidewalk.

We met frequently with President Shirley. He wanted to hear our concerns and opinions. For instance, when I first joined the advisory council, there was a metal door in front of the building which I think weighed a hundred to two hundred pounds. I think it was even hard for any single able-bodied person to open it, because the electric wheelchair button was always broken. I raised my hand and asked, "Mr. President, have you ever opened the door at the entrance of the building? I think it would be best to get a sliding door, to get innovative and live by the ADA regulations." The president agreed, but another guy spoke up, "So you want this building to look like Wal-Mart?" I told him, "Only if you can change the name, then it can be Wal-Mart also," and a lot of people just laughed.

As one of the technology specialists under the Division of Vocational Rehabilitation in the state of New Mexico, Kathy worked with assistive technology in her Santa Fe office. Under this division they had board members. Kathy brought a letter of interest for me to fill out to see if I could become a member of the New Mexico Technology Assistance Project. At the time, I did not hesitate to write any kind of letters of interest or resumes to become a board member when I was asked. I filled out the paperwork with my niece's assistance and mailed it back. I was elected to be one of the members in 2004. Some members wanted me to be one of the officers, but I told them I couldn't do it because I didn't have a consistent helper and I belonged to other boards in the state, if I became an officer I would be missing many meetings. But I enjoyed being a member of this board. I resigned because I was on too many boards such as the Navajo Nation Advisory Council, Statewide Independent Living Council, and the Governor's Commission on Disability.

I resigned from the Navajo Nation Advisory Council on Disability in 2006. I had been on the board for more than the three-year term, including being vice-president for a while and then president. I served an extra six months and nobody said anything to me. While at a meeting in Window Rock I approached all the members and told them they had to find themselves a new president because I was just too worn out. Being a president and being severely disabled really got to me. I began dreaming and talking in my sleep about the meetings. I told them I was quitting and that would be my last meeting. Most of them didn't want me to go because I made a great many changes.

The members told me that I was the first president to put up meetings at the five agencies on the reservation. They also told me that we could do those meetings again. But I knew there was no funding. The director had hired a new worker for herself and that was where all the money went. The Advisory Council was at a standstill for a year and a half, flat broke. Finally they got enough funding and started looking for board members again. The same members applied, but the vice president and I knew it wasn't going to work unless the director and her assistant stepped down. They didn't have a heart for the disabled. They only knew how to use "disability" in a sentence. They could talk about it all they wanted to and go to conferences and meetings and still have no clue how to work with somebody with a disability. Until someone in their family or themselves experienced disability, they would not wake up to what it's like going up against so many obstacles and barriers.

My first meeting with the Statewide Independent Living Council was at the end of January 2005 at the Mariott Hotel in Santa Fe. I had received an invitation from the Governor of New Mexico, Bill Richardson, and I was happy to be chosen to serve the Northwest region of New Mexico and to be the only Native American to serve on this board. I served two terms on the SILC, which is six years and all you're allowed to serve. September 2011 was my last month to be a member, but they didn't figure that out until March of 2012.

The RSA (Rehabilitation Services Administration, part of the U.S. Department of Education) in Washington finally realized that I had already served six years, so they wrote telling me that I could no longer be a member. I wasn't too happy about how that happened, but I was pleased to get off the board. While serving on the SILC board we never had a consistent Executive Director. We'd get a director for a year or two and then it would change again—the executive committee would give the directors poor evaluations, so they were out. I served on this board with four executive directors. Some were intelligently good, and the last one I didn't really know.

In 2009 I had finished writing my autobiography, and I wondered what I wanted to do for my next project to keep me occupied and motivated, that would help me thrive and succeed in becoming the man that I always wanted to be. I thought about going back to school on-line but I needed a consistent helper to be there for me when I was doing my homework. I was about to enroll but I was too busy with other things, like being on the Governor's Commission on Disability. By the time I'd get home from traveling, my body needed to rest, so going back to school was not going to work out. I committed to attending quarterly meetings of the commission and I was able to attend most meetings that were mandatory. I attended meetings that were closer to home in Albuquerque, Farmington or Santa Fe but not as far south as Las Cruces or Phoenix. For other meetings I did telephone conferences that averaged about an hour or two. These are the things that kept me occupied so I would not get too bored and go crazy staring at the ceiling and looking at the television.

In 2010 I resigned from the Governor's Commission because it was hard for me to attend the meetings. The bylaws said that the board could meet all over the state, but they mainly met in Santa Fe and Albuquerque. I also didn't have a consistent caregiver, which is why I missed some of the meetings. A lot of the members were from departments like DOH, DVR, the Governor's office and some others. I noticed that most of them were Anglo and Hispanic and I was the only Native American. I felt there was a prejudice against Native Americans; as I write, there is no Native American on the board. The negative feelings I attracted from some of the members got to me. I put in my resignation and didn't attend any more meetings, but my name remained on the Governor's Commission on Disability website, maybe just to get more funding for the commission.

< >

I would like to say what an effective advocate I was to have served on all these boards for the severely disabled, while meeting some nice people who reside in a rural area of the Navajo reservation. I did enjoy serving on all the boards, but to be honest there are a lot of rude people from our diverse populations of New Mexico. If only people would get along with one another, this world would be in better condition. I know that later on I might change my mind, but after some of my negative experiences, I'm not interested in being on any more boards. Right now I'm just an author, at home doing my writing and living with all my experiences and knowledge that I gained from being an advocate and sometimes a board member.

28

OUR PAST AND FUTURE

Moving forward with my life has brought me back around to living here on the reservation. The reservation here can't be any better, this gorgeous day and beautiful evening. I start looking at these four sacred mountains surrounding the sacred reservation and I think of many things. This land is where all my ancestors lived and walked freely. I think of the history of our people when we had some pretty negative times, like when they moved people from these beautiful areas. That is called The Long Walk. The Navajo people who were called at that time Diné were prisoners at army camp Bosque Redondo in Fort Sumner with other Native tribes. The Diné were among the last to sign the treaty of 1868. They were not released until they made the agreement with the U.S. government. Across the nation all the Native tribes signed treaties that stopped us from doing some traditional activities, which meant that we couldn't sing, we couldn't dance, and sometimes we couldn't even pray and have ceremonies because it was illegal.

When they were released from the army prison camp, most of the Navajo tribe made it back to their land, but some of them had passed on and some of them were adopted by the Pueblos or the Hispanic people. That is one of the reasons why most of the younger generations have a Hispanic last name. However, that didn't turn a lot of Navajo people away from what's right and the knowledge of what was given to them at the time they signed the treaty, things like free health care and free education. To this day the federal government has not lived up to their obligations and promises—all that was on their minds was just greed. They took all the resources off the land and polluted the water and the land. Today we walk on the land trying to look for a place where it is not polluted. All we see is a bunch of erosions and dry arroyos and fewer plants. It is extremely sad to think and talk about this. What kind of lie will they tell us next? How much money they will offer us along with other empty promises? Above all, my grandpa told me to never believe a white man.

My mom tells me that grandpa had over three thousand sheep and over one thousand head of cattle. The federal government came in to reduce the number of livestock to a certain amount around the 1930s when the Open Range Act was adopted on the reservation. They gave the Navajo people what they called a sheep permit to graze only a few cattle and sheep. This is when most of the Navajo stopped being self-reliant, and the federal government gave the Indian tribes what they call today welfare. I would say that the federal government should be ashamed, because the Navajo people used to work for themselves while raising their own livestock, and they didn't have to depend on the government to provide commodities of all sorts. We know what has happened. They can look at us like we're stupid but we aren't.

I don't think there is a full-blooded Navajo anymore, in the sense of keeping our traditional life. We are losing our language and religion which my culture desperately needs. We are losing our language and culture and tradition because we are losing a majority of our medicine men who perform the traditional ceremonials. These healing doings are slowly and sadly fading away like the dry land that once was filled with vegetation. They may one day be extinct like those of the Anasazi, the Ancient Ones. Now we only have our memories of them sadly written in textbooks.

When an in-law brings in someone from the outside world who isn't Native American, here is another reason for the loss of the religion and language. Some say the Navajos are betrayed again when the non-Native men leave their wives, and the women and children are left behind without support. That is how our population becomes diverse. I can forecast the future from this, and I don't see a reservation anymore. Most teenagers who reside on the reservation only speak English. When they grow up, what do you think is going to happen? Pretty soon we are going to lose our language, which played a big role in America's freedom when our elders, who we all know as the Navajo Code Talkers, outsmarted the most intelligent people in the world who couldn't break the code of the Navajo language. As we lose the values of the language, the whole reservation is going to change. We may even have a different purpose for residing here.

In years ahead, a lot of our children will not know the Navajo language, and it will fade away like snow melting in the desert, becoming no more than a memory. It will be referred to as a dead language, possibly known only to linguistics scholars. We will probably lose most of our Native culture and customs along with it, as these things are not being taught at home now. Our Native traditions will only be known in textbooks because the practices will die out. Sometimes, looking at this bleak future for the Navajo culture is frightening to me because we will be losing the traditions that have kept us strong.

Living in the Navajo Nation on the largest Indian reservation, the only thing that people have is sovereignty, which is self-government. But sovereignty rings hollow when you do not have a connection with your culture to protect and to benefit you. I don't know how others feel or think about it. Maybe someday in the future the mixture of Anglo people, Hispanic people and other minorities might become the dominant population on the reservation. I think that's why the Navajo Nation is trying to protect their land, the land guaranteed them in the Treaty of Bosque Redondo.

I found the reservation to be almost comparable to a third-world country, with minimal public transportation for the physically challenged; a lack of communication, as not every household can afford a telephone; and no opportunities for people with disabilities to interact, as disabilities are still seen as taboo subjects. Mexico is a poor country but a very different place because there are people always willing to help you and to converse with you even when you can't speak their language. The majority of the people in Mexico are unemployed, and they are willing to do any kind of work for whatever little pay they can get. That is the way they live from day to day just to feed their families so they can survive.

I had been eager to get home to the reservation, but then when I first came back, I wanted to move back to the city. That was the environment I was used to, where I had more friends that came by to visit. Here I was isolated. I was not used to being in a place that was so confined with family members. I just wanted to move away again, but I did not know where.

I had been away from home because of my rehabilitation and higher education. I guess this is why a lot of Natives on the reservation get alienated when they move to another city, losing their language little by little until before they know it they don't know anything. They no longer recognize their own culture or language or even their clans. The thing that keeps them away is employment. Once you step into a city environment, you get used to it right away and don't want to come back because of the hardship on the reservation. I once ran across another person in Albuquerque who was from the reservation and hadn't gone back for twenty years. He didn't know if he had any relatives or if his parents were still living. That was strange and shocking to me, and to top it off I tried to talk to him in our native language. He did not know much, just yes and no. This is one of the main reasons I came back to live on the reservation. I had gone to Mexico to see what the conditions were like down there. The environment was nice and I kind of liked it. I wanted to move down there. That's what I thought to myself when I was coming back to the States. If I hadn't run across that guy in Albuquerque, maybe I would be living in Mexico.

This is the land where I grew up. Ever since I came home from the city, I have enjoyed living here on the reservation. Although you have to travel to get to town or to a local store, I don't mind because that's how it was in my teenage years. I still go visit the places where I was raised, and some of my siblings still live there. I like spending the whole day and sometimes spend the night with them. It's nice and quiet. I can see the clear sky and bright stars when I recline in my wheelchair. It brings back a lot of memories of when I was in Mexico and visited the beach and slept a couple of nights out beside the Pacific Ocean near Acapulco.

In the daytime I go behind the mountains to see if everything is at the right place—like it was when I was young riding my horse around hills and slopes, out and about. I realize there are fewer trees there now than before, when it used to look like a forest. There's not too much shade to cool down the land from the hot sun. The land is bare with a lot of erosions which have gotten bigger. It has changed a lot since back in the early 1970s when we had more rain and snow. There are not as many homesteads, but some of the places have running water, electricity and telephone lines. Back in my teenage years when I was able and living at the place where I was raised, it would have made a big difference if we'd had electricity and running water. It would have made everything easier, but I was used to all these places and the way things were. My grandma had lived like this for decades, along with my mom and dad.

Despite the many changes, I still like to go see this area. It brings back a lot of memories of when my grandma would name some of the places in Navajo. She used to tell me not to forget these names; some of these places are sacred and named after her grandparents or some medicine man who used to do the blessing there. I can only remember some but not all of it. Sometimes I asked my mom what these places were called, and she could answer some but not all, because she'd forgotten some of the names too.

My grandpa would sometimes tell me how the animals used to talk, like the mischievous coyote. I used to love and admire the way my grandpa told me the coyote stories. I would ask him to tell them over and over, but he would wait until another day. I miss my grandpa a lot. Sometimes I dream about him, that he is around. He was a very nice gentleman with a lot of humor.

During all the years I have been living with my severe disability, a lot of people have confronted me with comments about religion. Countless numbers of people have remarked, "Your faith must be a great help as you cope with your condition, it must be what keeps you going day after day and year after year being in your position." One individual actually told me, "If I was in your position I would just commit suicide immediately. I don't think I would want to be in your shoes, or be able to laugh and joke all the time like you do." I always tell everybody who asks about my condition, if I'm in the mood to talk to them, "You can take my dignity away but not my faith and patience." Then they ask, "What is your religion?" That used to put me in an uncomfortable position, because I could tell they wanted to hear that I am not a deeply religious person. But they are wrong.

The truth is that I'm not biblically educated and only found a real religion, the Church of Jesus Christ of Latter Day Saints, when their people would come to my bedside in the hospital and at home and talk to me about the word of God. I have knowledge about the

Christian bible and its teachings, too. The scriptures from John in which Jesus says to the infirm, "Wilt thou be made whole? " and "Rise, take up thy bed, and walk" give me plenty of patience. Every day is a new day and I only take it one day at a time.

The end of my routine involvement with religion marked the beginning of an ongoing search for the meaning of spirituality in my life. It had taken many years, many well-intentioned but misguided detours, and ultimately a near-fatal accident to get me to that point. To this day I have not found an answer. I have cheated death several times trying to commit suicide and let go of life, but I don't know what kept me alive. After all these encounters I woke up in the ICU unit not knowing where I was.

I detest when other people talk about religion. I always tell them, "If religion is real, why do people get hurt, die and live in poverty?" Most of the time, I'm puzzled about the word religion. Yes, I'm a believer, but the subject is too full of endless questions and endless answers, and sometimes concludes in an argument. I would ask a minister or a priest, "Who is Jesus?" They would tell me that he is a savior who went back to live with his father, he is amongst us but we can't see him. It really bothers me when I hear that God is around us. Look at the world, everything that's going on. When I was little it was like this and I think that it is getting worse by the decades. So, I don't have an answer for that, the only answer I get from that is to just pray daily, nightly, and to sometimes read my Bible. To really understand both sides of the traditions and the Bible is very difficult. It's not like math or English. It is also not science. You have to read the Bible regularly to understand all the scriptures.

Today I don't separate my Native American traditional culture from either of my religions, the Word from the Bible and the Book of Mormon, which is another testament of the Holy Bible. The only thing that matters to me is that both of these religions, and many other churches also, talk about God and we all pray to one Almighty, our father in heaven. I can reconcile them all with a lifelong journey for the meaning of spirituality. I can talk about many testaments that I have come across and honestly believe.

I encourage people to never, ever forget about the past. But we must also continue to have tremendous hope for the future. Our children can play side by side without fear no matter what color they are, no matter what language they speak and no matter what background they come from. If we try, we can get away from the terms and activities that lead to racism and prejudice. Terrible events like 9/11 and the terrorism our young men and women are fighting today can truly bring us together as human beings so that again we are one people, we are equal. We are equal to walk on this earth, we are equal to be free in America. So with those thoughts in mind, I encourage you to keep teaching your children about who you are. I don't care what color we are, we shouldn't forget our cultures and traditions. I don't care if we are American-Indian, American-Arab, Hispanic, African-American and so forth. Firstly we are human beings, secondly we are Americans, and above all that we are free.

29

ROLE MODELS

When a person becomes disabled, the need for accomplishment and desire to fit into the normal traffic of life does not end. Within the first years of living with disability, family plays an important role in the disabled individual's physical, mental, and emotional rehabilitation. The initial reactions a person has to a severe impairment may forecast the possibility of future survival. Family and friends can soften the rage and apathy that usually manifests during the first trials of rehabilitation. This allows a pathway to a healthier state of mind for the disabled individual to look beyond the immediate challenges before them.

I know that there is a purpose for me still being in this world, a survivor of a tragic accident. Younger people with recent spinal cord injuries have no knowledge about how to deal with the challenge of their new lives confined to a wheelchair. These young individuals may believe that this is the end of the world for them. Once they recover from the initial pain and shock of their spinal cord injuries there may be nothing for them to do to keep their minds occupied. If they are coming out of the reservation, there is the added possibility of culture shock—which works both ways as I have personally learned and experienced. They may not comprehend that even though they can't move a leg or an arm, they still have a mind to utilize. It is my understanding that a mind is the only element needed to do almost anything.

When I first got injured there was nobody to give me advice. My own native people ignored me because of the traditional taboos about being physically challenged and being in a wheelchair. Nobody came forward to talk to me about my situation as a physically challenged individual. I wanted someone to give me guidance and support, to say: this is the way it goes, this is how it is to live with paralysis, this is what it's like living in a wheelchair.

I lived in a world of red tape, barriers and obstacles that I had known nothing about. The obstacles that I'm talking about are not mountains, canyons or rivers. The barriers are people who think that you can't do anything once you are paralyzed. I encounter these attitudes almost every day, and I want to prove them wrong. I am just a human being who wants to live life to the fullest.

I truly understand that it was because of the traditional taboos that go with being a Native American that I was ignored in college by my own people. No Native American in the reservation knew how to deal with an individual who is disabled. This made me feel kind of bad but never brought me down from my new perspective about life: to keep moving on to another day.

I cannot say that I understand exactly what other people with spinal cord injuries like mine are going through. Anyone who is living with paralysis has his or her own way of accomplishing tasks. People with spinal cord injuries need inspiration, motivation and guidance from someone who has experienced similar situations. However, each person must be open to hear and believe that the greatest force in the healing process is their own attitude. Yes, it is tough to live with paralysis through the years and to deal with the thoughts that run through your mind every day of what life could have been like if you weren't paralyzed. Life must be lived one day at a time, and it takes a lot of endurance. It's up to the individual to accept some guidance to keep on living in the challenging world of the physically disabled. I know that advice is easy to give. I know from my own experience the many obstacles and barriers ahead of you. However it's not the end of the world; you can live with your disability. All I can tell you is to move on and not dwell on the past. You cannot know what the future holds.

Throughout my stay at the rehab hospital I observed all kinds of medical devices that aided people living with disabilities and allowed them to become independent. This gave me an idea about how the biomedical engineers' inventions might be successful in the future. I had seen demonstrations of robots that were being designed to aide people, but I was never interested in these machines, I imagined other kinds of inventions. Many things I thought about in the rehab center are available today. You can talk to a computer and it will type and do a lot of things for you. Sometimes it makes me wonder if there will be a mind boggling new technology that will help paralyzed people to walk again. Hmmm—if I see one it will amaze me. Imagine just one paralyzed human being walking without a chair, walking miles and miles, climbing up hills— Maybe in the next generation. Hmmm—

You hear of a recent experiment in a laboratory described as "an exciting breakthrough": paralyzed rats treated with X were able to climb a few steps up a rope ladder six weeks later. You think, "Terrific, what does it mean to me or any of the rest of us?" Christopher Reeve and some neuroscientists were looking into this.

I always wanted to visit Mr. Reeve at his residence just to find out how his house was made wheelchair friendly and to meet his family, but I did not have a chance to meet him before he passed on. I especially wanted to know how he coped with his condition mentally and physically. I've read some of his books. He sounds like a extraordinary and interesting individual. I would have loved to visit with him when Robin Williams was at his home joking around with him about his catheter. I also would've liked to meet his helpers while they were there and while he was dictating to his writer, writing his autobiography. He's the one that inspired me to write about myself and my life, just by reading his autobiography. A man one day walking and the next moment paralyzed. He overcame great obstacles and barriers and he never gave up; he is a big inspiration for people who have spinal cord injuries.

Here is someone else who inspired me: I had seen a movie that caught my attention when I was trying to recall my life story. The movie was called *La Bamba*, and was about a teenage Mexican-American singer named Ritchie Valens who was told that Mexican folk music couldn't be made into rock-'n-roll. He sang it anyway and made a number-one hit on American Bandstand. His agent was skeptical of Ritchie Valens' use of folk songs in mainstream American music. But after seeing the immense talent that Ritchie had, he was willing to take a risk against the racial prejudice that existed during that time. Somewhere, in the middle of a concert of various artists, when it was his turn to perform, Valens announced, "Here's a bit of rattlesnake!" before he started. He came to mind when I was thinking of how I can overcome all these transitions and obstacles. Ritchie's rock-'n-roll influence came from a mentor, Buddy Holly, another great musician, who died with Ritchie in the fatal plane accident resulting from a winter storm in 1959. Ritchie was seventeen years old, the same age I was when I had my fateful accident.

I gained a lot of knowledge about being in a wheelchair and especially about depending on others by going to the two biggest universities in New Mexico. I had to change my attitude totally around, which made me meet new people and make a lot of friends. I lived with people who helped me out with anything I needed. I was not ignored, and I felt comfortable and at ease around them. No one from the reservation helped me with any funds to pay for my caretakers. I paid them with free room and board. I had just enough money for what the caretaker and I needed for the apartment with not much left over.

Sometimes I used to get petrified about my living conditions from the culture shock of the real world and college life. I was barely over twenty years old and felt lonely sometimes, but this got me prepared for the future and the life I'm living right now. I gained the confidence and endurance that made me the strong man I am today. I can move anywhere at any time whenever I want. Today I still think about the hard times I went through while I was living in the big city. I think about what I accomplished and I try not to think about being disabled. That's the only way I get things done. I've been living forty years being quadriplegic and I can see that I've made more progress than a younger able-bodied person.

When things are really bad you have to laugh. We use humor to relieve tension and cope with many things in life that are whimsical and even weird. Humor and laughter can cover up jealousy, prejudice and intolerance. It can show people what they have in common, which was one of the reasons I enjoyed doing presentations, keynotes and master of ceremony, also doing many chores like serving on boards. My injury gave me firsthand knowledge that humor is also one of the best ways, if not the best way, to re-route anger. Humor and laughter are the best things that you can ever learn and employ every day. These two things are not exactly the same, and everybody should at least have one.

Have a sense of humor or at least have the ability to laugh. Too many people that I have met at some of the conferences on the reservation do not have either one of these. All they do is criticize one another about how they did their presentation or how they are dressed. This is life in the world of a sovereign nation. But outside of the reservation, people are different. They don't look at how you are dressed, how you talk and what you look like. All they are looking for is some knowledge and wisdom to gain and something new to learn from the conference, and also what they can lean on in the future. They listen carefully to you during your presentation so they can use the tools you are sharing and take them back home to use there.

My sense of humor has gotten me through a lot of painful and embarrassing encounters. One time, a nurse from a state on the East Coast visited me. She asked me if I liked my new wheelchair. She'd never seen a wheelchair that did all sorts of things, like reclining. I told her I didn't particularly like it, but it was my only means of getting around the house. Plus, I said, it was a good way to legally drink and drive at the same time, instead of getting a designated driver. She laughed, showing me she had a good sense of humor.

That was such a weird transition for me, having to depend on a machine as the only means of transport. Jokes about the wheelchair help mollify my anger about being in one. I quickly discovered that when I appeared in public it was best to begin with a light remark to put the audience at ease. I'd comment on how far everyone had to come to hear my talk, and then tell them my own joke about how my personal transportation doesn't use any gas.

In my new life I've slipped into the "numb zone" many times. That's when creating humor and appreciating it becomes very difficult, but even more necessary. It doesn't matter if you're not that funny. The point is that the numb zone can become dangerously comfortable. If you get stuck in it for a long period of time you may end up going back to square one, when life after a catastrophe has no meaning. This reminds me of another of my heroes, the multi-talented Navajo entertainer—comedian, singer, songwriter, actor and creator of the "Mutton Man" cartoon strip—Vincent Craig. He was the subject of a text message saying he'd died. The story goes that he said, "Dying is easy, comedy is hard." What a gifted individual he was.

Many of us live in the numb zone whether we are disabled or not. In fact many people who are suffering from some condition look at others who are not ill but seem to be unhappy all the time and wonder what gives them the right to complain. I ask them when I am around them, "What side of the bed did you wake up on?" They turn around and strike me with words: "It doesn't matter what side I woke up on. Everything's relative. No one gets to corner the market on misery." Okay, but I agree with any dying comedian anywhere in the world: sometimes humor is hard but it's worth it. Let's get out of the numb zone and live like we mean it. Live like tomorrow is not promised, because—it's not.

A tragic horrifying accident changed my life without warning. I was walking ably ten minutes before, and the next moment I was laid out on a stretcher headed for the hospital not knowing what the outcome of my life was going to be. I was drifting in and out of consciousness, with a tremendous pain in the back of my neck. I never realized that I could not feel the rest of my body until I got into the emergency room and was waiting for the radiologist to do my x-ray. My doctor came by and asked me a lot of questions, like if I could still move my arms and legs. I tried to say what I knew but I was drifting in and out of consciousness. I asked for some pain medication. The nurse responded, "It's too early to give you any kind of pain medication until your doctor writes an order for you." The pain I had was so unbearable that I could not concentrate and converse with anybody. No one knew what I was saying, I kept being told that they could not understand the language I was speaking.

At first after my accident all I wanted was to go back to what I used to do when I was able, to do some silversmithing and to participate in rodeo; to this day I can't do either. But I did go the white man's way—through rehab, completing high school and higher education until I finished my bachelor's degree. From that experience and the knowledge that I gained, I know a little about my second language English, and my first language that is Navajo which I speak and understand well, along with some Spanish that I picked up in college and when I was residing in Mexico.

Today I am the first Native American Navajo author to write about my disability. I have done so despite the taboos and myths warning against it. My autobiography was first published in August 2009 after I'd been working on it for six long years, reminiscing about all the things I did during my youth and up to the present. I had looked for Native American mentors who survived their severely disabled life and had written about how they struggled and coped with their disability. I couldn't find one, so I decided to write that book. At first it was just an idea.

From the time I wrote and published my book, I was already thinking about writing some more. I wanted to go into more depth about my life story and include what I missed, because I wrote the first book in such a rush. To be honest, I didn't know what I was doing. It was very hard for me to start a paragraph or start any sentences, but as I progressed I got more familiar with the work and got comfortable with it. I do not know what I will be doing next, but I know I will be doing some sort of writing again because I love to write, which is to me a romantic thing to do.

Sometimes I get a phone call asking if I'm available to do a presentation about my book. Every time, the talk has to be "about yourself, what to do so you don't quit, and how there is always a light at the end of the tunnel." They ask me to tell how I got started, what gave me these ideas and who inspired me to write such an amazing book. I do not know if it's amazing, but to them it is. All I am doing is writing from the bottom of my heart about my truthful and hard experiences and my life on the reservation and off the reservation. My hope is that somewhere somebody will pick up a book and get inspired when they read it, and pass along the knowledge that I am trying to express to them.

Postscript, 2016

LIFE WITH NO BOUNDARIES:
TRIUMPH OVER TRAGEDY

A young Native American man faces all different kinds of transitions and tries to raise himself from the sovereign nation and to struggle out of poverty from the southwestern desert of northwest New Mexico. The striving of life is not chosen by gender, race, custom, culture, religion or whether one is blessed or despised. It goes searching for a better life. He commits himself to the challenge by embarking on a higher education at a big university, knowing little about his disability or what the future holds for him. How will his disability affect him at school, in class and living away from the reservation, the place he calls home?

Somewhere between starting his first semester and the middle of the semester, he sees the difficulties that he faces and thinks he will have to give up sooner or later and forget about going forward. No curbs on sidewalks, no door openers or any kind of technology is available for disabled people. He's too shy to ask anybody for help because he's by himself in this big world at the university. He just continues attending class every day, but he has to prepare for the class early, and arrive before any student gets to the doorway. Then he will ask someone nicely to open the door for him. Sometimes he is there first or sometimes with friends he knows from class. He finds a way to enter a class or lecture room. He often sits in the front of the class or in the back of the whole classroom. He asks a professor if he can record his lecture. The professor denies him and tells him that he has office hours twice a week—if he has any questions he can go visit him there. But this young Native American does not stop there or listen to the professor. He goes to the local electronics store and buys a small portable tape recorder to give to one of his friends so he or she can record the lecture for him. Some of the students get to share tapes of the lecture. Alongside he continues reading his textbook and asking for lecture notes from other students that he attends class with so he can prepare for the next class session. These are obstacles that he never thought he would ever face.

In a world of challenges, he's a quadriplegic, paralyzed from the neck on down, cannot move any limbs, only a finger or two. Even when there's an itch on his face, there's no way that he can scratch it himself for relief. He doesn't give up. He just keeps on going, talking with the friends that he made in college about what would be best for him, to go to class or just to drop out of school. One problem is that the grocery stores and restaurants are so far away from the campus, as well as the fast food joints, and his wheelchair battery does not hold that much charge. The idea to transfer to a different school in a cooler environment runs through his mind, another university would be more wheelchair friendly and have everything up to date like door openers and other technology.

He transfers, and finds more big challenges, even more than he had imagined. Too many curbed sidewalks between classes, and just like at the other school he has to ask somebody to help him down the curb. Another big challenge is the weather, the cold temperatures, rain and snow. Frozen sidewalks. Sometimes his wheelchair won't move on a sidewalk covered with ice, not forward or backwards. Some students walk by with a smile but without offering any kind of help. But nothing will stop this young Native American man who has set his mind on the future. One day he was in his room at the rehab center watching a commercial about students being able to go to school anywhere in the world. He doesn't remember if it mentioned disability, but he set his goal and kept on going whether the university was accessible or not. He was going to put himself on a road to success and be a positive role model for others who must struggle like him to get a higher education. Whether rain or shine, day or night, he attends class. He is not crazy but just eager to learn the white man's knowledge.

While I was going to school at the University of New Mexico, I was the first Native American with a severe disability to attend UNM. I did not think of myself as being disabled. I made a lot of friends from out of state and from different countries. All these students lifted up my spirit, they got what I projected out of myself. Sometimes I even forgot that I was in a wheelchair, until I was going to reach for a pair of tickets to go to a basketball game and remembered I was not able to get my own wallet. The power wheelchair was my only means of getting around and going places, but no obstacles or barriers could stop me from watching any sporting event.

I think being in a wheelchair really changed my attitude so that I became a lot nicer and friendlier. A lot of my friends asked me if I could go back with them to their homestead or their countries, and without thinking about that question I would say yes. That is one reason I went to Mexico, just because I wanted to see the country and the environment where they live, and some awesome places and beaches. It was good that I took this opportunity to see another place in the world.

I didn't know how much effort it might be for these people to take care of me, but now I know how much work it takes, living here at home on the reservation where my family alternates in looking after me. It has really got me thinking, having all this technology in my room, that if all these technologies had been available when I went to school I would've gone higher with my education. Still, the education that I gained from the university was worthwhile. The bachelor's degree opened a lot of avenues for me and kept me going and exploring the world. I made a lot of friends from outside of the reservation. It would've been very simple to go to school from home if I had today's technology, but I probably would not have met a lot of friends the way I did by going to school every day with my wheelchair.

Living with no boundaries here on the reservation, another day, the early dawn morning light touches the eastern sky all over the reservation. Oh, how does it feel to live here in what we call a sovereign nation? For me, it is unlimited freedom. But what does freedom really mean when you have to struggle to live, especially being disabled? I am living in a remote area in the largest Native American Indian Nation where every day my people face poverty and struggle to survive.

The Americans with Disabilities Act was passed and signed into law by George H. W. Bush on July 26, 1990. The law did not come into effect across the nation until 1992. Little by little, all buildings had to be built according to the ADA standards, but the old buildings from the 1950s and 60s are protected by the historic preservation act and do not have to comply. These are most of the buildings in Santa Fe; some were built in the 1800s and early 1900s.

Most of the Navajo Housing Authority residences are not wheelchair friendly, yet the agency gets funding from the U.S. Department of Housing and Urban Development (HUD). Instead of getting help to improve their homes, the people that are in wheelchairs are put in an institution where they cannot voice their opinions. They are made to be more dependent on others when everything could be accessible. The ADA was amended in 2008, and again revised by President Obama on its twentieth anniversary in 2010. I don't know how many years it will take to be implemented fully for those of us dependent on wheels for mobility in this great state of New Mexico.

I wonder where all these acts were when I was going to school. Most of the campus was not wheelchair friendly and I had to struggle a lot. Some of the people on campus tried to put me down and said it was not hard to go to class. I told them to walk the walk and talk the talk: be in a wheelchair for a day and see how it is trying to get to class with your arms tied behind your back. I guess all the lawmakers were waiting for me to finish with my school so they could pass the ADA and put it into law. Now when I go back to UNM in Albuquerque, there is a great difference. It looks like a brand new university. Everything is accessible, door openers and handicap parking areas, even accessible drinking fountains. When you go to the library there is an accessible computer for disabled people. Almost everywhere on campus and in the city is wheelchair friendly now. I don't know how many wheelchair frames I broke trying to jump the curb, acting like Evel Knievel jumping the Snake River Canyon in Idaho. Jumping curbs is fun, but not when you break a frame.

Living here on the Navajo Reservation, I am content. I can get hold of almost anyone from my own room with technology, and I can do a lot of research. This is what I love about all the new innovative technology that is available today. I do not look at myself as being disabled as long as I can reach out to somebody from a different country or another city by email or a phone call from my little room, where it is nice and quiet and cool and my thinking cap resides. It seems like I can hold the world in my hand by just looking at the map. When I'm on my computer I do not get bored because it has mind-boggling information. My computer is what keeps me going from day to day, and that's why I like to keep it updated with the little money I get. I'm in a clean and quiet environment, without traffic and pollution. I'm making good use of what my ancestors have left for me.

Even though the house I live in is not wheelchair friendly, I'm fond of living this way. The only time I see a boundary around me is when I think about my disability, but I don't think about it too much. There are times when someone wants to ask a stupid question that puts me down, or when I'm feeling low and don't want to do anything but sleep and waste a whole day. How nice it is to be teased, but sometimes I don't like to be over teased. So I just quietly leave the area to avoid any kind of dispute about my condition, as I might burst out in anger because I can't hold myself back. I don't want to erupt, I just like to be direct.

Most of the time I just eat in my room where strange people won't stare at me. My own family doesn't bother me while I eat, so I can join them and tease them and joke around. I love it when I approach the dinner table, which I occasionally hit as I try to park my wheelchair as close as possible. Too much joking sometimes isn't good for me because I can't hold my food down from laughing and trying to swallow at the same time and tend to choke. Since I'm dependent on everything I don't want to be picky, but sometimes I am. I am trying to work on that, but sometimes I have to get things the way I want. Usually I just take whatever is brought to the table or my bedside. Coming from the Southwest, I love beans, green chili and tortillas, especially bean burritos with hot chili. It's my favorite food and I can live on it.

I don't think anyone understands what it's like to be fed or go to a dining table sitting amongst strangers and someone will be helping me eat. That is the reason I don't go to restaurants anymore. I'd rather go for fast food or to the grocery store and get some fruits and drinks. When I go into a restaurant I always ask the waiter if there's a table somewhere away from the crowd where nobody will look. Sometimes the waitresses will tease me and say they'll sit by me and help me eat. That kind of cheers me up, but the feeling fades very quickly. I think they are trying to get me to stay in the crowd. They also tell me it doesn't matter how I eat because I'm the one who will be paying for the food, but I tell them that people seem to stare at me to see what's in my thoughts, with their eyes as big as softballs looking straight at me. I tell them that their remark is very kind and they've made my day.

Since the beginning of my new abnormal uncomfortable life being in a wheelchair, I've always wanted to be as average as possible. The longing for normality applies to every aspect of living with a disability, from health to relationships, work, travel, study and play. It's been difficult to find the right balance between managing my own needs and meeting my obligations and reaching out to others.

Some days I don't realize how seriously heavy I am. It is one of the reasons why I don't like to go too many places where I have to be lifted and transferred into a vehicle using portable ramps to load my chair in the back of the pick-up truck. It does more damage to the wheelchair and is time consuming to do all this stuff required for traveling. In my younger days it didn't bother me. I don't like to go somewhere unless it is really necessary and if there is a wheelchair ramp. It's also easier for my caretaker.

I'm home most of the time but occasionally I will go out to the mall, some stores or my best hang out place, Fire Rock Casino. I'm not a big gambler but I just like to go over there and maybe donate and sometimes I'll win a few dollars. I like to see new faces and meet people who chat with me and lift my spirits. Most of all I like to eat there and discover people that I used to know back from high school. To be honest, I cannot recognize them when they come up to me and say hello. I always have to ask, "What's your name and where are you from?" I was not around this area after I got hurt and

I forgot how they looked, plus they are changed from aging. Sometimes there are local bands playing and I just listen in and watch.

I like to go to the movies during the day only if there is a movie that I like showing in Gallup, or I may just get too relaxed and kick back and go to sleep during the shows. Gallup is not a big city, just a little town that is growing a little at a time. The population is diverse, which I like. I think Native Americans are the majority of the population in Gallup. There's always some kind of event going on during the week as well as on weekends. There are lots of rodeos in Gallup and also the surroundings areas. I used to love to go to rodeos when I was able, but now I've lost much interest in it. It just brings up too many memories, so I try not to go although my brother always asks me to go with him. Rodeos out here haven't changed too much. I think today more females participate in all events and all age categories. Even my niece participated in barrel racing.

Occasionally I will go into town to get something that I need for myself and my work here as an author and maybe some clothing. In the meantime, I'm here at home doing what I want to do. I go to sleep and wake up when I want to wake up, though sometimes I'm not comfortable sleeping. Sometimes I wake up in the middle of the night thinking that I can walk again, especially when I'm thirsty and tired. I do not want to wake anybody up just to ask them for a glass of water. I just let them sleep while I try to put myself back to sleep. Sometimes when I need a glass of water I think positive and try to move my legs, but that's never worked for me. Sometimes when I'm trying to go back to sleep I end up praying and that's a good way to go back to sleep. The next day I wake up wondering where I was and who I was talking to.

Sometimes I just sleep as though I have never slept before, like a bear snoring, and I wake up the next afternoon with a dry mouth. I don't know if I really do snore like a bear but I don't care as long as I get my rest for the next day, even though it is just going to be another harmonious day for me to look forward to. I'm always eager to open up my email to see who wrote me and to get on social networks. I save that for later on during the day, but one thing is, I don't like to talk on the phone much especially when I am busy writing. Just when I am really bored or when I want to bug somebody to get attention.

The transition of aging has taken its toll but has not gotten the best of me. Living here on the reservation is hard for me, especially during winter times with my body not able to adapt to the intense cold temperatures. Everywhere I want to go is challenging; I have to make appointments ahead of time so I will be prepared for anything. What I really want even though I'm quadriplegic is to live a life without barriers. I don't want to give up this idea.

Sometimes it seems like the only things I have left in me are my faith and lots of patience. No one can take those away from me. I also think about the great amount of experience I have gained living many years being disabled and serving as an advocate. It was hard for me to utilize all this knowledge due to not being able to write and having to rely on my memory. There have been a lot of people who wanted me to work with them in a workplace environment, but due to my condition as a quadriplegic I could not see myself being in a workplace. I cannot sit constantly in one position for a long period of time. I might be in a workplace for a week, then start having problems physically, and that is when it becomes hard for me to cope mentally, too. So I did not want to take the chance of being in the hospital with a nasty pressure sore. Most of all I always try to stay away from hospitals, but they are like my second home and I still continue to go for necessary treatments and visits.

From time to time, I run out of medication, and this brings me back to the clinic to visit with my primary doctor who prescribes further medication and evaluates my condition. These visits with my doctor at least twice a year are not something that I look forward to, but I know that they are necessary. Boy, do I despise going to the doctor's office! The smells in the clinic—the odors of alcohol and the cleansers used inside the building—create an environment that can make anyone depressed. I think this is the reason for nurses being upbeat and cheery most of the time, to temper the bleak nature of a clinic. I can't wait to get out of such an environment—to get away from the clinic and be back at home where I can be more comfortable and contented without fear of any medical staff. Doctor appointments and clinics make me dwell on the possible outcome of my visit, fearing admittance and confinement to the hospital.

There have been several times that I have gone to the hospital for treatment and been admitted for a long stay, to my disappointment. When sitting in a wheelchair for long periods of time, circulation of blood in the muscles and tissue is cut off by the pressure of body weight on bone, and this can create huge pressure sores in a short period of time. To avoid such sores, I have my attendant shift my weight every hour or so to assume a different position to alleviate the pressure points. This is the most common ailment that causes me to be admitted to the hospital. The common technique of curing these huge pressure sores is surgery. Every day and in every situation, I try to stay out of the hospital, keeping myself in a healthy state and being aware of the everyday requirements for my physically challenged body.

With the immense load of stress stemming from living in a hospital, I have attempted a couple of times to take my own life. I had a close encounter with death by way of overdose of medication. As a result of my decision, I was treated in an Intensive Care Unit followed by a long rehabilitation stay in Albuquerque. To make matters worse, I had distanced myself from my own family. I felt guilt tapping on my shoulder, knowing that I had thrown my family into a strenuous tribulation, fearing the worst possible conclusion. In my head it seemed as if I heard every other voice on earth and I was unable to hear my own. It soon became so intense and the pressure became unbearable to the point that I wanted to let go of myself and let nature take its course, to have the peace and quiet once again where I did not hear any demanding voices.

Despite all the issues I face every day, I try to put them behind me and keep going forward with my life. I have been in the pits, the lowest place in life, so for me there's nowhere to go but up. I don't know how or where I got the motivation to write, but it came naturally to me just like talking to a person in a conversation. Every once in a while I like to write little stories here and there, but I never kept a diary. If I had, it would speak of many untold things that would add more detail to my story. I'm not the greatest writer but my goal is to someday be up there with the greats. It keeps me busy and my mind occupied and alert. It keeps me out of trouble. When I'm not writing, it's like my mind is full of ideas that I can't keep to myself, I have to get them down in black and white. But then when it's time for me to write, everything just goes away into thin air like vapor steaming out of a hot teacup.

I look back today at the obstacles I've faced, and they are nothing to me now. I had challenged myself in many ways, and I know that it is the challenges that keep me going from one day to another. That's why I keep on living and do not want to give up. Why give up when I still have my whole life ahead of me and a lot more patience and humor in me? The world is full of challenges whether you are disabled or not. I wonder what will challenge me next.

ABOUT THE AUTHOR

Gilbert John was born in 1957 in Gallup, New Mexico. He was named in Navajo Hashke' Yitaaswod—He ran amongst the warriors. Gilbert was raised on the Navajo reservation, where he was taught the traditional ways by his grandparents. He experienced a lifestyle that was close to nature, adventurous and full of challenges. He received his formal education at boarding schools, and then the local public high school. In September of 1975, Gilbert had just started his junior year when an accident left him with a severe spinal cord injury.

Gilbert finished his high school education at the Carrie Tingley Hospital rehabilitation school in southern New Mexico. Despite many obstacles and frequent hospitalizations, he went on to pursue higher education and more adventures. Quadriplegic in a pre-ADA world, he traveled, attended college and lived independently for a number of years. He earned his Bachelor of Science degree from the University of New Mexico in 1988.

After returning to his family on the Navajo reservation, Gilbert began writing his autobiography by dictating into a cassette tape recorder. His efforts to obtain better technology and the assistance he needed to complete his project, along with his firsthand experiences both in the city and on the reservation, led to him becoming an advocate for Native Americans with disabilities. He has served on the boards of the Navajo Nation Advisory Council on Disability; the Governor's Commission on Disability, New Mexico Technology Assistance Project of the Division of Vocational Rehabilitation; and the Statewide Independent Living Council, representing Northwest New Mexico.

Gilbert is currently based in Farmington, New Mexico.

CPSIA information can be obtained
at www.ICGtesting.com
Printed in the USA
LVHW081913210421
685132LV00015B/467